REFORMATION READINGS OF THE APOCALYPSE

OXFORD STUDIES IN HISTORICAL THEOLOGY

REFORMATION
READINGS OF THE
APOCALYPSE

GENEVA, ZURICH,
AND WITTENBERG

Irena Backus

UNIVERSITY PRESS

2000

OXFORD
UNIVERSITY PRESS

Oxford   New York

Athens   Auckland   Bangkok   Bogotá   Buenos Aires   Calcutta
Cape Town   Chennai   Dar es Salaam   Delhi   Florence   Hong Kong   Istanbul
Karachi   Kuala Lumpur   Madrid   Melbourne   Mexico City   Mumbai
Nairobi   Paris   São Paulo   Shanghai   Singapore   Taipei   Tokyo   Toronto   Warsaw

and associated companies in
Berlin   Ibadan

Copyright © 2000 by Irena Backus

Published by Oxford University Press, Inc.
198 Madison Avenue, New York, New York 10016

Oxford is a registered trademark of Oxford University Press.

Library of Congress Cataloging-in-Publication Data
Backus, Irena Dorota, 1950–
Reformation readings of the Apocalypse : Geneva, Zurich,
and Wittenberg / Irena Backus.
p.   cm—(Oxford studies in historical theology)
Includes bibliographical references and index.
ISBN 0-19-513885-6
1. Bible. N.T. Revelation—Criticism, interpretation, etc—
History—16th century.   2. Bible—Criticism, interpretation, etc.—
History—16th century.   3. Reformation.   I. Title.   II. Series.
BS2825.2.B34   2000
228'.06'09409031—dc21   00-026356

1 3 5 7 9 8 6 4 2

Printed in the United States of America
on acid-free paper

ACKNOWLEDGMENTS

I should like to thank all the people who made this book possible: first and foremost, Cristina Pitassi, Enrico Norelli, Olivier Fatio, and Guy Backus, all of whom have, over the years, encouraged my interest in the Apocalypse and whose critical remarks have often acted as a spur. I should also like to thank David Steinmetz, who encouraged me to completely transform a short pamphlet I wrote in 1996, *Les sept visions et la fin des temps*, into a comprehensive monograph, and Marlène Jaouich, who provided extremely valuable technical assistance, as always. My thanks also go to the Lutheran Brotherhood Foundation Library in Minnesota, without whose help I could not have gained access to Selnecker's commentary.

Geneva, Switzerland   I. B.
April 2000

CONTENTS

ABBREVIATIONS

Apc   The Apocalypse of John.

ASD   Desiderius Erasmus. *Opera omnia*. Amsterdam, 1969.

CCL   *Corpus Christianorum*. Series Latina.

CPG   *Clavis patrum graecorum*.

LB   Desiderius Erasmus. *Opera omnia emendatiora et auctiora, ad optimas editiones, praecipue quas ipse Erasmus postremo curauit, summa fide exacta doctorumque virorum notis illustrata.* Leiden, 1705.

PG   Jacques-Paul Migne, ed. *Patrologiae cursus completus.* Series graeca.

PL   Jacques-Paul Migne, ed. *Patrologiae cursus completus.* Series Latina.

WA   *D. Martin Luthers Werke.*

Z   Ulrich Zwingli. *Huldreich Zwinglis sämtliche Werke.*

INTRODUCTION

Early Exegesis of the Apocalypse

Although much has been written already on the Apocalypse text itself and on its early exegesis,[1] some preliminary remarks are useful. As we shall see, some problems inherent in the text and methods of exegesis which were developed between the second and the twelfth centuries were known to sixteenth-century commentators and did, to a greater or lesser extent, influence their approach.

The Apocalypse, or Revelation, of John is the sole Christian apocalyptic writing to enter the biblical canon. Apocalyptics as a genre was quite unknown in the sixteenth century, and none of the authors we shall be discussing was ever aware of Jewish or Christian apocalyptic literature as a specific genre, although, as we shall have occasion to see, all were aware of the elements of Daniel and Ezekiel imported into the text of the Apocalypse. According to most scholars, the origins and growth of Jewish apocalyptic literature reflect the history of Israel's conflicts with other nations and the conviction that trust in military power was useless. As the nation continued to be subjected to foreign domination, it despaired of attaining political supremacy, and the conclusion was drawn that God would eventually intervene, destroy Israel's enemies, and set up his kingdom on earth. Apocalyptic literature proper begins with the book of Daniel, probably written during the persecution of Antiochus Epiphanes (175–164 B.C.). Important Jewish apocalyptic writings outside the Old Testament canon are the first and second books of Enoch, the Apocalypse of Baruch, the

Assumption of Moses, and the Ascension of Isaiah. All, with the exception of the very slightly later Ascension of Isaiah, are dated as originating in the second half of the first century, after the destruction of the Temple in A.D. 70, and are therefore roughly contemporary with the Apocalypse of John, normally considered to have been written in the reign of Domitian (A.D. 81–96). The chief characteristic of apocalyptic literature is its recourse to one or several visions of the past, the present, and the future (both real and eschatological). The vision is normally granted to the seer by God himself, but it is mediated by one or several angels. This enables the author to transmit new prophecies without fearing accusations of excessive self-importance. For the same reason, most of the Jewish apocalypses appear under the names of great prophets such as Moses, Enoch, or Isaiah. Their real authors remain unknown.

Apart from the Apocalypse of John, the most important Christian Apocalypse is that of Peter, which never entered the canon. John's work contains one interesting feature which was to earn it much criticism in the sixteenth century and which distinguishes it sharply from the Jewish apocalyptic literature: It is written under the author's own name. In Apc 1.9, he says quite openly that he is the brother of the seven churches in Asia Minor and that he has shared in their suffering. Whether John was in fact John the Evangelist or, most likely, another John is without importance. He above all wanted to make his identity known to the communities he was addressing, as they could thus decipher what lay behind the deliberately cryptic language of the visions. The Apocalypse was not intended for general consumption. Its visions hide all sorts of allusions to the particular situation of particular Christian communities in the second half of the first century.

As is well known, the Apocalypse (as we shall call it from now on) was held in great esteem by the millenarian ante-Nicene Fathers who took it to be the work of John the Evangelist. Justin Martyr praised it in his *Dialogue with Trypho* (chap. 81), and Irenaeus used it (together with other writings) to defend chiliasm against the doctrine of spiritual resurrection put forward by the Valentinian Gnosis. However, as millenarianism began to lose hold in the Eastern, and particularly the Alexandrian, church, the respectability of the Apocalypse was challenged. Dionysius of Alexandria questioned its apostolic authorship, ca. A.D. 250, on grounds of difference in style and content from the Fourth Gospel. Eusebius of Caesarea admitted its place in the canon with some reluctance. Some subsequent Eastern writers and councils (Cyril of Jerusalem, Council of Laodicea, John Chrysostom) did not include it in the canon.

In the West, the attribution to John the Evangelist was maintained in the Muratorian Canon and also by Tertullian and Hippolytus, so that the Apocalypse was viewed more favorably. It is no accident that the most influential commentaries on the text were Western.

The Spiritual Interpretation

The commentaries of Victorinus of Poetovio (d. ca. 304) and Tyconius (d. ca. 380) shaped in different ways, and for different reasons, the exegesis of the Apocalypse in the West in late antiquity and the early Middle Ages. Victorinus, bishop of Poetovio in today's Slovenia, suffered martyrdom under Diocletian. His commentary on the Apocalypse was "revised" by Jerome. Although there is some disagreement among scholars about the number and the nature of corrections Jerome introduced into the body of the text, there is no doubt that the translator of the Vulgate rewrote the millenarian ending of Victorinus' commentary, bringing the heavenly Jerusalem down to the realm of ethics.[2] Victorinus' original commentary with its millenarian ending remained quite unknown until 1916, when Y. Haussleiter discovered a fifteenth-century manuscript of it at the Vatican (Ottobonianus Latinus 3288A, fol. 1–22). However, Jerome's version of the commentary circulated throughout the Middle Ages and was published in the sixteenth century in two recensions, the shorter[3] and the longer.[4] Victorinus saw the Apocalypse not as a prophecy but as an unveiling by Christ of the true sense of Scripture. He was also the first exegete to apply the principle of recapitulation to the text; according to him, the Apocalypse relates the same events in different ways, so that, for example, the bowls do no more than elaborate on the persecutions, which have already been revealed by the trumpets. It is not chronology but understanding that is of crucial importance in John's Revelation.

Tyconius' commentary is no longer extant, and its contents can only be reconstructed from later commentaries that made extensive use of it, notably those of Beatus, Primasius, and the Venerable Bede. We do know that it was written after a persecution of Donatists during a period of relative tranquillity. As a Donatist, Tyconius found in the Apocalypse a prophecy of the suffering and hopes of his church. The Satanic forces in the text represented to him the sum total of the ecclesiastical powers of the Catholic Church, which he found to be worldly and decadent. Openly spiritual in his interpretation, Tyconius rejected, for example, the idea that the two witnesses should be identified with persons past or present; he preferred to interpret the passage as referring to the church holding the two testaments. More important, the Antichrist ceased to be a person but became identified with the *corpus diaboli*, the omnipresent evil, and the false Christians, not easily distinguishable from the true and the good. Tyconius completely neutralized the millenarianism of the Apocalypse by referring the *thousand years* of the chaining up of Satan to the Incarnation. However, while doing away with the messianic interregnum, the Donatist did not minimize the importance of the Apocalypse as the text of the latter days, seeing himself as living at the end of time. Taking the cosmic week as the basic scheme of the duration of the world, he thought that Christ was born halfway through the sixth day, the seventh day being already situated after the Last Judgment. The three and a half years of Apc 12 thus stood for 350 years, the period of the church's testimony. By the time Tyconius was writing, 850 years of the "sixth day" had passed, which meant that around 150 years were left until the Last Judgment.

It is not useful to speculate on whether the influence of Tyconius on the later Apocalypse commentaries would have been as great had Augustine not made so much use of Tyconius in his *De ciuitate Dei* 20.7–20. In his sermon 259, Augustine adopted a millenarian position and envisaged an earthly period of peace for the just before the final resurrection. In the *De ciuitate Dei*, he adopts Tyconius' interpretation of the *thousand years* and situates the chaining up of Satan at the same time as the Incarnation. The *thousand years* thus simply denotes a period from the Incarnation until the Last Judgment. However, it is important to remember that Augustine, like most of his contemporaries, considered himself to be living in the last days and also followed the scheme of the cosmic week, although what interests him most in *De ciuitate Dei* is not the number of years left until the Last Judgment but the identity of "the devil" and the relative nature of both his captivity and his release. For Augustine as for Tyconius, "the devil" represents all the wicked and the enemies of the Christian church, whose power is contained by Christ. His release does not mean that he will be able to seduce the Christian church, the true faithful, but that during that brief release there will be no more new converts, with the exception of newly born Christian infants, who will still be able to undergo the baptism of regeneration. The first resurrection was to Augustine the life of true believers during the chaining up of Satan, which was equivalent to some sort of spiritual millennium.

The spiritual school of the exegesis of the Apocalypse which was to dominate the Western interpretations of the book for several centuries was thus born. Among its most eminent and influential representatives were Primasius (d. ca. 560), bishop of Hadrumetum in Africa, and the Venerable Bede (672–735), the English Benedictine monk. Both made extensive use of Tyconius, while adapting his work to "catholic" use. Bede's chief innovation was to divide the Apocalypse into seven sections or summaries ("periochae"), which gradually became seven visions, the standard division of the text. Bede explains how he proceeded in his prefatory epistle to Eusebius (PL 93:130–131). The first section comprises the address to the seven churches which represent the church universal and the promise of the return of the Son (Apc 1–3). The second section describes the opening of the seven seals of the book in which the Lamb will read the conflicts and triumphs that the church has been confronting since the Incarnation. The order of opening is maintained until the sixth seal; the contents of the six seals are then recapitulated in a narrative section, before the narrator moves on to the seventh seal (Apc 4–8.5). The third section follows the same pattern, depicting the same events in the form of seven trumpets (Apc 8.6–11.19). The fourth section (Apc 12–14) describes the joys and tribulations of the church, while the fifth "afflicts the earth with seven plagues" (Apc 15–16). The sixth section describes the judgment on the great whore, Babylon (Apc 17–20), and the seventh (Apc 21–22) describes the heavenly Jerusalem and the eternal peace after the Last Judgment.

As we shall see, several Protestant commentators in the sixteenth century took over Bede's division. As well as "conveniently" dividing the text into easily distinguishable sections, it had the advantage of concealing any millenarian tendencies of the text and of focusing the reader's attention on the trials and tribulations of the church since the Incarnation. In other words, it provided an ecclesiological as well as a spiritual framework. It was also flexible enough to be adapted by, for example, Joachim of Fiore.

Bede also included in his preface Tyconius' seven rules for the interpretation of Scripture (the *Liber regularum*),[5] which, if applied to the Apocalypse, were apt to accentuate its spiritual implications even more. As the rules were to be cited again by some of the Protestant commentators that we shall be considering, it is worth reminding the reader of their content. The first rule is that of the Lord and his body; it allows us to distinguish propositions concerning Christ himself from those concerning his church. The second rule concerns the Lord and the communication of his body via the communion; it allows us to correctly pick out the eucharistic content of the Bible. The third rule is to do with relating law and grace, in other words, the Old Testament and the New Testament. The fourth rule is that of the genus and the species; it shows us how to distinguish what is said about an Old Testament person—for example, Salomon—as a historical figure from what is said about him as a prototype of Christ. The fifth rule is to do with the interpretation of times and tenses, and the sixth is the rule of recapitulation. As a representative example of the latter, Bede cites Gen. 10.32–11.1, which appears to state that the tribes of Noah had one common language when they were dispersed. It is only further on in Gen. 11 that we learn that the linguistic division was completed before the dispersal. The seventh rule is to do with the devil and his body; according to Tyconius, the Scripture often attributes to the devil actions which are committed by the wicked, that is, by the members of his "body." The Apocalypse was thus stabilized in the spiritual and ecclesiological realm. However, changing social conditions soon dictated a different way of reading the text.

The Historico-Prophetic Interpretation

Kamlah's book[6] sketches out the chief features of the historico-prophetic method, which, by the sixteenth century, became integrated into the spiritual hermeneutic. We shall therefore confine ourselves to some remarks on two of the most characteristic and influential representatives of this school of interpretation, Rupert of Deutz (d. 1129) and Nicholas of Lyra (d. 1340), both of whom were much used in the sixteenth century. The basic feature of the historical approach was to divide the Apocalypse into six rather than into seven parts and to read it as a history of salvation from Adam until a certain date. Depending on the *terminus ad quem* chosen by the exegete, John thus became either a historian or simultaneously a historian and a prophet. For Rupert of Deutz, John was basically a historian and the Apocalypse a history of salvation from Adam until the Council of Nicaea, although the commentary also contains numerous references to Rupert's own time and to the life of the church in general. Rupert was the first commentator to have recourse to ecclesiastical histories of Eusebius and Flavius Josephus in order to establish parallels between events in history and prophecies in the text. As an example of Rupert's method, we shall cite here some of his comments on Apc 4, where the celestial church service receives a historically based inter- pretation. John's vision of the door in heaven thus signifies heavenly life, which Christ on his Resurrection guaranteed for the church, which also rose with him. The first resurrection is the Resurrection of Christ, which also caused the church to rise to life. The twenty-four ancients around the throne pose a problem to Rupert, as he notes that the figure was variously inter- preted by the church Fathers; Jerome saw the twenty-four ancients as repre- senting the twenty-four books of the Old Testament. Others, notably Primasius and Bede, took the figure to symbolize twelve patriarchs and twelve apostles, the church of the New Testament and its precursor in the Old Testament. Rupert, for his part, sees in the twenty-four ancients a represen- tation of the history of Israel. There are twelve judges (Rupert includes Samuel) who preceded David; the other twelve are those who succeeded David's direct descendent, Christ—in other words, the twelve apostles.

The sea of glass evokes to Rupert the crossing of the Red Sea in the Old Testament, and baptism in the New Testament. Both denote liberation. The Christocentric nature of his commentary coupled with his interest in the Old Testament and his interest in the history of the early church in general was probably what made Rupert's commentary popular with reformers like Sebastian Meyer.

Nicholas of Lyra's postill on the Apocalypse (ca. 1329), which reproduced portions of the commentary of Alexander of Bremen and of other Franciscan commentaries, was much more grounded in historical events which took place between the Ascension of Christ and his own time. The seals thus refer to Domitian's reign, and the trumpets symbolize the era of heresies, particu- larly the Arian heresy. The first beast of Apc 11 is Kavat, the son of Cosdroes (the Persian enemy of the emperor Heraclius), and the second beast is the Islam. The seven bowls stand for the first Crusades. According to Lyra, Apc 19.11 (white horse with its rider, Faithful and True) refers not to Christ but to Baldwin, the Christian king installed in Jerusalem (after the First Crusade of 1099) who finally capitulated to Saladin in 1187. Even Apc 20.1

is interpreted historically, as a symbolic account of the investitures quarrel between Pope Calixtus and the emperor Henry V. The tying up of Satan thus simply means the limiting of imperial power by the 1122 Concordat of Worms. Nicholas of Lyra's commentary was not original. However, it had the merit of being easily accessible, and, although few Protestant commentators followed it in every detail, they did draw on it for historical facts which fitted into their own exegetical framework.

Joachim of Fiore (d. 1202) and the Spiritual Franciscans

It is difficult to estimate the extent of the influence of Joachim's commentary on sixteenth-century exegetes. His major work on the Apocalypse was published in Venice in 1527[7] but was not reissued in the course of the century. Due to the papal condemnation of the Franciscan Gerard of Borgo San Donnino in 1254 for his proclamation of the *Eternal Gospel* (excerpts from Joachim's works), intended to supersede the Old Testament and the New Testament, and due to the condemnation of Joachim's own doctrine in 1215 by the Lateran Council and in 1263 by the provincial Council of Arles, the Calabrian abbot enjoyed a dubious reputation. However, his hermeneutic implicitly underlay some of the ideas expressed in the commentaries that we shall be studying and therefore deserves some consideration.

Joachim wrote his commentary around 1195. He divided it into eight parts. Unlike Bede, he begins part 7 with Apc 20 and not with Apc 21, and he ends part 7 at Apc 20.10. Apc 20.11 to the end of chapter 22 thus represents the eighth part or book, treating of the eternal rest.

To Joachim, the Apocalypse encapsulates the latter two *status* in history, the Age of the Son and the Age of the Holy Spirit. The first six parts of his commentary cover the Age of the Son (forty-two generations, each lasting about thirty years), and part 7 covers the Age of the Holy Spirit. The eighth part, extremely short, treats of the metahistorical heavenly Jerusalem. Thus, part 1 (Apc 1–3) contains seven generations and treats of the struggle of the apostles against the synagogue. Part 2 (Apc 4.1–8.1) treats of the struggle of the martyrs against pagan persecutions. Part 3 (Apc 8.2–11.18) deals with the struggle of the doctors of the church against heretics and lasts until the Constantinian settlement. Part 4 (Apc 11.19–14.20) is the struggle of the monastic orders against the Islam, and part 5 (Apc 15.1–16.17) represents the conflict between the church of Rome and the Holy Empire. Part 6 (Apc 16.18–19.21) represents the struggle of the spiritual men (represented by two new religious orders), first against the dragon, then against the two beasts, which represent, respectively, Saladin (Joachim's contemporary) and the "maximus Antichristus," a person who combines the heresy of Islam and all the Western heresies.

Joachim wrote his commentary at the end of the twelfth century. The Age of the Son would, according to his calculations, come to an end in 1260. It would be succeeded by the Age of the Holy Spirit depicted in part 7 (Apc 20.1–10), when Satan would be chained up and the church freed from all persecution after the final conflict. At that point, the contemplative order would take possession of the church and there would be a complete spiritual renewal. Although Joachim's commentary is characterized by his underlying conviction of spiritual progress in the history of the church, it would be naive to consider him a hard and fast millenarian. Indeed, he himself was very careful to relativize his interpretation of Apc 20 by distinguishing between the chaining up of Satan, which could not begin in earnest until the defeat of the beast and the false prophet, and the *thousand years*, which had begun the moment the Resurrection of Christ took place (Joachim considers the actual number *thousand* to be symbolic) and during which Satan's power was to some extent limited. His seventh age is an age of full monastic spirituality prior to the Last Judgment.

Two features of Joachim's hermeneutic would have been of interest to the Protestant commentators of the Apocalypse—first, his idea that after a series of struggles there would emerge an age in which the faithful would be in some sense "closer to God" than hitherto, and, second, his idea that the Antichrist was an unspecified individual (emanating from Rome) who would combine all the heresies. The latter idea in fact captured the imagination of the spiritual Franciscans long before the Reformation.

Thus, Petrus Joannis Olivi (ca. 1248–1298),[8] writing nearly a hundred years after Joachim, also describes six periods in the church corresponding to six parts of the Apocalypse. However, unlike Joachim, he saw part 4 as the era of the Greek monks, part 5 as the era of the monastic orders under Charlemagne, and part 6 as Franciscan reforms, which were in his eyes equivalent to Joachim's Age of the Holy Spirit. There was thus no part 7 in Olivi's *Lectura super Apocalypsim*, as the transcendent age was already to take place in the sixth part. The teachers of the sixth *status* were, according to Olivi, totally successful in combatting the forces of the Antichrist. The immediate precursor of the *Antichristus magnus* was the *Antichristus mysticus*, or the papacy, thus named because it was opposed to the strict application of the Rule of St. Francis. The *Antichristus magnus* designated, for Olivi, the emperor Frederick II together with a pseudopope.

Ubertino de Casale, who wrote his *Arbor vitae crucifixae* at the beginning of the fourteenth century, was even more explicit in his designation of the beast and the Antichrist. To him, the first beast of Apc 13 was Pope Boniface VIII (1294–1303) and the second, Benedict XI. Slowly, the idea of the Roman Antichrist took shape and was ready for use by the reformers. However, at the same time, the Franciscan exploitation of the Apocalypse certainly did not improve the reputation of the book. By the time of the Reformation, there was a general aura of unease surrounding it.

The aim of the present book is to examine commentaries on the Apocalypse produced in or around Geneva and Zurich between 1539 and 1584 with the

aim of analyzing their methods and their views of the status of the Apocalypse and its place in the religious and cultural context of the Reformation.
In chapter 5, two commentaries produced in the Lutheran context are intended as a point of comparison.

I have concentrated on authors who made an effort to produce a commentary on the Apocalypse, irrespective of what else they wrote, and I have
ignored authors such as Piscator, Pareus, or Flacius Illyricus who produced
a commentary on the Apocalypse as part of a commentary on the whole of
(or almost the whole of) the New Testament. I have also deliberately excluded
English commentators, who were the object of a very good study by Richard Bauckham in 1978[9] and whose works were in any case to some extent
dependent on the commentaries we analyze here. With the exception of
Bullinger's *Sermons*, sixteenth-century Protestant commentaries on the
Apocalypse are not easily available. The same goes for Lutheran commentaries. The desire to write the present book was partly the result of frustra-
tion. Only too often one reads a statement in secondary literature such as
"Meyer's commentary has been unavailable to me,"[10] which apparently does
not stop the author from pronouncing on Meyer's exegesis. The resulting
analysis is unreliable by its very nature.

The other reason for writing the present book was the wish simply to
examine whether there was such a thing as a single Protestant approach to
the Apocalypse or whether varying social, linguistic, and political conditions
determined the way that different writers read the text. The choice of Zurich,
Geneva, and Wittenberg was thus deliberate.

I first examine the issue of canonicity, which resurfaced in the sixteenth
century after being initially raised in third-century Alexandria. As for the
commentaries themselves, I chose, for Geneva, that of Antoine du Pinet
(Pignet), a commentator considered by some modern authors as Calvin's
mouthpiece,[11] which is studied here in the light of sources du Pinet claims
to have used, especially François Lambert and Sebastian Meyer. I also examine, for Geneva, the commentaries of Augustin Marlorat and Nicolas
Colladon. Marlorat constitutes something of a methodological exception,
seeing as his *Expositio in Apocalypsim* is a part of his *Expositio ecclesiastica* on
the whole of the New Testament. I included it deliberately, however, as it
provides an excellent indication of the way Meyer's commentary left an
imprint on the Calvinist conception of the Apocalypse. Colladon's commentary has never been the object of any detailed study[12] and is particularly
important, as it claims to mirror Calvin's own views on the Apocalypse, of
which Colladon apparently had inside knowledge.

Among the Zurich commentaries, those of Heinrich Bullinger, Theodore
Bibliander, and Leo Jud are considered. The choice of the Lutherans David
Chytraeus and Nikolaus Selnecker was dictated by the circumstances in which
the two wrote their commentaries and also by their proximity in time to the
mainstream of the Protestant commentaries. In Chytraeus' case, as I shall

show, there are definite traces of Bullinger's exegesis, whereas Selnecker with his desire to make the Apocalypse comprehensible to the common man can be considered a Lutheran counterpart to du Pinet.

So as to avoid a patchwork effect and in order to show the varying degree of the different commentators' dependence on tradition, I have concentrated my analysis on the exegesis of Apc 12 and 20—on Apc 12 because of its ecclesiastical connotations and because many ancient commentators saw it as the central vision, and on Apc 20 because of the variety of interpretations that were sparked by the famous passage on the *thousand years* of Satan's imprisonment. However, I have also devoted some attention to the commentators' global approach to the text and to the interpretation of the seven seals in the more historically inclined commentaries. The resulting work will, it is hoped, throw light on how different groups and individuals within the Reformation establishment viewed the Apocalypse.

REFORMATION READINGS OF THE APOCALYPSE

I

THE PROBLEM OF CANONICITY

Erasmus

Although, by the early sixteenth century, the Apocalypse had acquired a dubious reputation due partly to the use that radical Franciscans and Hussites[1] made of it, no one since the third century had questioned its place in the canon. The first to do so was Erasmus in his 1516 *Annotations*. His low view of it was to do partly with the nature of the text itself and partly, no doubt, with the difficulties he had in obtaining a copy of it in 1516. He had previously seen some manuscripts and made notes on them during his visit to England in 1505, but it was only through Johannes Reuchlin that he finally managed to obtain the incomplete twelfth-century manuscript that he published in his *Nouum Instrumentum*. Reuchlin himself had borrowed the *Kommentartext* to the commentary of Andreas of Caesarea from the Dominican monastery in Basel. The manuscript, as is well known, lacked Apc 22.16–21, which Erasmus reconstructed. It is commonly supposed that he supplied the missing Greek verses from the Complutensian Polyglot in 1527.[2]

Erasmus' terse textual annotations make no mention of any practical difficulties to do with obtaining the manuscript, and it is only his very final note (on Apc 22.12: "yes, I am coming soon . . . I am the Alpha and the Omega") that gives us an insight into his hostility to the book. The note was expanded in 1522 by roughly two-thirds of its original size, as Erasmus provided more evidence for his doubts about the apostolic origin of the Apocalypse and about its place in the canon. The 1516 version of the note concentrates on the linguistic argument and contains very few patristic testimonies. Erasmus does, however, refer to Jerome's famous letter to Dardanus (ep. 129) to make the point that the Apocalypse was rejected by the Greek church in Jerome's time.[3] As his second argument against the book he invokes the authority of (anonymous) "learned men" who have found the text to be lacking apostolic weight (*apostolica grauitas*), a mere historical account (*historia rerum*) expressed in allegorical terms. After recounting this opinion, Erasmus refuses to take up a position on it. He does, however, consider two factors as quite decisive in undermining the authority of the book: Both are to do with the name *John*. First, he repeats his name, *ego Johannes*, as if he were writing "a promissory note" instead of divinely conferred revelations, whereas he refers to himself only periphrastically when he describes far more down-to-earth things in his Gospel, while Paul writes about his own revelations as if they were someone else's. Second, notes Erasmus, the Greek manuscripts of the Apocalypse that he consulted bear the name, not of *Ioannes Euangelista* but of *Ioannes theologus*. As if those two arguments were not enough to seriously damage the authority of the book, Erasmus adds a third: The style of the Apocalypse is quite different from that of John's Gospel and Epistle, and it would be easy to disprove Johannine authorship from the passages which some have maligned, "suspecting them of certain heretical doctrines."

While only three points are made explicitly, a great deal has been insinuated not only about the heretical contents of the Apocalypse but also about its reputation among the learned. However, instead of drawing the inevitable conclusion, Erasmus takes a step back and asserts that the arguments of John's name and style would have inclined him to disbelieve that John the Evangelist was the author of the book, had the consensus and the authority of the church not approved the book as fully canonical and written by John the Evangelist.[4] The 1516 version ends on two pieces of (not very authoritative) patristic testimony, further damaging the credibility of the Apocalypse. Dorotheus, "bishop" of Tyre, notes Erasmus, does not say in his *De vita prophetarum et apostolorum synopsis* that John the Evangelist wrote the Apocalypse, although, unlike Eusebius, he is of the opinion that John wrote the Gospel in Patmos (which would make it a priori likely that he was the author of the Apocalypse, also written in Patmos). That Dorotheus' work is of doubtful authenticity does not even occur to Erasmus, or perhaps he chooses to ignore that possibility deliberately.[5] Moreover, he continues, Anastasius the Greek in his *Catalogus* (i.e., in the *Synopsis Sacrae Scripturae*) does *not* say that the Apocalypse is the work of John the Evangelist; he simply admits that it was received thus. The text Erasmus has in mind here is the pseudo-Athanasian (and *not Anastasian*) canon dating from the fourth or fifth century and formerly ascribed to the bishop of Alexandria.[6] Even though Erasmus in this instance does not seem certain of his source, he certainly reproduces its contents correctly. The 1516 edition of the annotation ends on a noncommittal note: Jewels are not all of equal worth; some gold is purer than other gold; in sacred matters, some things are more sacred than others. As Paul would have it (1 Cor. 2.15), "[H]e who is spiritual judges all things, yet he himself is judged of no man."

This very radical view of the Apocalypse did not provoke an outcry straightaway, no doubt because the caveats voiced by Erasmus echoed the reservations felt by the more conservative Roman theologians in the first quarter of the sixteenth century, who tended to be suspicious of the Apocalypse. Stunica, in his criticism of Erasmus' annotations, did point out, however, that *Ioannes Euangelista* and *Ioannes theologus* were one and the same person, an objection Erasmus curtly dismissed in his *Apology* against the Spaniard.[7]

Why did Erasmus not include more patristic testimonies in 1516? A sentence which disappeared in 1522 shows us just how dismissive he was about the whole issue of the Apocalypse: "Indeed," he said, "I see that former theologians cited testimonies [in favor of the Apocalypse] more by way of an ornament than to prove something serious."[8] By 1522, however, he had changed his mind and decided to quote a large number of patristic testimonies showing that the Apocalypse occupied a dubious place in the canon and implying that it was tinged with heresy. Particularly, Erasmus decided to explore the question of millenarianism on the strength of evidence supplied by Eusebius of Caesarea in his *Historia ecclesiastica*.

Erasmus begins by examining the judgment of Dionysius of Alexandria as expounded by Eusebius in *Historia ecclesiastica* 7.23.[9] Although apparently agreeing with Dionysius that the Apocalypse could not have been written by Cerinthus in an attempt to pass off as apostolic his heretical doctrine of the millennium as a hedonistic paradise on earth, Erasmus dwells at great length on the details (drawn from hostile sources) of Cerinthus' doctrine and is obviously strongly tempted by the hypothesis. Resisting the temptation, however, he gives his assent to Dionysius' judgment: The author was a man called John but not John the Evangelist, who would not have repeated his name so often. Erasmus' note makes clear that he knew the opinion of Gaius of Rome (also cited by Eusebius, *Hist. Eccl.* 3.28.1–2), who attributed the Apocalypse to Cerinthus in his controversy with the Montanists. However, the details of the disagreement are not known to the Dutch humanist; indeed, Eusebius being his sole source, he does not know who the Montanists were or what the nature of their eschatological beliefs was. However, the mere fact of Gaius "pius quidam author" putting up a plea for Cerinthian authorship suffices to set Erasmus off on his speculations about Cerinthus as author, prior to regretfully discarding the hypothesis, "as it seems difficult to believe that God would have permitted the devil's tricks to delude the Christian people with impunity for so many years"[10] A non-Cerinthian authorship, however, did not mean canonicity, especially as Erasmus was quick to spot that Eusebius himself placed the Apocalypse (together with 2 and 3 John, James, Jude, and 2 Peter) in the category of books whose place within the canon was disputable (*Hist. Eccl.* 3.25) and was inclined to attribute it to "Ioannes presbyter" (*Hist. Eccl.* 3.39).

As Erasmus himself admits, it is clear that the problem which confronts him is the very one expounded by Jerome in his commentary on Ezek. 36.[11] From the late third century onward, the Greek church, particularly, rejected the Apocalypse. Yet the text was very ancient and apparently not only accepted but also commented on by the ante-Nicene Fathers such as Justin, Irenaeus, Tertullian, and Lactantius. However, Erasmus is fully aware that all those ante-Nicene Fathers were chiliasts, as were Victorinus of Poetovio and Apollinaris. After all, he had just edited Jerome and would have had his commentary on Ezekiel still fresh in his mind. He also notes that the Apocalypse is itself a chiliastic text and that the word *chilias* appears very frequently, especially in Apc 12 and 20.

After this historical excursus that further undermined the authority of the book he had already condemned for its recourse to allegory, its barbarous style, and the dubious person of its author constantly compelled to justify his authorship, Erasmus ends his note with what he had already said in 1516: Among holy things, some are holier than others; the Apocalypse, it is implied, is in the category of the less holy.

The two versions of Erasmus' annotation made it quite plain that only the *consensus ecclesiae* made it necessary to keep the book in the canon. However, while the 1516 version of the annotation trivialized the issue, the 1522 version, with its recourse to patristic testimonies, made Erasmus' strictures seem very serious. The 1516 version of the note fell quickly into oblivion. The second version put in doubt the book's canonicity, with some consequences for its commentators.

Martin Luther

A vast amount of work has already been done on Martin Luther's two prefaces to the Apocalypse (1522 and 1530) in his translation of the Bible.[12] Without intending to add anything original to the debate on whether Luther fundamentally changed his mind on the Apocalypse, we shall now briefly examine the two prefaces so as to situate Luther's views of the status of the book in relation to Erasmus' remarks.[13]

On reading the 1522 preface, one is quickly aware that Luther was familiar with the 1516 version of Erasmus' *Annotations*, but that his own problems with the Apocalypse had nothing to do with those of the Dutch scholar. Luther states quite openly that he considers the book neither apostolic nor prophetic, because no Old Testament prophet, let alone a New Testament apostle, speaks about Christ quite so obscurely, with the possible exception of the apocryphal 4 Esdras. He also finds it offensive that John should threaten with God's punishment anyone who adds to or takes away from the prophecies (Apc 22.18–19). Although the problem of clarity did also figure in Erasmus' note of 1516, it was more the problem of discrepancy of style and lack of apostolic *weight* that was emphasized by the Dutchman. Moreover, while considering the book a mere history expressed in allegorical terms, Erasmus never dwelled on the theology of the Apocalypse—that is, on the way it teaches or does not teach Christ. Yet, this turns out to be the principal reason for Luther's condemnation of the text in 1522. "My mind cannot reconcile itself to this book," he says, "and for me it is reason enough not to value his [the author's] mind when I see that Christ is neither taught nor recognized in this work."[14]

Similarly, it is not the stylistic defect—John's frequent repetition of his own name—that Luther criticizes but the author's excessive recommendation of his own book. "Those who listen and go by what is written there are supposed to be blessed, but as no one can understand it, let alone go by it, this amounts to the same thing as the book not existing, and there are many more noble books that do exist and that we should go by."[15] In other words, the author's recommendation of his own book is both morally and pastorally dubious. Luther is also aware of the doubts cast upon the book's authenticity by the early Greek church and of Jerome's rather ambivalent attitude toward it. However, unlike Erasmus, he does not appeal to tradition to either vindicate or discredit the book. He discredits it solely on the evidence of its lack of Christian message, as compared to the canonical literature.

Contrary to what might be expected, this radical dismissal of the Apocalypse did not completely stop the production of commentaries on it in Wittenberg. The Apocalypse was indeed obscure and did not teach Christ. It could, however, teach the Antichrist, who could be and indeed had been identified with the pope in many of the radical fourteenth- and fifteenth-century commentaries. When one of those came to light in Wittenberg, Luther apparently forgot his earlier caveats and wrote an enthusiastic preface in 1528 to the *Commentarius in Apocalypsin ante centum annos aeditus*.[16] He wrote the preface, he says, especially to show everyone "that we are not the first to interpret papacy to mean the reign of the Antichrist."[17] It is plain that he feels that he and his contemporaries live in a better age than the author of the *Commentarius*, when Christ is more fully revealed and waging a more open (and, it is to be hoped, final) war on the pope and his lackeys. Luther's preface has very slight eschatological overtones but expresses no overt eschatological expectations.

Having put his name to a *Commentary on the Apocalypse*, Luther could hardly carry on voicing such a negative view of it in 1530. Erasmian-like considerations were left behind. Questions such as the author's exaggerated praise of his own work as proof of nonapostolicity no longer played any part. Without going into the authorship question, Luther combined the problem of obscurity and that of the book's prophetic value into one. He begins the

1530 preface by outlining three types of prophecy. The most explicit, need-
ing no further explanations, are the prophecies of Christ uttered by Moses,
David, and other Old Testament prophets, as well as prophecies of the final
Antichrist and false teachers uttered by Christ and the apostles themselves.
The second type of prophecy consists of figures or symbols which are interpreted by the prophet himself—the best examples here are Joseph's and
Daniel's interpretation of dreams and Daniel's interpretations of symbols
or visions (Dan. 7). The third type of prophecy consists of uninterpreted
figures or symbols visited upon saints by the Holy Spirit, in accordance with
Peter's prophecy in Acts 2.18. The Apocalypse, according to Luther, should
be placed in the last category, but, contrary to what might be expected, this
time this placement does not make it a nonapostolic text. Going back somewhat on his categorical affirmations of 1522, and referring to Eusebius of
Caesarea's *Historia ecclesiastica* 3.25, the reformer decides to leave the question open:

> Because of the uncertainty of its interpretation and its hidden meaning,
> we have so far abstained from commenting on it, especially as some an-
> cient Fathers considered it not to be the work of S. John the Apostle, as we
> can read in the *Ecclesiastical History* 3.25. We persist in this doubt, but this
> should not stop anyone from considering it the work of John the Apostle,
> or whatever they wish.[18]

Despite this tolerant counsel to his readers, it is plain that Luther considers the Apocalypse an inferior and difficult prophecy on which nothing
of any value has been written.[19] It is important to note a shift of emphasis
between the 1522 and the 1530 prefaces. In the latter, Luther no longer insists openly on the text's capacity to "convey Christ" (*Christum treyben*) as a
criterion of canonicity. In fact, he seems to have lost all interest in the problem. He has, however, picked up on the problem of apostolic authorship.
Although he leaves the matter open and, unlike Erasmus, does not get caught
up in disentangling the identities of John the Theologian and John the Evangelist, he now openly questions the authorship of the book. Having once
decided to comment on the contents, however briefly, he could no longer
use the book's total absence of the Christian message and its obscurity as
arguments for noncanonicity. Yet, he obviously did not want his readers to
think that the Apocalypse could now be handled like any other book in the
New Testament, or that allegory, which he was driven to using in his own
preface, could be used indiscriminately. He instead fell back on questioning
the authority of the person who wrote it.

Luther's 1530 preface thus sets out to be an interpretation of an inferior,
obscure prophecy. Luther adopts a historical method. Seeing as John was
supposed to be prophesying events that were future to his own time, that is,
future troubles and disasters for Christianity, it seems only reasonable to look
at church history from John's to approximately Luther's time and to com-

pare the disasters that have befallen the church with John's prophecy. It is important to note that the exegetical details of the 1528 anonymous *Commentarius* are vastly different, and, although it does not at any time cast a doubt on the apostolic authorship of the Apocalypse, it too sees the text as a prophecy by John of future disasters for the church, beginning with the apostle's era and finishing *after* 1380 (the date of composition of the *Commentarius*).

> This book contains things that God revealed to John and that John revealed to the church; it tells us how great are the tribulations that the church suffered in its early days and suffers now and will suffer at the time of the Antichrist.[20]

Whatever the fourteenth-century commentary did or did not do for Luther's appreciation of the Apocalypse, it at least provided the reformer with his basic hermeneutical scheme. Although the rest of his 1530 preface does not touch overtly on the question of apostolic authorship, we shall nonetheless analyze it here, as the very fact of interpreting the book meant that Luther, *volens nolens*, reevaluated its status. Indeed, to write a preface which would be at all coherent, Luther had to have recourse to allegory—the very thing he reproached the book for.

Interpreting the angels in Apc 1 to mean bishops or teachers of Christian doctrine, Luther takes Apc 1–3 to be a representation of the coming to be of the seven churches of Asia and an injunction to those churches to grow and improve, despite the false and heretical bishops and shepherds who prevail in the book. Apc 4 and 5 depict all of Christendom and its future suffering. The four riders depict future troubles in detail: persecution by worldly powers, war, hunger, and pestilence for all those who despise God's word. In Apc 7 and 8, all the future spiritual troubles—in other words, main heresies—are revealed under the guise of the four wicked angels (out of the total of seven) of Apc 7. However, Luther notes, there is also the good angel holding a golden censer and offering up prayers, who is in possession of the pure word of God. "Such angels are the holy Fathers such as Spiridion, Athanasius, Hilary, the Council of Nicaea, and their like."[21]

The four wicked angels represent what to Luther are the four main heresies. The first angel is "Tatian with his Encratites," who combined the worst of all worlds with their marriage ban and emphasis on good works, "just like the Jews." Luther thus places the belief in the saving power of good works at the very beginning of all Christian heresies, "forever reborn with new teachers and under new names such as Pelagianism, etc." The second angel represents Marcion "with his Cataphrygians, Manichaeans, Montanists," etc., who elevate their spirituality over the Scripture and are hurled down from heaven to earth like the blazing mountain (Apc 8), just like Müntzer and his fanatics in Luther's own day. Having thus identified the central doctrine of the Roman Catholic Church with Encratism and Müntzer and his disciples

with Marcion and the Gnostics, without paying much attention to historical accuracy, the reformer cannot but identify Origen, "the third angel," and
his philosophy with the scholastic theology of his time. Equally inaccurate
is his identification of Novatian, "the fourth angel," and "his" Cathars with
the clergy of Luther's time "who want to be purer than all the others."

In other words, the four wicked angels of Apc 7 and 8 are a symbolic
representation of the four main evils in Christianity—good works, spiritual understanding of Scripture, philosophy, and excessive power of the
clergy—which recurred in various guises up until Luther's own time and
his Reformation.

Indeed, as the sequel of his preface shows, the subsequent chapters of
the Apocalypse represent a steady worsening of Christendom. The three woes,
or the three remaining angels out of the total of seven, are phenomena so
well known that they do not require any specific correlates from Luther's
own time. The first woe (fifth angel) is Arius, the second (sixth angel) is
Mahomet, and the third (seventh angel) is the papacy as an institution.
However, so as not to plunge his readers into total despair, Luther interprets
the two witnesses of Apc 11 and the pregnant woman of Apc 12 as symbols of
pious Christians who remain steadfast despite the woes visited upon them.

For Luther, Apc 13 describes the flowering of the papacy with all its
imperialistic designs, and Apc 14–16 tells of the storming of the papacy by
the Gospel. Apc 17 is simply a history of the papacy, and Apc 18 and 19 depict the downfall of Roman supremacy and the victory of God's word.

Luther does not make it clear at what stage Satan was chained up for a
thousand years. All he says in commenting on Apc 20 is that Satan has been
chained up for the past *thousand years*, and that the *thousand years* are to be
counted from the time that the Apocalypse was written: "[A]t the same time
the devil too was chained up." Luther is well aware that the Messianic period does not literally cover a *thousand years*, as he quickly says that "the
calculation does not have to be exact minute for minute." The concept of
the millennium is reduced to the very minimum in Luther's exposition of
Apc 20. What matters to the reformer is that Satan is about to be released
again and will march across the earth with Gog and Magog, or the Turks,
whereupon the Last Judgment will follow. The heavenly Jerusalem is in
heaven and offers eternal consolation to the good Christian.[22]

Leaving open the question of the book's canonicity served Luther's
purpose: Resorting to allegory, he made it correspond to the chief points of
his reforming program while sketching out a conception of church history
that was later to be adapted and developed by the *Centuries of Magdeburg*.[23]
While the whole of the period from the beginning of Christianity until the
Last Judgment (Luther's own era) could be considered the millennium, that
is, the chaining up of Satan, the period from the second until the fifteenth
century could only be seen as one of steady decline, reaching its lowest ebb
when the power of the papacy was at its height, and then recovering its pu-

rity at the time of the Reformation, just as Satan was about to be unleashed prior to the Last Judgment. Luther's 1530 preface did contribute to the rehabilitation of the Apocalypse as a source of prophecy. However, it is important to bear in mind that nearly all its prophecies referred to events that were already in the past by the time Luther was writing. The only future event was the forthcoming Last Judgment. Luther thus confirmed the eschatological value of the book and also used it as a programmatic work for the development of his conception of church history.

François Lambert (1528)

Before the appearance of Luther's 1530 preface, in the climate of general suspicion about the Apocalypse generated by Erasmus, there appeared what is nowadays considered the first major Protestant commentary on the Apocalypse. Its author, François Lambert, shared neither Erasmus' nor Luther's views about the book's apostolic authorship and canonicity. We shall be referring to the commentary at some length in subsequent chapters. Here we shall give the reader a brief reminder of Lambert's life and career and examine his preface to the first edition.

François Lambert was born in 1486 and entered the Franciscan order in Avignon at the age of fifteen, very quickly acquiring a name for himself as a preacher. In 1522, he met Ulrich Zwingli during one of his journeys and converted to the Reformation as a result of the meeting. In 1523 and 1524, he was in Wittenberg, where he wrote several works, including commentaries on Hosea and Luke. In 1524, he moved to Metz, then to Strasbourg, where he produced more biblical commentaries.

In 1526, he was summoned by the Landgrave Philip of Hesse, who wanted to call a synod with a view of reforming the church of Hesse. Lambert was assigned the task of drawing up the theses for the debate. The synod took place in Homberg on 2 October 1526 and lasted until 23 October; Lambert successfully defended 158 Reformation theses, encountering very little opposition. In May 1527, he was appointed professor of theology at Marburg and, shortly after his appointment, gave his lectures on the Apocalypse, which he subsequently wrote up as a commentary. In 1529, he took part in the Marburg colloquy, where he defended Zwingli's doctrine of the Eucharist, thus losing many of his Lutheran friends. His theology was in general rather idiosyncratic, and historians are divided as to the date of his conversion to Zwingli's doctrines: Some consider him to have passed into the Zwinglian camp in 1528; others think that he ceased to be Lutheran the moment he set foot in Wittenberg in 1523.[24]

His commentary on the Apocalypse appeared for the first time in Marburg, in 1528. It was entitled *Exegeseos Francisci Lamberti Auenionensis in sanctam Diui Ioannis Apocalypsim libri VII. In Academia Marpurgensi praelecti*. The printer was Franz Rhode. The commentary was reissued in Marburg in the same year, then reedited in Basel by Nicholas Brylinger in 1539.[25] Contrary to what is generally supposed,[26] Lambert's commentary was *not* cannibalized by Antoine du Pinet for his *Familère et briefve Exposition sur l'Apocalpyse de sainct Jehan l'apostre* (1539), as we show later.

Did Lambert know Erasmus' and Luther's doubts when he started lecturing on the book? He certainly knew something about them when he wrote up his lectures in commentary form; otherwise, it is difficult to explain the rather ostentatious title (*holy* Revelation of *saint* John) and above all his second preface, which is a plea for the canonicity of the book of Revelation as a book of prophecies by John the Evangelist in person. In all, the commentary contains two prefaces and a short *argumentum*. The first preface, addressed to Landgrave Philip, presents Philip as leader of the heavenly Jerusalem come down to earth, just before the Second Coming. Some passages are sufficiently explicit to make the reader think that Lambert sees Philip's Reformation as the blessed period preceding the Second Coming. Thus he declares:

> You wish sincerely to rule by your word over the people entrusted to you as steward of the holy church of your kindom. For this book talks about the government of this kingdom from the death of Christ until the end of the World. Thanks to the gift which is granted rarely to princes by God's mercy, you have become one of those kings who have gloriously transported into his own state our holy Jerusalem which is coming down from heaven, in accordance with the prophecy of the Holy Spirit in chapter 21 of this book: *And the kings of the earth shall bring into it all their splendor.* (Apc 21.24)[27]

We shall be discussing the question of Lambert's probable millenarian tendencies elsewhere. Still, after stating that Philip's Reformation of Hesse contributed to bringing the heavenly Jerusalem down to earth, he could hardly go back on his word by questioning the canonicity of the Apocalypse! On the contrary, as the first "orthodox" Protestant theologian to see its potential as a text prophesying the Reformation as the messianic period, he had to show that its place in the canon was fully justified. The second preface to his commentary is thus best considered as an attack on both Erasmus and Luther.

Lambert begins by defending the prophetic status of the book. Just as God revealed to the Old Testament prophets his judgment against the wicked, and also salvation, peace, and victory for the pious believers, in the same way, once the Gospel had been announced by Jesus and the apostles, the Lord himself revealed the contents of the Apocalypse to the apostle John. The allegories, considered by the ex-Franciscan as "most fortunate" (*iucundissimi typi*), were intended as consolation for all the faithful and depicted everything that would come to pass after the Passion until the end of the world in all the Christian churches. Without dwelling on any historical details, in contrast to Luther, he asserts that the book describes—in what manner; by what wonderful providence, virtue, and order; and with what wisdom, glory, and power—Christ the King, Lord, and Almighty Ruler governs his kingdom. Lambert is quite happy to admit that the book is unclear and difficult to interpret and that it needs to be compared with other books in the Scripture to enable us to understand it. However, he finds this not merely acceptable but, again unlike Luther, commendable. Mysteries of such great importance should only become clear to those who are prepared to study the Scriptures in depth. After some practical advice to his readers on how to make sense of figures and visions of the Apocalypse (they should elucidate the meaning of figures by looking at the meaning of similar figures found in other biblical books; they should not attempt to search out the symbolic significance of every detail of every vision but interpret each vision as a whole), Lambert has almost succeeded in assimilating the Apocalypse to any other biblical book. Contrary to Luther, he finds that the prophecies of the Apocalypse should be interpreted like all Old Testament prophecies: Overinterpretation of symbols is to be avoided but so too is the interpretation of symbolic expressions as literal statements. There is no hint of the three-tier system of prophecy, the linchpin of Luther's second preface, which had not been written when Lambert published his lectures. However, Lambert did know Erasmus' *Annotations* of 1522, as he very briefly counters it in the final section of his second preface. Yes, he says, referring indirectly to Jerome's commentary on Ezek. 36, he shares Justin Martyr's and Origen's opinion that it was written by the apostle John, the author of the Gospel.[28] As proof of authorship, he adduces not merely the *spiritus scribentis* ("the author's inspiration")—thus making very short work of Erasmus' stylistic arguments—but first and foremost "a very ancient Greek manuscript, without the usual breathing signs of which many copies were made in the famous Academy of Alcala, in Spain." Lambert says he owns one of the copies, which is very clearly entitled "The Apocalypse of the holy apostle, John the Evangelist *and* Theologian."[29] Lambert had obviously very little patience with the doubts about John's identity expressed by Eusebius, Erasmus, and others and felt that they could be easily silenced by a reference to the *Complutensian Polyglot*. His brief and naïve philological arguments, when read together with his sophisticated theories about how to interpret the book's symbols and visions, show that Lambert had sensed the danger contained in Luther's first preface and in Erasmus' annotation: To him, the Apocalypse was the text that clearly prophesied the Reformation, and so it had to be maintained in the canon.

Frans Titelmans

Lambert had not overtly sought to provoke a quarrel with either Luther or Erasmus. However, unlike both of them, he was convinced of the theological value of the Apocalypse: It contained what Christ had taught would happen between the Passion and the end of the world. What theological value was imputed to the book by Frans Titelmans is not clear. Yet, it was he who, in his *Libri duo de authoritate libri Apocalypsis*, published in 1530, openly attacked Erasmus' pronouncements.[30]

Frans Titelmans (1502–1537) was, as is well known, one of Erasmus' fiercest enemies and opposed practically all that Erasmus stood for. Although a good philologist, he was a partisan of allegorical exegesis, as witnessed, among other things, by his *Commentary on the Psalms* (1531), his most popular work of exegesis. He launched his first attack on Erasmus in his *Commentary on Romans* (1529).[31] Was his defense of the canonicity of the Apocalypse only a year after his *Romans* simply the reflex of a man who thought that everything that Erasmus did had to be attacked? This does not seem likely, given that, as has been shown, Erasmus' annotation on the Apocalypse provoked only a slight reaction from his Roman Catholic adversaries, who did not view the book with any great favor in the first half of the sixteenth century. It is more likely that Titelmans read the annotation in its 1522 version and sensed the likelihood of the Apocalypse disappearing from the canon. There is no indication that the Franciscan would have wished to keep it there because of its prophetic significance. However, he feared quite legitimately that the removal of the Apocalypse from the canon or even just its weakening on philological grounds constituted a threat to the established tradition and therefore to the authority of the church. Verbose and tendentious though his attack was, it certainly did not miss its mark, hence Erasmus' letter to the Friars Minor of Louvain complaining of virulent attacks.[32]

What Titelmans aimed to do was to exploit Erasmus' hesitancy to break with the *consensus ecclesiae*, despite the evidence provided by the church Fathers. He therefore had to show his adversary that he was mistaken in his reading of the Fathers and that the *consensus* was unbroken from the apostolic era onward. If his demonstration proved successful, Titelmans could then use the work of any theologian from any period to refute Erasmus' doubts. Thus, referring to Jerome's *De viris illustribus* and to Johannes Trithemius' *Catalogus scriptorum ecclesiasticorum*, Titelmans notes that the first commentaries on the Apocalypse go back to the second generation of Christians. Among the earliest commentators, he naturally singles out Justin Martyr and Irenaeus. He means, obviously, Justin's *Dialogus contra Tryphonem*, chapter 81, and Irenaeus' *Contra haereses* 5.31.2–5.36, neither of which he would have known firsthand. Justin's *Dialogue with Trypho* was unpublished in 1530, and Irenaeus' work, which had appeared in Erasmus' edition in 1526, ended at book V, verse 31.2, and lacked the millenarian ending, which did not come to light until 1575.[33] The millenarianism of the ante-Nicene Fathers, as attested by Jerome, made Erasmus doubt the value of their testimony. Titelmans, however, ignores the issue completely. What matters to him is the sheer quantity of very early commentaries on the Apocalypse.

Basing his information on Jerome's *De viris illustr.*, he adds to the names of Justin and Irenaeus those of Melito of Sardis, Hippolytus, and Victorinus of Poetovio. It was the first book of the New Testament to receive a commentary, he adds triumphantly, before going on to list later commentators: Tyconius, Cassiodore, Apri[n]gius, Isidore of Seville, the Venerable Bede, Alcuin, Haymo of Halberstadt (in fact, of Auxerre), Rabanus Maurus, Rupert of Deutz, Richard of St. Victor, Alexander of Hales. Although it in fact contains several inaccuracies and misattributions, the line is to all intents and purposes unbroken. Titelmans takes no interest in his authors' theological biases, nor has he any firsthand knowledge of most of the commentaries he lists. Furthermore, unlike Erasmus, he does not distinguish between the Greek church and the Latin church, although he must be aware that most of the authors he cites are Latin, late and respectable. Less universally respected medieval commentators such as Joachim of Fiore and his, as it happens, Franciscan imitators are simply left out.

However, Titelmans was not naïve and knew that any consensus established thus did not answer Erasmus' point about the Greek church's doubts about the apostolic authorship of the book. Neither Dionysius of Alexandria nor Eusebius of Caesarea could be included, and it was plain that the consensus that Titelmans was attempting to establish was incomplete. To remedy this, he had to find a guarantor earlier than Justin Martyr or Irenaeus, one who went back to the time of the first apostles and who had known John the Evangelist personally. Who better than Dionysius the Areopagite?[34] Ignoring the doubts justly cast upon Dionysius' identity by Lorenzo Valla and by Erasmus himself, Titelmans refutes the Dutch humanist's point that recourse to allegory in the Apocalypse constitutes proof of nonapostolic authorship by citing the famous *Letter Nine* by Paul's companion, who was also a contemporary and correspondent of John the Evangelist! It is just as well to bear in mind here that, despite the efforts of Valla, Erasmus, and several Protestant theologians, the authenticity of "Dionysius the Areopagite" was not finally disproved in most Roman Catholic circles until well into the eighteenth century.[35]

Titelmans begins by citing (pseudo-)Dionysius *a contrario* prior to showing how his pronouncements on allegory fully vindicate the apostolic authorship of the allegorical Apocalypse. The relevant chapter in Titelmans' book is entitled "Ex Dionysio Areopagita causa assignatur ob quam videntur nonnullis hae reuelationes in contemptum venisse" (From [the work of] Dionysius the Areopagite we give the reason why some have come to despise these revelations). It begins with a citation from pseudo-Dionysius' *Letter Nine* to Titus:

> Those Fathers who teach arcane wisdom leave untrained minds imprinted
> with great absurdity if they expose mystical truth, inaccessible to the pro-

fane, by resorting to daring and abstruse puzzles. That is why so many of
us find it difficult to believe in divine mysteries. For we study them only
with the aid of linguistic and corporeal symbols, whereas we should be contemplating the mysteries in themselves, which are bare and transparent.[36]

Titelmans' choice of passage is tendentious. In *Letter Nine*, the pseudo-
Dionysius actually says that the unskilled are unable to cope with the supreme noncarnal unity of God, having been taught to apprehend it only via
a multiplicity of symbols, all of which are perceptible to the senses. He makes
not the slightest reference to the allegorical nature of the Apocalypse. In fact,
the passage, if read with Erasmus' strictures in mind and out of context, would
seem to condemn the allegorical nature of the book of Revelation. However,
Titelmans expounds it in such a way that it ends up refuting Erasmus' point.
Instead of following on logically and denying allegory in the teaching of
theology, the Franciscan specifies that symbolism and allegory constitute even
greater obstacles to the understanding of the sacred science if students are
not simply unskilled but also perverse, "as is only too often the case in our
unfortunate times." He then explains Dionysius' dual theology, which makes
a distinction between "the arcane and mystical theological tradition . . . symbolic and pertaining to mysteries, and the philosophical and demonstrative
theology."[37] The former sort, naturally available only to the initiated few,
includes the Apocalypse. According to Titelmans, all those who understand
Dionysius' words correctly "will have no problem in understanding that the
allegorical nature of the book makes it a very worthy representative of apostolic weight and dignity."[38] That the pseudo-Dionysius does not refer to the
Apocalypse once in his *Letter Nine* is neither here nor there, so far as the
Franciscan is concerned.

By his medieval use of the Areopagite as an *auctoritas*[39] (i.e., by giving a
"benign" interpretation to a passage on an unrelated subject by a theologian
thought to be authoritative, so as to prove a preconceived point of doctrine),
Titelmans has proved his point, at least to his own satisfaction: The most
apostolic of the Greek Fathers and a contemporary of John the Evangelist
clearly granted his seal of approval to the Apocalypse and its allegories. Not
only is the book apostolic (and therefore fully canonical), it is also directed
at those who are "the most eager to be initiated into sacred mysteries." Any
historical investigation into its origins is thus quite irrelevant; Dionysius of
Alexandria and Eusebius were simply mistaken. The pseudo-Dionysius becomes the linchpin of Titelmans' consensus.

Once this framework has been established, Erasmus' individual arguments become very easy to manage by invoking any single author from the
consensus. Thus, refuting the argument regarding the frequent repetition
of the name *John*, Titelmans cites the testimony of Rupert of Deutz, the
twelfth-century commentator. Rupert notes that John does indeed repeat
his name three times, but that this is not to be taken as an attempt at self-
aggrandisement: John was simply trying to stamp the difficult revelations

he was about to expound with the mark of apostolicity. Titelmans notes further that, commenting on Apc 1.1–2 ("he made it known by sending his angel to his servant John who has borne witness to the word of God"), Rupert sees it as conclusive proof of apostolic authorship (and therefore of the canonicity) of the book, as the passage is a straightforward reference to the prologue of the Fourth Gospel. Having thus summarized Rupert's testimony, Titelmans dwells on it at some length and finds it conclusive.[40]

The choice of Rupert is by no means arbitrary, given that the monastic theologian was viewed favorably by the reformers not just because of his commentary on the Apocalypse but also because of his doctrine of the Eucharist, which discarded transubstantiation in favor of impanation. Rupert's defense of the Johannine authorship of the Apocalypse was not a part of any real twelfth-century debate on the subject but simply a reaction to Eusebius' strictures. By making the abbot a part of the all-encompassing consensus, Titelmans made it seem as if Rupert's prologue was an answer to the doubts of Erasmus and to any sixteenth-century commentators (of Protestant persuasion) who were dubious about the apostolicity and canonicity of the book.

What of the manuscript allegedly seen by Erasmus (Titelmans quotes the passage from the *Annotations*) which had the name of "John the Theologian" and not of "John the Evangelist" in the title? Once again, the Franciscan can use the consensus to some effect by invoking his guarantor, "Dionysius the Areopagite," whose *Letter Ten* is addressed to "John the Theologian, apostle and Evangelist exiled on the island of Patmos" (Ioanni theologo et apostolo et euangelistae in Patmos insula relegato). This superscript proves incontrovertibly that *Ioannes Theologus*, author of the Apocalypse, is the same person as John the Evangelist.[41] Added evidence from Ephraim of Edessa, Suidas, and Theophylactus stresses the uniformity of the consensus as against Erasmus' lone voice.

However, Erasmus' attitude to the consensus was not overtly critical but, as we saw, ambivalent. On the one hand, he brought forward historical evidence likely to invalidate it; on the other hand, he bowed to it. The weak point in Erasmus' ultimate acceptance of the consensus was his hypothetical phrasing ("if, however, the church approves of this work in such a way that it wishes that John the Evangelist be considered as the author and the book itself have the same weight as the other books in the canon"), and this was why Titelmans had to eradicate his opponent's scepticism (as he said himself) by showing his adversary that the church's approval was unanimous and total, and that this was the ultimate criterion of canonicity.[42]

It is with this aim in mind that he notes that several books of the New Testament such as the Epistle to the Hebrews, the Epistle of James, the Second Epistle of Peter, and the Epistle of Jude were at one time or another subject to doubt among isolated groups or individuals. These doubts, however, pale into insignificance when confronted with the *consensus ecclesiae* on the biblical canon.[43]

Erasmus and Titelmans have different criteria of canonicity. To the Dutch scholar, despite his weak demurrers, the authorship, the style, and the content take precedence over the consensus; to Titelmans, the consensus overrules all other considerations, possibly with the exception of authorship. As we have shown, it was important to him to demonstrate that John the Theologian was also John the Evangelist, while arguing that the church's approval was the final criterion of canonicity.

So as to finally move Erasmus from his skeptical position, Titelmans attempts to isolate him from his fellow humanists by citing at some length Jacques Lefèvre d'Etaples' preface to his edition of pseudo-Dionysius.[44] The Stapulensis, for whom Erasmus had a great respect despite their quarrel of 1517/18,[45] does indeed say in his preface of 1499 that the Gospels are the purest, as being the closest to their divine origin, and that they are closely followed by "the holy and arcane Revelations of Jesus, the Acts of the Apostles and their Epistles, and the works of the Prophets contained in the textbook of the Ancient Law."[46] There is no doubt in Titelmans' mind (rightly) that the "sanctae et arcanae Iesu reuelationes" is another way of referring to the Apocalypse and that therefore, in contrast to Erasmus, Lefèvre holds the book in high esteem on the authority of the pseudo-Dionysius and the rest of the consensus.

The choice of Lefèvre was likely to point up the isolation of Erasmus. The memory of their quarrel over Heb. 2.7 was still fresh. Moreover, by 1530, the Dutch humanist had been disowned by like-minded reformers such as Melanchthon and Oecolampadius[47] after refusing to depart from the *consensus ecclesiae* over the Eucharist, and after sounding a resolute no to the Reformation in his *Epistola in pseudeuangelicos* in 1529. He was in a difficult position, accepting the *consensus ecclesiae* on some points, for example, the Eucharist, but questioning it on the capital issue of canonicity. Titelmans certainly managed to show the isolated nature of Erasmus' position, but he did not manage to answer his very real questions about the place of the Apocalypse in the canon. Those were to occupy commentators for the best part of the century.

Sebastian Meyer

Sebastian Meyer was one of the staunchest and most explicit Protestant defenders of the canonicity of the book. As he had not read Lambert's commentary, his venture, entitled *In Apocalypsim Johannis Apostoli D. Sebastiani Meyer ecclesiastae Bernensis commentarius, nostro huic saeculo accommodus, natus et aeditus*,[48] can be considered completely independent,[49] even though Sebastian Meyer was, like François Lambert, a Franciscan. Born in Alsace, he exercised the office of reader at the Franciscan monastery in Berne between 1521 and 1524, while supporting from as early as 1515 the reforming movement initiated by Thomas Wyttenbach and the future reformer of

Berne, Berthold Haller. In 1523, Meyer was present at Zwingli's first disputation in Zurich. The following year, however, he had to leave Berne after a
quarrel with the reader of the rival (Dominican) convent. He left the
Franciscan order shortly afterward, settled in Strasbourg, and married. Between 1531 and 1535, he lived in Augsburg. He attempted to retire to
Strasbourg at the age of seventy but was called back to the ministry by the
Bernese Council after the death of Berthold Haller. It was at that time that
the Bernese church went through a period of bitter struggle. Erasmus Ritter
and Caspar Megander were inflexible Zwinglians, whereas Peter Kunz and
Meyer himself sought an agreement with the Lutherans. Kunz's aggressive
attitude was at least partly responsible for Megander's exile. Disillusioned
by the conflict, Meyer withdrew in 1541 and died four years later, in 1545.
According to Vuilleumier,[50] his commentary on the Apocalypse appeared
in 1541–1545. However, Wilhelm Bousset in the introduction to his classic
commentary of 1906, *Die Offenbarung Johannis*,[51] cites Panzer's *Annales
typographici* in favor of 1534 as marking the date of the *editio princeps*. Bousset
himself, however, used the 1603 Zurich edition and had never seen the 1534
printing. None of the copies of Meyer's commentary that I consulted bears
a date. However, the title of the work would suggest 1536–1545 as the more
likely date of publication, for it is extremely unlikely that Meyer would have
given himself the title of "ecclesiasta bernensis" prior to 1536.

As is shown by his preface, *De libri Apocalypsis autoritate, dignitate et
vsu*, Meyer took early Luther's and Erasmus' criticisms of the Apocalypse
very seriously and felt he had to counter them. Interestingly enough, the result
was that, although he almost certainly had no knowledge of Titelmans' work,
the method he uses to rehabilitate the Apocalypse is very similar to that of
Erasmus' adversary. In fact, it could legitimately be argued that it was due
to their Franciscan roots that both Titelmans and Meyer defended the Apocalypse in a similar way, despite their confessional differences.

Meyer begins by defending the apostolic authorship of the book, which
he separates from the issue of its canonicity. He notes with sadness that both
the author and the authority of the book proved to be matters of contention,
not only among recent authors but also among the ancients: Some have thought
that the author was John the Apostle, others that he was John the Theologian
or John the Presbyter, a disciple of the apostles (the allusion to Eusebius is barely
concealed). Unlike Titelmans, Meyer is aware that the condemnation of the
Apocalypse by the Greeks was harsher than its condemnation by the Western
church, for he notes that Latin churchmen have always tended to attribute the
book to John the Apostle. His guarantor here is, interestingly enough, the
millenarian Tertullian, who asserts against Marcion:

> We have churches which were founded by John. For although Marcion
> rejects the Apocalypse, the line of bishops, going right back to the origins,
> agrees on John as the author.[52]

Tertullian guarantees the consensus, which in turn guarantees the apostolic authorship of the book. However, apostolic authorship is not, in Meyer's eyes, synonymous with canonicity, for he insists:

> But it is a matter accepted so generally among ecclesiastical authors that this book is not just the work of the apostle John but also part of the canon of the Scripture, that its authority is fully recognized in all the churches throughout the world, and several famous men have commended it with fulsome praise and have clarified it in commentaries that they published.[53]

Although the consensus that follows naturally does not include the pseudo-Dionysius, it is nonetheless nearly as massive and all encompassing as the one constructed by Titelmans, beginning with the second generation of Christians, Justin and Irenaeus, and moving through chronologically to include Augustine, Venerable Bede, Tyconius ("a very worthy author except for his Donatism"), Haymo of Halberstadt (i.e., of Auxerre), Rupert of Deutz, "and some others"—not to mention "a multitude of more recent commentaries and annotations, containing very many useful things." Although the names mentioned are numerically fewer than those in Titelmans' work, Meyer strives for a similar impression of universal agreement against which any individual view seems eccentric and inconsequential. However, unlike Titelmans, Meyer never once mentions Erasmus (or, for that matter, Luther) by name, even when there is no doubt that his appeal to Jerome's letter 129 (to Dardanus) is meant to provide an antidote to Erasmus' use of the same source to damage the credibility of the Apocalypse. Jerome's testimony in letter 129 is indeed rather more favorable to it (and to the Epistle to the Hebrews) than Erasmus' note would lead his reader to suppose. That is no doubt why Meyer cites it *in extenso*:

> [A]nd nonetheless we accept both the texts, following not the custom of our time but the authority of ancient authors who have cited extensively from both, not as if they were apocryphal—seeing as exceptionally they also cite from pagan authors—but treating them as fully canonical and ecclesiastical.[54]

The Bernese preacher thus shows that not only was Jerome favorable to the Apocalypse but that he too, like Meyer himself (and Tertullian), was dependent chiefly on the consensus for establishing its canonicity. As might be expected, Meyer does not refer to Jerome's condemnation of the chiliasm of the early Fathers or to the link between their chiliasm and their high opinion of the Apocalypse, which Jerome (and Erasmus after him) had spotted so well. Jerome's condemnation of chiliasm naturally relativized his approval of the Apocalypse. Indeed, it is well to remember that Jerome rewrote Victorinus of Poetovio's commentary on the book in such a way as to neutralize its millenarianism.

Meyer, like Titelmans, prefers to ignore the question of chiliasm. In the second half of his preface, he raises, in a somewhat disorderly fashion, different points to do with the *consensus ecclesiae* and the apostolic authorship of the work before moving on to its style and content and a more detailed refutation of Luther and Erasmus. Meyer has already established that all (to all intents and purposes) ecclesiastical authors have written commentaries on the book and that great churchmen such as Tertullian and great biblicists such as Jerome established its canonicity on the basis of the consensus. He now notes that all Fathers who wrote on the canon of the Scripture included the Apocalypse (he refers particularly to Jerome, Eusebius, and Origen, as cited by Eusebius in *Hist. Eccl.* 6.25) and that even Dionysius of Alexandria, who disputed its apostolic authorship, had a high opinion of it. Moreover, he notes, all histories report that John the Apostle was exiled to Patmos under Domitian and then returned to his own church at Ephesus. Given that the author of the Apocalypse says that he is in Patmos at the moment of writing and that his name is John, would those who deny that the Apocalypse is the work of John the Apostle like to suggest another candidate?[55]

Despite this rhetorical flourish, Meyer obviously has not yet managed to convince himself that he is dealing with a biblical book like any other, for he concludes somewhat lamely:

> From all that has been said so far, it follows we should consider this book as authoritative in such a way as to be able to use it when appropriate instead of rejecting it wholesale, as some do, while abusing its authority in matters of controversy.[56]

What Meyer is asking his readers to do is to ignore issues such as the rejection of the Apocalypse by the Greek church, its chiliasm, and, above all, doubts about the identity of its authority when referring to the Apocalypse. In other words, on the strength of the consensus, the book is to be given the benefit of the doubt.

Still without explicitly naming either Erasmus or early Luther, he criticizes their grounds for what he considers to be their rejection of the book: It is too obscure for a book of the New Testament, its author sings his own praises far too much, some church Fathers rejected the book, it does not teach Christ, John repeats his name as if he were writing a promissory note. We saw that neither Luther nor Erasmus rejected the Apocalypse outright. In fact, their questionings might be considered rather timid by modern standards. To Meyer, however, they put forward "arguments which remove the authority of the book" (*argumenta . . . quibus huic libro autoritatem adimant*).

Having thus dealt with the consensus and the author's identity in the first part of his preface, Meyer now addresses the problems of the book's style and content. Dealing with Luther's arguments (still without naming him) first, he notes that the Scripture often disguises by figures and metaphors things that it most wants its readers to remember and learn as divine. He also warns Luther and his followers that one of Satan's designs is to render suspect those very things which should be honored most. (Here, Meyer gives the example of Jews who should have welcomed the announcements of Christ by the prophets instead of fearing them; the Antichrist of the Apocalypse, on the other hand, should be feared and not found suspect.) The obscurity of the author's style is further accounted for by his status as prophet. "They say" ("they" being, of course, Luther) that only Old Testament prophets, and not apostles, speak in riddles. However, Meyer retorts, no New Testament passage that touches on last things is clear, be it Matt. 24, 2 Thess. 2, or 2 Pet. 3. The author's *constant* use of figures is to be explained by the circumstances of the time he lived in: It was advisable to predict the forthcoming fall of the Roman Empire in terms of allegory, so as to avoid persecution. As for the author's inordinate praise of his own work, he has Meyer's full support: Why should he not praise a work that would be of very great use to the churches if only they went by it? He is also right, in Meyer's view, to threaten those who want to add to or subtract from the prophecy, seeing as apostolic doctrine must not be adulterated. Irenaeus of Lyon (Meyer cites Eusebius, *Hist. eccl.* 5.20) did after all exhort all future copyists of his treatise *De Ogdoade* to exercise the greatest possible care and to transcribe it as accurately as possible, an authorial sentiment which met with Eusebius' (who cites Irenaeus) full approval. John is doing no more than Irenaeus did: exhorting to precision so as to avoid any falsifications in the transmission of his work. Luther's last two arguments get very short shrift: It may well be that one or two church Fathers denied the canonicity of the Apocalypse, just as there were one or two Fathers who denied the authority of other canonical books. Most ancient theologians, from Dionysius of Alexandria to Jerome, praise it, and fulsomely at that. As for the Apocalypse not teaching Christ, Meyer flatly contradicts Luther's assertion: "On the contrary, throughout the text, Christ's priesthood, reign, and his power to judge is described as grandly and magnificently as in hardly any other book."[57]

It is interesting to note that although Meyer takes apart, point by point, Luther's preface of 1522, he seems to have no knowledge of Luther's preface of 1530. As has been noted, it is likely that Meyer's commentary was first published between 1536 and 1545. Is it at all conceivable that it was written between 1524 (Meyer's conversion to the Reformation) and 1530? Meyer's reference in the second part of his preface to Anabaptists "who share the opinion of those who teach that the visible kingdom of Christ should be established in the present century by force of arms, and all wicked men destroyed" could refer equally well to the Münster siege of 1535 or to Thomas Müntzer's peasant revolt ten years earlier. The one certain landmark is 1528, the date of publication of Lambert's commentary, which Meyer said he had not seen. Given that no more specific indication of the date of composition is to be found in the text of the commentary, we shall assume that the commentary was written sometime during Meyer's Bernese period and that it was published sometime before his retirement in 1541. Indeed, given his wish to seek agreement with the Lutheran party during his time in Berne, it would have been strange for him to publish at that very time a commentary that contained such overt criticism of Luther. On the other hand, however, Meyer ran no risk of provoking a controversy, given his great age. It is not inconceivable that he simply never read Luther's 1530 preface.

Luther, at any rate, as has already been shown, was not Meyer's sole adversary. However, it was only Erasmus' argument about the frequent repetition of the name *John* that the ex-Franciscan chose to refute in any detail. Either he had not read the whole of Erasmus' annotation or he decided that it was not worth the trouble of a detailed refutation. Refuting Erasmus' criticism of John's repetition of his own name, he simply cites a few examples of Christ's and Paul's locution "ego dico vobis."

Meyer is aware that he has just been arguing for the canonicity of a biblical book by invoking the *consensus patrum*.[58] This put him in a rather anomalous position as a Protestant commentator of the Apocalypse but seems to have had no ill effects on his reputation among other Protestant commentators of the book. It is also interesting that Meyer is the first commentator to distinguish between the issue of canonicity based on the consensus and the question of the identity of the author. Although the distinction is not very clearly drawn, it does exist: Dionysius of Alexandria is part of the consensus because he praised the Apocalypse (and therefore admitted it as canonical) while denying apostolic authorship. Historical evidence points to John the Apostle as author, and indeed, Meyer implies, most of the Fathers who make up the consensus do think that John the Apostle is its author, but this question is not of overwhelming importance. Yet, Meyer finally cannot see the book as a biblical book like any other, and his attempt to situate it within the genre of prophecy is a lot more hesitant than the attempt of François Lambert, or, as we shall see, of Theodore Beza. When all is said and done, the Apocalypse is to him a book whose authority needs to be defended and which must be used with caution. That is why the section on the book's authority is followed by a section entitled *De dignitate et vsu*, which we shall discuss in chapter 2.

Antoine du Pinet

Antoine du Pinet was born around 1510 and studied at Orléans at the same time that Calvin did. Between 1537 and 1543, he was a pastor at Ville-la-Grand near Geneva. He then moved to Lyon, where he spent the rest of his life in the service of "important people." It was during his time at Lyon that he translated Pliny's *Natural History* from Latin into French. He died in 1566 and is no doubt best remembered for his commentary on the Apocalypse which went through no fewer than five editions in the author's lifetime (1539, 1543, 1545, 1552, and 1557). The commentary has an interesting particularity of being composed in French. Its last edition (1557) contains by way of a preface the French translation of Theodore Beza's reply to Erasmus on the subject of the Apocalypse, which appeared in Latin in Beza's edition of the annotated New Testament in the same year.[59]

Du Pinet did not explicitly raise the question of canonicity in the first (1539) edition of his commentary. However, the second edition, published after the author had read Meyer's commentary, does contain a section entitled *De l'authorité et vsage de l'Apocalypse*. As might be expected, this turns out to be simply a French summary of Meyer's preface. The way du Pinet abbreviated it throws an interesting light on his conception of himself as popularizer of erudite commentaries. The Genevan clergyman leaves out anything to do with the *consensus ecclesiae*, which as we saw constituted the cornerstone of Meyer's defense of the Apocalypse. Du Pinet has nothing against the doctrine itself, but he obviously prefers to reduce it to its simplest common denominator:

> All the doctors are so in agreement over this that they attribute it to
> him [the apostle John] with one voice. And the church, be it Greek or Latin,
> also accepts it, given that certain readings from this book are part of the
> church service under the name of St. John.[60]

All the references to the Fathers who in one way or another pronounced themselves on the status of the Apocalypse disappear from du Pinet's preface, which becomes much easier for the uninitiated reader to follow: Not only is he spared the trouble of painfully stumbling through lists of obscure names, he does not need to worry about working out the distinction between canonicity (based on the consensus) and apostolic authorship, which also preoccupied Meyer.

How much of Meyer's original preface is left? The short answer is: very little. By establishing from the outset that all the doctors agree that the book is by John the Apostle and that both the Greek and the Latin churches attribute it to him, du Pinet has effectively assimilated the problem of canonicity to that of apostolic authorship and has, so to speak, drawn the teeth of Meyer's preface. He does, however, keep all of Meyer's statements on the obscurity of the language: The Scripture often resorts to metaphors to encourage us to strive for a better understanding of the mysteries of faith; when John was writing the Apocalypse, it was much more appropriate to resort to allegory in a description of the fall of the Roman Empire, so as to minimize the risk of persecution; despite the obscurity of its language, the book is not so obscure that it cannot be recognized as a prophecy of what would happen to the faithful and their adversaries after the Passion (du Pinet avoids tying the Apocalypse down in time). Du Pinet insists that the book teaches Christ, but there is no indication that he knew that Meyer's preface was directed against Erasmus and particularly against Luther.

After studying du Pinet's preface, the reader is left with the impression that the Apocalypse is the work of John the Apostle and that it is a useful book.

However, all the complexities of Meyer's position are erased. Du Pinet makes no contribution at all to the debate on canonicity; nor was it his purpose to do so, seeing as he intended his commentary for fairly untutored readers.

It is therefore interesting to note that in 1557 a French translation of Beza's note was appended to du Pinet's commentary. Beza's note was a monument of erudition refuting, point by point, Erasmus on the Apocalypse. Although it would have proved far too difficult for the public du Pinet had in mind, it nonetheless supplemented his commentary in at least one important aspect: It settled the canonicity question.

Theodore Beza

Beza's actual annotations on the Apocalypse were practically as scant as Erasmus' own; only the preface gave away the author's intentions. Why did Beza undertake to refute Erasmus' doubts in preference to Luther's? Several reasons could be given here, the main one being that, as is well known, Beza's *Annotations* and new Latin translation of the New Testament were intended to counter and supplant Erasmus.

Second, by 1557, Luther's doubts and objections carried no great weight in the Protestant camp, seeing as Luther's 1530 preface had managed to domesticate the Apocalypse, even if it did not actually rehabilitate it. However, the persistence of Erasmus' sceptical note meant that, despite the appearance of Protestant commentaries on the book by, for example, François Lambert, Sebastian Meyer, Antoine du Pinet, Theodore Bibliander (1545), Leo Jud (1542), and Heinrich Bullinger (1557), doubts lingered. Some Roman Catholic theologians persisted in thinking, mistakenly, that one of the hallmarks of the Protestant heresy was its rejection of the Book of Revelation. This could have been no more than a polemical device, given that Thomas de Vio Cajetan was quite open about his mistrust of the Apocalypse, and even a conservative theologian such as Jean de Gagny accepted it only grudgingly. Still, the polemical device persisted, and in 1566, Sixtus of Siena noted in his *Bibliotheca sancta* that the Protestants considered the Apocalypse neither as the work of John the Apostle nor as a part of the canon.[61] Beza's note, which stilled all lingering doubts within his own camp, obviously did not silence the opposition.

How does Beza's method of tackling Erasmus[62] differ from that of his Roman Catholic "predecessor" Titelmans, whose work he would in any case either not have known or deliberately ignored?

Although he relies extensively on the testimonies of the early church, Beza makes no attempt to establish any sort of *consensus ecclesiae*. What he aims to do first is select the most reliable testimonies, not necessarily with a very fortunate result, as we shall see. Second, he devotes more space to proving the apostolic authorship of the book than to arguing for its place in the canon. However, as we shall show, apostolic authorship is not synonymous with canonicity in Beza's eyes, and he does show that the book is indeed part of the canon not by virtue of what it teaches but by virtue of representing a particular literary genre (prophecy) which is also represented by other (fully canonical) books in the Bible. Needless to say, (pseudo-) Dionysius the Areopagite plays no active part in Beza's argument, having been relegated to the realm of the apocrypha by all Protestant theologians since Zwingli.

The actual note is structured so as to constitute a point-by-point reply and includes a full summary of Erasmus' criticisms. Yes, the apostolic authorship of the book was questioned by the Greeks (according to Jerome's testimony in his letter 129); yes, Dorotheus of Tyre makes no mention of John's having written the Apocalypse in Patmos or anywhere else; yes, Athanasius (Beza partly corrects Erasmus' error here) has doubts about the author's identity, as do Dionysius of Alexandria and Gaius, the latter considering the Apocalypse to be the work of Cerinthus. Granted that some church Fathers doubted the apostolic authorship of the book, there were many others who found it to be fully apostolic and a part of the canon. Beza cites by way of example the *Panarion* of Epiphanius of Salamis (365–403), who condemns (*haeresis* 51) as heretics all those who deny the canonicity of the Apocalypse. He then particularly insists that the book was not only approved but also commented by Justin Martyr and Irenaeus,[63] both "very ancient authors" (*antiquissimi scriptores*) who "adorned it with their commentaries." Beza would have known the *Dialogus contra Tryphonem*, in which Justin gives a chiliastic interpretation of the Apocalypse in chapter 81.[64] He most certainly would have known too the *Aduersus haereses*, at least up until 5.31.2, where Erasmus' edition ended. By reading those authors, but also by reading Jerome and Erasmus, he would have been aware that Justin's and Irenaeus' respect for the Apocalypse was due to their chiliasm. However, not wishing to damage the credibility of his guarantors, Beza makes no mention of it.

On the other hand, he rejects with total and undeserved contempt the testimonies of Dionysius of Alexandria and Eusebius: Dionysius is only known via Eusebius, and the latter, according to Calvin's successor, is not worth taking seriously, "as all learned men find that he lacks judgment in many of his writings" (*in quo docti omnes iudicium in plerisque scriptis requirunt*).[65]

Pursuing then the argument of the book's presumed lack of *apostolica grauitas* as proof of nonapostolic authorship, Beza takes as his authority Arethas, a tenth-century Greek compiler of a commentary on the Apocalypse, and notes that although (as Erasmus would have it) several *eruditissimi viri* have indeed argued that the book lacks apostolic weight, Arethas names several other equally learned men within the Greek church who have attributed it to John the Apostle. Indeed, Beza notes rightly that the book contains very little over and above what is to be found in the Old Testament prophecies.[66]

Beza also replies to Erasmus' objections to John's repetition of his own name "as if he were writing a promissory note, and not a book." Beza finds this indictment "weak and incoherent" (*infirmum ac imbecile*) and turns directly to the text in order to show his readers that the Apocalypse is not a historical account but a prophecy: As the truth of a prophecy depends entirely on the authority of the prophet, it is only natural that John should have found it necessary to repeat his name, just as did Jeremiah, Daniel, or Isaiah. Had the Apocalypse been a historical account, its truth would have been dependent on the truth of the events related, irrespective of the authority of the narrator.[67]

Beza could thus be said to kill two birds with one stone: He implicitly integrates the Apocalypse into the biblical canon while discounting the Lutheran view of the book as a history of the church. But then he returns to the problem of the author's identity: John the Evangelist was usually called John the Theologian by the ancients, and so manuscripts with the latter attribution seen by Erasmus are irrelevant to the debate. As for the difference of style between the Fourth Gospel and the Apocalypse, Beza's reply to Erasmus happens to be identical to Titelmans': Different subject matter calls for a different style. However, unlike the Franciscan, he adds as an afterthought that on purely stylistic grounds he would have been tempted to attribute the Apocalypse to Mark, who was also called John (in Col. 4.1).

Having proved to his own satisfaction that John the Apostle was indeed the author of the Apocalypse, Beza then returns to the question of canonicity, although, as we saw, the two questions are never clearly separated in his mind. The rough style of the Apocalypse is to Beza a proof of its canonicity: The book is an imitation of an Old Testament prophecy for which only Hebrew models were available to John. "Therefore no one should be surprised that his style is not particularly polished, seeing as he did not wish to depart from the prophets who wrote in Hebrew either by his vocabulary or by his style."[68]

We saw that Beza refused to discuss the chiliastic views of Justin and Irenaeus, whom he selected as privileged witnesses of the book's apostolic origin and canonicity. He was, however, prepared to discuss Erasmus' suspicion that the book postulated a millennium, as well as the Dutch scholar's thinly veiled wish to attribute it to Cerinthus. Subjecting the latter hypothesis to a careful scrutiny on the basis of *Panarion* (*haeresis* 28) of Epiphanius of Salamis, Beza concludes firmly that he finds no resemblance between the hedonistic earthly paradise postulated by Cerinthus and the *thousand years* of the Apocalypse.[69]

Thus reducing the question of chiliasm to that of Cerinthus' heresy on the basis of one hostile source, Beza effectively neutralizes the issue and avoids going into the delicate question of possible links between the *thousand years* and millenarian doctrines in general. Was he aware that this maneuver, although successful in the short term, was easy to see through and that he was implicitly opening the door to the chiliasm of Justin and Irenaeus? Probably. What mattered to him, however, was first and foremost to refute Erasmus' doubts, and there he was successful. The Apocalypse did not require any special handling. It was simply a continuation of Old Testament prophecies, written after the Ascension and containing for the most part prophecies that had already been fulfilled by Beza's time. In common with Old Testament prophecies, it was obscure and difficult to understand. "I would think," says Beza, "that the Holy Spirit wanted to assemble in this most precious book those things which the previous prophets had predicted would come to pass after the advent of Christ, and to those he added some that he knew would concern us."[70] The question of canonicity was thus, to all intents and purposes, settled: A biblical book dictated by the Holy Spirit and bearing the name of John could not have been written by anyone other than John the Apostle and was therefore a part of the canon.

Augustin Marlorat

Augustin Marlorat (1506–1561), author of *Noui Testamenti Catholica Expositio ecclesiastica* (1561), a sort of *catena aurea* of Protestant commentaries on the New Testament, was a contemporary of Beza's. He certainly would have known the latter's annotated New Testament (although he did not include it in his *Expositio*) and was indeed much admired by Beza as a commentator.[71] The first edition of the *Noui Testamenti Catholica Expositio ecclesiastica* was published in Geneva by Henri Estienne, only four years after the publication of the first edition of Beza's Latin Bible and the fifth edition of du Pinet's commentary on the Apocalypse with Beza's preface in French.

Marlorat was aware of the doubts surrounding the Apocalypse and was convinced that the book was canonical. However, he defended its canonicity mainly by an appeal to its content. His *argumentum* does contain implicit references to Beza's note, but the method adopted by the Frenchman was very much his own.

He begins the *argumentum* by admitting that many have doubted the status of the book; some have even obstinately refused to admit it into the canon. However, according to Marlorat, it would be a crime (*nefas*) to dispute its truth and authority, seeing its immense usefulness in the construction of the church and bearing in mind its reception by most of the ancient Fathers by a common consensus.[72] He also discounts all doubts cast upon the identity of the author, considering that they have already been proved to be unfounded by "many men famous for their great learning" (*multis summa eruditione praeclaris*). He much prefers to follow those who attribute the book, "full of consolation," to the apostle John or indeed to Mark, who was also called John. It is quite obvious that Marlorat is referring to Beza's note here. In his view, so he implies, Beza had already rehabilitated the

Apocalypse on historical and textual grounds. He, Marlorat, is more interested in its doctrine.

All prophecies are obscure so long as they are unfulfilled. This is especially true of the Apocalypse, as John could not speak plainly, at the time, of persecutions of Christians by the Roman Empire (Marlorat echoes Meyer here). Marlorat recommends that his readers carefully compare the Apocalypse to approved historical accounts of the church, so that they can see that he relates nothing but pure history. The French commentator is seen here to adopt Luther's 1530 interpretation of the Apocalypse, without Luther's mistrustful attitude. Indeed, Marlorat expands Luther's conception of the Apocalypse as key to church history, to include the fundamental doctrine of the Resurrection and the Last Judgment:

> For he [John] teaches us (typologically but more clearly than the prophets) about the state of the kingdom of Christ, the fate of the church, and the persecutions to which all those who seriously follow the Christian religion are exposed. . . . He reveals heaven itself to us and explains beautifully the veritable hope of the faithful; he also affirms the true resurrection of all flesh. He sketches out in detail the final end of the elect and the reprobate, the faithful and the unfaithful . . . and under dictation of the Holy Spirit, he demonstrates and convinces us.[73]

Marlorat was not the first Protestant theologian to see that the object of the Apocalypse was to provide an answer to the problem of how to cope with the present in view of Christ's first (past) and (future) Second Coming and his intervening presence "elsewhere."[74] He was, however, the first Protestant theologian to formulate the problem succinctly and to see that the Apocalypse of John provided a better solution to it than did any other biblical book. Its capacity to relate soteriology to history sufficed to guarantee its place in the canon. However, unlike Beza, Marlorat was not afraid to openly voice his conviction that the Antichrist was the papacy and that his reign was shortly to come to an end with Christ's glorious descent to sit at the Last Judgment.[75] The question of the canonicity of the Apocalypse was thus intrinsically linked to Marlorat's own experience as a persecuted Christian.

The Zurich School: Leo Jud, and Theodore Bibliander, and Heinrich Bullinger

As is well known, Ulrich Zwingli did not accept the Apocalypse as canonical. Overly influenced by Jerome's letter 129, he did not think that it was held to be canonical in the early church and regarded it as nonapostolic and lacking the heart and spirit of John.[76] However, Zwingli's opinion was not shared by his colleagues, and the void left by his silence on the subject was quickly filled. In 1542, Leo Jud published his German translation of Erasmus' *Paraphrases* on the New Testament. As Erasmus had left out the Apocalypse,

Jud simply added his own *Paraphrase* of it in German, thus making it available to the larger mass of the Swiss faithful.[77] The year 1545 saw the appearance of Theodore Bibliander's highly original commentary on the Apocalypse in Latin.[78] Heinrich Bullinger, who had attended Bibliander's lectures, was for his part greatly attracted to the Apocalypse from very early on, although his famous *Sermons* did not appear until 1557.[79]

Although Bibliander was the only one of the Zurich commentators to undertake a systematic defense of the book's canonicity, all three assumed that the text was a revelation divinely conferred upon the apostle John and as such automatically part of the canon. In his preface to the Latin Bible of 1543, Bullinger stated:

> The last book [of the Bible] written by the same apostle [John] bears a Greek title, for it is called the Apocalypse, which means Revelation. For in this book he depicts in prophetic style the fate of the church which the Lord revealed to him and all that would happen to the church until the end of time. You will find much here that has been borrowed from Ezekiel, Daniel, Zachariah, and other prophets. For it has so pleased God's goodness to admonish the church early and in good time of evils to come so that it might more wisely take care and pray more ardently to God. The New Testament canon contains no more books.[80]

Jud incorporated a statement on canonicity into his paraphrase of Apocalypse 22.18–19, which he interprets as a warning to all those who reject the book as apocryphal on finding that they cannot understand parts of it. He notes that to do so is a sin. Jud was the sole Protestant commentator to argue that the use of the Apocalypse in church liturgy provided a proof of its canonicity. Were it an apocryphal book, as some have claimed, it could only be read privately,[81] he asserted.

As we said, only Bibliander put forward a detailed and reasoned defense of the canonicity of the Apocalypse, using an impressive range of arguments. Addressing the Christian princes, he uses the Apocalypse to demonstrate that nothing is clearer and more authoritative than the Word of God. If the Apocalypse is the Word of God, it must be both authoritative and clear. Bibliander therefore divides his preface into two parts, the first part designed to show the book's authority or canonicity, and the second part to show its clarity. The second part is, as we shall see, less convincing, so Bibliander has to carry his demonstration over into the commentary itself. In the first part he sets out to show (against Erasmus) that the authority of a biblical book is not to be measured by any consensus of the church. To do so is to act like those half-hearted believers who declare that "they believe what their king believes." It is true, he continues, that many church Fathers accepted the Apocalypse as canonical, but there are just as many Fathers and councils (a reference to the canons of Laodicea) who condemned it. However, in Bibliander's view, neither a general approbation nor a general condemnation is enough to approve a biblical text as canonical or to remove it from the canon:

> We follow the judgment of men and we are under the sway of human
> authority, so long as we do not courageously approve the text because of
> itself and because of the majesty of God, whom we recognize and feel to be
> speaking here.[82]

Having eliminated the consensus as a criterion of canonicity, Bibliander
offers his reader the alternative criterion of Scripture as the exclusive vehicle
of divine revelation. But how is his reader to know whether the Apocalypse
contains divine revelation? Bibliander establishes several tests that can be
applied to the book. In accordance with Paul's injunction in 1 Thess 5.19–21
and John's injunction in 1 John 4.1–2, we must first test its spirit. If its spirit
confesses that Jesus Christ came to us in the flesh from God, then the book
is canonical. We must then examine it thoroughly sentence by sentence to
see if it breathes the glory of Christ and God the Father, and then see if it
conforms to the Decalogue and the Apostles' Creed in its teaching. Having
done that, we must check whether it accords with Paul's description of the
use of Holy Scripture in 2 Tim. 3.16–17, whether its style is the same as the
apostle John's style in writings known to be his, and whether the Christ it
represents is the Christ of the Gospels.

However, it is interesting to note that, having given an affirmative answer to all the questions concerning the divine origin of the text itself and
its conformity to other canonical texts, Bibliander does have recourse to
historical proof. His plea for the authority of the Apocalypse ends with an
interesting adaptation of Irenaeus' argument of apostolic tradition: The canon
of the Scripture—and, more particularly, the canon of the New Testament—
was determined by those who knew the apostles in person. Irenaeus and
Tertullian attest that the Apocalypse was written at the time of the apostles,
asserts Bibliander. Moreover, Irenaeus (*Adv. haer.* 5.30.1), when he criticizes
as forgers of the Scripture those who changed the number 666 into 616,
depends on the authority of his brethren who knew the apostle John and
heard him preach. Thus, apart from its intrinsic qualities, we know the
Apocalypse to be canonical because it was known as such to those who knew
the apostle. Arguments about John's exile in Patmos and the style of the
Apocalypse (especially the opening) being identical to that of John's other
writings close the first part of the preface devoted to the authority of the book.

Bibliander has found his own criterion of canonicity: the intrinsic qualities of the text and its attested link with apostolic times. What about the clarity
of the text? Here he is forced to admit that even commentators close to apostolic times found it difficult and were driven to reading Papias' commentary on it. However, Bibliander is quick to qualify this statement: Only the
sections on the Antichrist were a source of difficulty; the patristic commentators found all the other passages to be perfectly clear. Augustine himself
(in fact Caesarius of Arles) found the Apocalypse clear enough to make it
the theme of sermons to the common people. Epiphanius did call it apocryphal but only in the sense of its being recondite. Realizing that his assertions

in the preface are somewhat confused, Bibliander decides to show the clarity of the book in his chapter-by-chapter commentary:

> "But it will be best to go through the whole book, so that the clarity of the Word of God may appear more manifestly even in this book which all judge to be extremely obscure."[83]

Bibliander's arguments taken by themselves are not very convincing. If the Word of God was to be part of the canon *and* clear, why did the Apocalypse require a whole commentary to prove its clarity? However, by separating the issue of canonicity from that of clarity, Bibliander avoided falling into the trap that Erasmus and indeed Beza had fallen or would fall into, which consisted of arguing for the authority of a book that they had to weakly confess they did not understand. After 1545, the Apocalypse, at least in Zurich, was considered canonical because its clarity, which posed something of a problem to Bibliander, was indisputable for Bullinger.

Heinrich Bullinger

Bullinger attended Bibliander's lectures on the Apocalypse in 1544 and was deeply influenced by them, as he admits himself in his preface to his *Sermons*, dated January 1557:

> Thirteen years ago, he [Bibliander] read publicly upon this book of the Revelation of St. John, praising it greatly; and I would be mean and ungrateful if I did not confess to having been very much helped by him. He is the author of the *Relatio fidelis* printed in Basel in the year 1545, in which he explains this book chapter by chapter and gives it brief annotations.[84]

According to Bullinger, two features of the text show it to be divinely revealed and of apostolic authorship, first, what it says, and second, the clarity of its style and presentation. Obviously convinced by Bibliander's demonstration of the book's clarity, Bullinger can take it for granted.

His account of the canonical nature of the contents is, however, different from that of Bibliander, in that Bullinger links the Apocalypse expressly with the Lord's promise in John 14.16–26 to send the Holy Spirit to the apostles once he was back in heaven. The Apocalypse is part of the mission of the Holy Spirit: It was intended to show the apostles what would happen after the Ascension. It shows, according to Bullinger, that the church militant will always suffer but that Christ will always govern it by his Spirit and the Word of the Gospel. There is no doubt in the Zurich reformer's mind that the Lord himself is the author of the Apocalypse and John the Apostle is the Lord's mouthpiece. The Lord's message is thus announced to the seven churches, which represent the church universal. Because of this association of the Lord and the apostle, Bullinger considers the book as completely evangelical and apostolic, in other words, as representative of both the Gospels and the Epistles.[85]

The canonicity of the book thus became self-evident. However, Bullinger was not naïve and knew that no less a scholar than Erasmus had contested both the apostolic authorship and the canonicity of the book, and that Luther's and Zwingli's reception of it had been extremely unenthusiastic. It was not Bullinger's intention to counter Erasmus point by point, nor did he want to engage in any controversies in the preface to what were supposed to be sermons (albeit artificial ones) on a book which was completely canonical and completely clear. It was therefore in his first sermon that he listed the opinions of Erasmus, Luther, and Zwingli and refuted them, not by an appeal to the book's subject matter, but by an appeal to the *consensus patrum* (starting with Justin and Irenaeus), the very thing that Bibliander had deplored and that played no part in Bullinger's own conception of the book's canonicity, as outlined in his preface. Why this double standard? The very title of the work, *Sermons*, gives us a clue to Bullinger's real intentions. Naturally, Bullinger had not delivered his sermons on the Apocalypse in their printed form. Not only were they far too learned for the average faithful, they were written in Latin and not in German. In publishing them in that form, however, Bullinger did provide Protestant clergy with *material* for sermons on the Apocalypse. If they were to preach on it at all convincingly, they had to be sure that the book was clear and canonical, but they also had to know what had been written about it; how its canonicity had been questioned, by whom, and for what reason; and why those doubts were no longer valid. They were no longer valid, in Bullinger's opinion, for the simple reason that he and his contemporaries lived nearer the end of time and so could benefit from a fuller revelation of the prophecies of the Apocalypse. If those Fathers who accepted its canonicity (i.e., the majority, in Bullinger's view) could expose it to the faithful of their time, his own *Sermons* should be all the more convincing, being the work of one living just before the Last Judgment.[86]

The intrinsic value of the contents and clarity of the Apocalypse was thus conditioned, for Bullinger, by the temporal setting of its readers and interpreters. If in doubt, those latter could indeed seek solace in the consensus and ignore the lonely voices of dissent such as Erasmus, Luther, and Zwingli.

The End of the Century: François du Jon and David Pareus

By 1560, the canonicity of the Apocalypse was no longer an issue. Even though Erasmus' and, to a much lesser extent, Luther's doubts were still being refuted by commentators such as François du Jon in 1591 or David Pareus in 1618, no one had seriously questioned the authority of the Apocalypse since the 1520s, and therefore its commentators did not have to think up new arguments. That the authority and canonicity of the Apocalypse were being defended at all as late as 1618 was a tribute to the pertinence of Erasmus' attacks.

Chiefly known for his religious irenicism, François du Jon (Junius) was born in 1545 at Bourges and studied in Lyon and Geneva. After a brief phase of atheism, apparently brought on by reading Cicero's *De natura deorum*, he became a minister in Antwerp in 1565 and took part in the revision of the *Confessio belgica*. In 1567, he moved to Schönau, where he looked after the Walloon congregation until 1573, when the elector Frederick III called him to Heidelberg to assist Tremellius with the new Latin translation of the Old Testament. He had to leave Heidelberg after the accession of the Lutheran Ludwig VI and spent the next eleven years at Neustadt an der Hardt and Otterberg. He spent the last years of his life teaching theology at Leiden, where he died in 1602. His *Apocalypsis methodica analysis notisque illustrata* constitutes an infinitesimal part of his immense literary and theological output.[87] Published for the first time in 1591 in Heidelberg, it underwent second and third editions in 1599 and (posthumously) in 1607 as part of his *Opera omnia*.[88] The author himself translated the commentary into French and had it published in 1592 and 1598. Moreover, the English Geneva Bible adopted Junius' text and commentary of the Apocalypse from 1599 onward.

Du Jon's defense of the canonicity of the Apocalypse in the preface to his very succinct commentary combined arguments from Marlorat and Bullinger. Like Marlorat, he emphasized the importance of the Apocalypse as the only biblical book that encompassed the time between the two comings of Christ. Like Bullinger, he insisted that (due to the person of its author) it combined the elements of the Gospel and the Epistle, the two main genres of the New Testament canon.[89] He also stressed that the Apocalypse was composed against a background of persecutions and was thus particularly apt for teaching the virtue of Christian patience. He globally dismissed as *rhetores* all those who questioned the place of the book within the canon, and, while admitting that some orthodox theologians in the past had entertained doubts, he maintains that the opinions of isolated individuals are not enough to "overthrow the republic of faith." Du Jon obviously took the consensus for granted and did not find it necessary to go into it in any detail.[90]

The commentary of David Pareus (Wängler) was in a way a synthesis of all the commentaries written in the course of the sixteenth century. Pareus was born in 1548 and studied philosophy and theology at Heidelberg. After serving in various parishes in the Palatinate, he became professor of the Old and New Testaments at Heidelberg, a post which he held practically until his death in 1622. He was in favor of the union of the reformed and Lutheran churches. His complete works were republished by his son, Johann Philipp Pareus, in 1642. Volume two of the posthumous edition contains, among other works, Pareus' commentary on the Apocalypse, which had come out for the first time in 1618.[91]

His assertion of the book's canonicity is lengthy but purely automatic and rests on the proof that John the Theologian was the same person as John the Evangelist and that no other John was exiled in Patmos. Pareus had read his Eusebius and indeed many other church Fathers, to whose works he gives accurate references.[92] The consensus was not to be ignored. Pareus does know that Erasmus had assembled an impressive range of ecclesiastical authors who disputed the authority of the book, but he considers Erasmus' arguments refuted by Beza.[93] Pareus also discusses the author's style and justifies the obscurity of some passages by the fact that the book is a prophecy.

Some late sixteenth- and early seventeenth-century Protestant commentators such as Nicolas Colladon or Beza's associate Iohannes Piscator took the book's canonicity for granted and felt no need to defend it or to justify their own commentaries. Neither for that matter did David Chytraeus, whose *Explicatio Apocalypsis*, published in 1564, was one of the rare commentaries to emerge from Lutheran circles[94] in the latter half of the sixteenth century. Chytraeus took it for granted that the Apocalypse was the work of the apostle John and that it had been revealed to him by Christ himself.[95]

It is doubtful whether the Apocalypse was in real danger of leaving the canon in the early sixteenth century. However, it is interesting to note the efforts expended by a relatively large number of Protestant theologians to prove its authenticity and canonicity. These proofs took various forms; insistence on the *consensus patrum* continued until the early seventeenth century. The book's unique status as the sole text that relates the Lord's two comings to the earthly present, past, and future seems to have found favor with Marlorat and du Jon. The Zurich school of exegesis defended the book's clarity while stressing the canonical nature of its contents. Bibliander's set of literary and theological criteria for what constitutes a Scriptural text was particularly interesting and innovative, although it found no imitators.

The Protestant theologians were particularly interested in defending the authority of the book. Roman Catholics tended to consider it canonical while distrusting it. Lutherans tended to treat it as a book revealing the history of the church, in conformity with Luther's second preface.

The most famous reformers either condemned the book (Zwingli, Luther) or ignored it (Melanchthon, Bucer, Calvin). Only Bullinger attempted to make it suitable reading for the faithful, no doubt due partly to his encounter with the English refugees whose enthusiasm for the book is well known and has been studied in detail by Richard Bauckham and others.

The rejection of the Apocalypse in the early part of the century and its progressive rehabilitation have often been noted, without ever being adequately analyzed. Was this phenomenon simply due to the post-1520 reformers' concern not to dismantle the canon? On the evidence examined here, I should like to venture the view that, as the century wore on, Protestant theologians saw the interest of the Apocalypse as a New Testament prophecy, a book of consolation, a book that could answer the question of what happened between the two comings of Christ. However, Erasmus' (not Luther's) objections proved a stumbling block, and all the Protestant commentaries tend to be somewhat embarrassed (or else overly aggressive) in their defense of the book. No one wanted to tackle Erasmus on his own ground and to review seriously the doubts raised by him. To do so would have meant admitting the justice of some of his objections and *then* deciding on the place of the Apocalypse in the canon. This procedure would have been quite alien to precritical Scriptural exegesis, which was linked indissociably with theology.[96]

2

ANTOINE DU PINET AND
HIS MODELS

The identity of Antoine du Pinet remains uncertain to this day.[1] A certain Antoine Pignet was minister at Ville-la-Grand in the Chablais, near Geneva, in October 1538. Judging by the correspondence between him and Calvin in the years 1538–1540, Pignet was the corrector of Calvin's works during the reformer's exile in Strasbourg. On 4 October 1539, he wrote to Calvin to say that he had just read the Latin version of the latter's *Reply* to Sadolet and was so struck by its elegance and importance that he proposed to translate it into French so as to make it available to a wider public.[2] On 27 October of the same year, in a letter to Guillaume Farel, Calvin made it quite clear that two translators of the *Reply* were working in competition with one another and that one of them was Pignet. The French translation finally appeared in Geneva in 1540 from the presses of Michel du Bois, with nothing to indicate whether it was the work of Antoine Pignet or of his competitor.[3]

In 1539, Pignet published, also in French, the first edition of his commentary on the Apocalypse, entitled *Familiere et brieue exposition sur l'Apocalypse de sainct Jehan l'apostre*. The commentary was substantially revised, as we shall see, between 1539 and 1543, when its second edition appeared under the title *Exposition sur l'Apocalypse de sainct Jean*.[4] The third edition, printed (like nearly all the others) by Jean Girard, in 1545, contained no changes in the text. The fourth edition,[5] printed presumably in Geneva, was again anonymous and very likely destined for export to France. It appeared in 1552. Pignet was no longer at Ville-la-Grand or anywhere in the vicinity of Geneva after 1548. In a letter to Farel of 19 March 1548, Calvin alluded to du Pinet's having started a movement to curb the excessively admonitory preaching of some

ministers, including Calvin. However, the reformer announced triumphantly
that his opponents had been crushed and that du Pinet was about to be banished from the city (CO 12.667–668). Fourth and fifth editions of du Pinet's
work were due to the initiative of the printers, although it is not unlikely
that Beza himself would have wanted his preface translated into French and
made available to a larger audience in 1557.[6]

It is generally assumed that Pignet was a pupil of Jean Sturm from the
latter's Parisian period. He was born around 1510 and was a fellow student
of Calvin at Orléans.[7] After 1543, nothing was heard of Pignet until 1560,
when he resurfaced in Lyon "in the service of certain grand noblemen,"[8] who
probably employed him as private tutor. No fewer than nine works by du
Pinet (as he called himself after 1560), five of them translations into French,
appeared in Lyon between 1560 and 1566, the year of his death. Those were:
*Le troisième livre ou tome des Epistres illustres composées en espagnol par don
Ant. de Guevare* (1560); *Historia plantarum* (1561); *Caie Pline second: l'histoire
du monde* (1562, several editions until 1625); *Plantz, pourtraitz et descriptions
de plusieurs villes et forteresses* (1564); *La conformité des églises réformées de France
et de l'Eglise primitive* (1564); *Taxes des parties casuelles de la boutique du Pape*
(1564); *Les secrets miracles de nature et divers enseignements de Lévin Lemnius*
(1566); *Les commentaires de Pierre Mathiole sur l'histoire des plantes de
Dioscorides* (1566); *Les lieux communs de la sainte Ecriture par W. Musculus*
(1577, published posthumously).

The nature of du Pinet's literary output after 1560 points clearly to him
being the same person as Antoine Pignet, Calvin's friend and author of *the*
sixteenth-century Genevan commentary on the Apocalypse, which we shall
now examine in greater detail.

Textual Changes in 1543

All the editions of du Pinet's commentary give the impression of clandes-
tine production. The first and fourth editions are completely anonymous.
In the second, third, and fifth editions, the author's name appears only in
his dedicatory epistle to Simon du Bois ("Antoine Pignet à Simon Silvius").
Was this discretion due to the book's being destined for export to France, or
was there something about the contents that made it not quite acceptable
reading?[9] Whatever the reasons, the reader cannot help but be struck by the
contrast between the elusiveness of the author and the notoriety of his commentary.

As I have shown elsewhere,[10] du Pinet's outlook on crucial theological
issues to do with the Apocalypse, such as the millennium or the identity of
the Antichrist, did not alter between 1539 and 1543. However, the commentary was substantially rewritten for the 1543 edition and was never touched
subsequently (although the 1552 edition did omit the prefatory material so

as to preserve total anonymity). We shall now examine the prefaces and analyze the main textual changes introduced into the 1543 edition in Apc 12 and Apc 20.

The preface to the 1539 edition, entitled *Argument ou diuision de l'Apocalypse de sainct Iehan* (argument or division of the Apocalypse of Saint John), is something of a puzzle in that it combines the standard division of the Venerable Bede[11] with an interpretation of the division that is redolent of Joachim of Fiore. Pinet classifies the Apocalypse as an epistle which begins at Apc 1.4 (John to the seven churches in the province of Asia), with the first three verses serving as a prologue. The epistle, according to du Pinet, contains seven visions.[12] The first vision begins at Apc 1.10 and finishes at Apc 3.22; the second vision encompasses Apc 4.1–7.17; the third, Apc 8.1–11.19; the fourth, Apc 12.1–14.20; the fifth, Apc 15.1–16.21; the sixth, Apc 17.1–20.15, and the seventh, Apc 21.1–22.21. The description of the content of the visions is no more than a French paraphrase of Bede. The first vision contains the seven letters; the second, the seals; the third, seven angels and seven trumpets; the fourth, the woman, the dragon, and the two beasts; the fifth, the seven bowls of the wrath of God; the sixth, the damnation of Babylon; and the seventh, the eternal Sabbath and the glory of the elect.[13] Where du Pinet departs from Bede, however, is in his strongly temporal conception of the time span of each vision. The visions together cover the period from the Passion until the end of the world, and in each vision seven things are revealed (e.g., seven letters, seven seals, seven bowls, etc.). These things were to happen one after another, with the second vision showing the understanding of the message of the Gospel; the third, its proclamation; the fourth, the persecution and steadfastness of the true faithful; the fifth, God's vengeance on the persecutors; the sixth, God's judgment of the persecutors; and the seventh, the eternal peace of the true faithful. "Each vision," continues du Pinet, "is divided into seven parts according to the diverse persecutions and persecutors and according to the seven ages from Christ until the end of the world." He sees himself as living in the sixth age. The first age was marked by the Jewish rebellion, the second was marked by the persecution of Christians by the Roman Empire, the third saw the rise of the main heresies, and the fourth saw the beast rising from the sea. The beast, or the Antichrist, was to begin its reign in the fifth age and was to be combatted by the faithful Christians in the sixth age, which would be followed by the seventh age of eternal rest for the church.[14]

The scheme of the seven ages of the world had nothing new about it and was not unrespectable, especially after having been used by Augustine in *De Trinitate* 4.4.7. Like du Pinet, Augustine considered himself as living in the sixth age, which preceded the end of the world and the peace of the heavenly Jerusalem. However, unlike du Pinet, Augustine saw the sixth age as the age of the birth of Christ. Joachim of Fiore, however, who took over the basic Augustinian scheme in his *Expositio in Apocalypsim* (which du Pinet might well have read, seeing as it had been published in Venice in 1527), started his history, as did du Pinet, at Christ's Passion, and, although he divided the book into eight parts and not into seven visions, he proposed a content for each of them which was not unlike that of du Pinet. For Joachim, each part of the book covered seven generations, seven generations making up each *aetas* or *tempus*. The first age (Apc 1.1–3.22) was the age of apostles; the second (Apc 4.1–8.1) was marked by the persecution of Christians by the pagans; the third (Apc 8.2–11.18) was marked by the rise of heresies; the fourth (Apc 11.19–14.20) was the struggle with Islam; the fifth (Apc 15.1–16.17) witnessed the fight of the Roman church against the German Empire; and the sixth (Apc 16.18–19.21) marked the victory of Christ over the beast. The seventh age (Apc 20.1–10) was the fully spiritual age, and the eighth age (or part) corresponded to the metahistorical phase of the heavenly Jerusalem.[15] Although du Pinet did not postulate any earthly millenniums, the formal similarity of his interpretation of the seven visions to that of Joachim is flagrant. However, unlike Joachim (if indeed it was Joachim and not a disciple that served him as model), du Pinet was not a great biblical commentator, and although he took over the classic joachite motif of seven visions, each containing seven things (generations, in Joachim's *Expositio*), he seemed not quite certain what to do with it. Were the seven ages supposed each to contain seven different types of persecution or persecutors? How was this statement to be reconciled with the one made by du Pinet in the early part of the preface, where he asserted that each vision contained seven objects such as letters, seals, trumpets, and so on.

All in all, du Pinet's 1539 preface was a hybrid product, combining the orthodox division of the book into Bede's seven visions with a sort of diluted Joachism, sharing the abbot of Fiore's conception of the seven ages but carefully eschewing his conception of the spiritual age. Even so, the preface bore the stamp of the exegesis of Joachim of Fiore or his school and, what is more, had strongly eschatological overtones.

It is no wonder that the undated, unsigned preface to the 1539 edition was replaced by three completely different prefaces in 1543:[16] the signed dedicatory epistle from du Pinet to Simon Silvius dated April 1543, a short piece entitled *De l'authorité et usage de l'Apocalypse* (for a partial discussion, see chapter 1), and an even shorter piece on the division of the book, obviously an attempt to present a more coherent schema than the one of 1539. As du Pinet's letter to du Bois shows, the edition of 1539 encountered only partial approval, although by 1543, there were apparently no copies of it left in shops:

> And so having seen the welcome given by the faithful to the first edition of this book and the judgment that several good people passed on it, I too thought that there was a great demand for it as you had attested several times and that it was not in bookshops. I did not pay heed to the calumnies of those who take pleasure in maligning others, nor did I care about making my name known publicly. . . .[17]

Was the disapproval expressed by "those who took pleasure in maligning others" due to the preface? Judging by the rest of the letter, it was rather the eclectic nature of the commentary that most annoyed some of du Pinet's readers.

> For you know [he says to du Bois] how many aspersions were cast upon the first edition of this book and what sort of potions those people used to sharpen their eyesight, all the better to search for something they could pick to pieces. I will not repeat all the things they said about it, most of them an affront to the Holy Spirit and to the apostle who is the author of this prophecy. For supposing this work cannot be interpreted without recourse to dreams and visions, and supposing that he who wishes to read it is a dreamer and a visionary, can we really say that the text it is founded on is anything other than dreams and visions? No one will be surprised to see them wax so eloquent in condemning others, when they themselves do not spare God's wisdom that they blaze abroad with their words. If they insist on dwelling on the fact that this commentary is compiled from those of several doctors, ancient and modern, whose work (so they say) cannot be mixed and confused so rashly, especially if one puts one's own name to it, let them be satisfied with the following reply: I do not deny but have always admitted and do so to this day that I have put together in this small treatise the opinions of all those whom I knew to have written on the whole of the Apocalypse or on some point or passage of it, and to have copied what they said word for word—from the moderns, such as François Lambert and Sebastian Meyer, more than from the ancients.[18]

Du Pinet himself considered his work impeccably ordered and did not see what harm there was in borrowing material from other authors. Indeed, as shown in chapter 1, the first part of his second preface, *De l'authorité et usage de l'Apocalypse* (on canonicity), was no more than a watered-down version of Sebastian Meyer's preface, *De dignitate et vsu libri Apocalypseos*. The second part of *De l'authorité* continues in the same vein. Du Pinet in fact does no more than translate and abridge Meyer's preface, including the "Bernese churchman's" condensation of Tyconius' rules into four.

The rules of Tyconius were known to Meyer and du Pinet through Augustine and through Bede's commentary on the Apocalypse. They were originally seven in number and concerned the interpretation of Scripture in general and not just the Apocalypse. The first rule, that of the Lord and his body, allows us to distinguish what in the Bible should be attributed to the Lord and what to the church. The second rule is to do with the church as a mixed body composed of the saved and the damned in the Old Testament and in the New Testament. The third rule is to do with distinguishing between statements of law and those of grace. The fourth rule is that of species and genus; it sets up the criteria for distinguishing between statements in the Old Testament that refer to an Old Testament person (e.g., Solomon) as such, and those that take Solomon (species) as a representation or foreshadowing of Christ (genus). The fifth rule is to do with the symbolism of time and number. Numbers seven, ten, and twelve in the Scripture tend to denote either "always" or the perfection of something. Thus, "seven times a day I praise thee" in Ps 119.164 means exactly the same as "I will bless the Lord continually" in Ps. 34.1. Similarly, the same numbers multiplied by themselves give the totality; the best example here is the 144,000 in the Apocalypse, which is simply twelve times twelve with zeros added. One hundred and forty-four thousand thus simply means *all* the saints. The sixth rule is the rule of recapitulation: Certain Scriptural accounts appear to follow a chronological sequence, whereas in reality they recount earlier events after the later ones. The best example here is Gen. 10.32–11.1, which gives the impression that the tribes of Noah had one common language when they were dispersed into separate nations after the Flood. It is only on reading Gen. 11.3–10 (the story of the Tower of Babel) that we realize that the languages were already divided before the dispersion. The author of the account is recapitulating how the division into languages came about. The seventh rule is that of the devil and his body: Very often, Scripture figuratively attributes to the devil bad actions that are committed by members of his body, in other words, by the wicked.[19]

In his commentary on the Apocalypse, Meyer collapsed into one rules one and seven (the Lord and his body / the devil and his body) and rules three and four (law and grace / species and genus). Moreover, he simply omitted the rule of time and number, thus reducing the total number of rules to four. Here is what Meyer said:

> [W]e should not lose sight of the rules of Tyconius mentioned by Augustine in book three of *De doctrina christiana* and by Bede in his preface to this commentary. The first of those is that things which refer to the head, Christ, should often be referred to Christ's body, that is, the church, and, conversely, things which are referred to the church should refer to Christ. The same applies to Satan and his body, that is, the church of evildoers. The second rule is that of the double body of Christ. One is the internal church, assembled in the spirit which is the church before God; it cannot be seen but only believed. The other is the mixed body because of the communion of the sacraments, as in the Song of Songs: I am black but comely etc. . . . The third is that genus can be understood from the species and the other way round. The same goes for the whole and its parts with synecdoche. The fourth is how to understand recapitulation and anticipation. Augustine and Bede explain all those rules in greater detail.[20]

Du Pinet took over the passage and simplified it, notably omitting the mentions of Augustine and Bede and tacitly suppressing all the references to the Bible. At no stage apparently did he stop and ask himself who Tyconius was, what exactly Bede and Augustine said about him, and whether the total number of his rules was in fact four:

[W]e should not lose sight of the four rules of Tyconius: the first is that that which belongs to Christ as head is often attributed to his body, which is the church, and vice versa. The same can be said of Satan and his body, which is the assembly of the wicked. The second rule is that Christ's church should be taken in two ways, that is to say veritably and spiritually—and as such, it is the church before God and we do not see it but only believe in it—and carnally, and as such, it is the visible church in which the Word and the sacraments are administered. The third rule is that by the special, the general is often understood and vice versa; similarly, the whole is sometimes taken for a part and a part for the whole. The fourth rule is that several things in this book are said by recapitulation or anticipation.[21]

Apart from the omission of references and of words such as *synecdoche*, which either du Pinet himself or his readers found too taxing, the passage is an almost word-for-word translation of Meyer. Why was the rule about the time and number symbolism left out? In Meyer's case, it was certainly no accident. In his commentary, the rules of Tyconius are included in a series of injunctions to the reader on how to read the Apocalypse. The first injunction has to do with the necessity of knowing the different types of biblical revelation (visions, as in the Apocalypse; dreams, as in Daniel; part of everyday events, as in Paul's conversion). The second injunction concerns the necessity of knowing what in any particular revelation is to be referred to the past, what to the present, and what to the future. The third injunction has to do with not dwelling too much on numbers, and the fourth injunction concerns different senses of the word *angel*. Tyconius' four rules are Meyer's fifth injunction, and his warning that the book has been variously divided, Meyer's sixth injunction.[22] He obviously left out Tyconius' fifth rule because he did not want his readers dabbling in numbers symbolism.

If we now turn to du Pinet's *Exposition* in its 1543 version, we find that he too has incorporated Tyconius' four rules into a series of injunctions to the reader (which follow immediately after his rather weak passage on canonicity). However, contrary to what might be expected, du Pinet has not blindly copied out Meyer's six injunctions (with the notable exception of the four rules of Tyconius!) but has combined a selection from Meyer with one precept taken directly from the preface of François Lambert. Like Meyer, du Pinet has six precepts but neither their content nor their order is quite the same as those in the commentary of the "Bernese preacher."

A synoptic table (table 2.1) is the best way of showing the similarities and divergences between du Pinet and Meyer. While sharing Meyer's dislike for dabbling in numbers symbolism, du Pinet felt that it was important to emphasize that the only good interpretation of the visions was a general one. He therefore added precept four, which consisted of two isolated sentences taken from Lambert's preface.[23] The first precept, simpler to grasp for an untutored reader than Meyer's subtle distinction of visions into three

Table 2.1. Similarities and Divergences of Antoine du Pinet's and
Sebastian Meyer's Commentaries on the Apocalypse

Apc	Du Pinet	Meyer
1	Revelation was granted to the apostle in figures and visions fashioned by the ministry of the angels.	Three different types of biblical revelation
2	It is necessary to know what is to be referred to past, present, or future.	Idem
3	Avoid too much superstitious delving into numbers.	Idem
4	Only the principal intention of every vision should be considered; no need to give an allegorical exposition of every detail. The literal and the figurative must not be confused.	Different senses of the word *angel*
5	The word *angel* has different senses.[1]	Four rules of Tyconius
6	Four rules of Tyconius	Different divisions of the book

1. *Exposition*, 1545, b1v.–b2r.: "Et premierement faut obseruer que ceste Reuelation a esté representée à l'apostre en certaines figures et visions, formees par le ministere des Anges. Secondement faut bien regarder les histoires des temps et diligemment considerer à ce qui est passé, present ou à venir. Tiercement, il ne se faut trop superstitieusement arrester aux nombres de ce liure. Quartement il conuient sauoir que toutes les choses contenues en ces visions n'ont pas besoin d'exposition particuliere, car aucunes n'y sont mises, sinon pour mieux monstrer la figure. Par quoy faut seulement regarder à la principale intention de la vision, sans trop s'arrester à allegoriser vne chascune chose qui y seroit figuralement proposee. Et sur tout, il se faut bien garder de prendre vn dit figuratif, pour vn propre et ouuert et vn propre pour vn figuratif. Quintement que ce mot ange est prins en ce liure aucunesfois pour Jesus Christ, aucunesfois pour un messager de Dieu et aucunesfois pour vn ministre."

types (in fact a reaction to Luther's 1530 classification),[24] was simply a reformulation of Meyer's definition of vision in the latter's first injunction: "There are three types of divine revelations; one is through visions or figures fashioned by divine virtue or by the ministry of angels."[25]

Meyer included a section on different divisions of the book, including his own (which happened to be also that of Venerable Bede), at the end of his preface. Du Pinet wrote, as we said, a separate short preface on the divisions of the book, probably so as to expunge the disgrace of his joachitic preface of 1539. The result differed from Meyer in only one respect. Instead of mentioning the possibility of dividing the book into seven seals, seven trumpets, and seven bowls at the end of the division into seven visions, du Pinet mentioned it at the very beginning of his *Division et partition de ce present livre*, which is otherwise no more than the translation of the corresponding passage from Meyer. Why did du Pinet alter Meyer's order? A wish to give at least an appearance of originality? Or a certain interest in the historical method as espoused by, among others, Nicholas of Lyra? Herewith the full text of du Pinet's *Division*:

Some divide the Revelation into three main things, that is, seven seals, seven trumpets, and seven bowls. And they mean by the seven seals the chief persecutions that the Roman emperors staged against the church of Christ, from the time of the apostles until the rule of Constantine the Great, in chapters 4, 5, 6, and 7. By the seven trumpets, they mean the chief heresies risen up in the church after the peace, heresies which greatly vexed her from the time of Constantine until Mahomet, who brought the last one; see chapters 8, 9, 10, 11, 12, 13, 14, 15, 16. And by the seven bowls, they mean the last plagues, which are yet to be visited upon the world by the beast, who is the Antichrist, chapters 17, 18, etc.

However, without despising this approach in any way, it is more reasonable to divide it into seven parts, according to the seven main visions which are described here. Of those, the first treats of what went on at that time in the seven churches of Asia in St. John's absence and what was going to happen shortly afterward, chap. 1, 2, and 3. The second treats of the exaltation, glory, and the universal Kingdom of Christ, the sure knowledge, victory, and present happiness of the people of God, chap. 4, 5, 6, and 7. The third treats of the diligence and constancy of the Lord's disciples when it came to the promotion and advancement of his kingdom and also of the usefulness of preaching. Also of diverse punishments of the unbelievers and especially of the Jews who scorned the preaching of the Gospel, chapters 8, 9, 10, and almost the whole of chapter 1. The fourth is about many afflictions and calamities that the church has had to suffer and about Gentiles and Jews, false apostles, and heretics driven by Satan and how she would be saved from all those by Jesus Christ her Protector and by the angels, chap. 12, 13, 14. The fifth part is about the last persecution that the church suffers and has yet to suffer under the tyranny of the Antichrist. Also of the diverse plagues with which God will strike those who abandon the faith of Christ, chap. 15 and 16. The sixth is of the judgment and final damnation of the great whore of Babylon, the church of the wicked, and of the joy that the faithful will experience on seeing her ruin, chap. 17, 18, and 19. The seventh is Christ's marriage with his church and the eternal happiness of the good after Satan and his kingdom have been triumphantly vanquished, chap. 20, 21, and 22.[26]

The joachitic preface to the 1539 edition was thus replaced by a letter to Simon du Bois and by two prefaces copied more or less verbatim out of Meyer's *De dignitate et vsu Apocalypsis*. The second and subsequent editions of the *Exposition* were branded as derivative but the prefatory material gave the work a minimal respectability. All the undesirable joachitic overtones had disappeared.

Apc 12 and 20

What changes did du Pinet introduce in the text? Apc 12 and 20 contain several additions, none of them apparently copied directly from Lambert,

Meyer, or indeed any of the older commentaries. As these additions throw an interesting light on du Pinet's method and on the way he modified the doctrinal profile of his commentary, we shall discuss them here in some detail.

Apc 12.1: *woman robed with the sun*

The interpretation of the woman as a symbol of the church went back to Victorinus of Poetovio and was a commonplace among Western commentators. Joachim of Fiore, Lambert, and Meyer all adopted it, even though Lambert, following Rupert of Deutz, admitted the Marial interpretation as a possibility.[27] Du Pinet naturally followed the majority in the general interpretation of the symbol but had already added his own details in 1539. Alone of the Protestant commentators, he asserts that the church is the wife of the Lord and that the marriage was concluded by the blood of Jesus Christ, so that all those who place their hope in anyone or anything other than God violate that marriage. The 1543 addition is in fact a development of Meyer's exegesis, which considered that the apostolic church was aptly compared to a woman—fragile, small, and sterile by nature, she is made powerful and fecund with multiple offspring by her spouse, Christ. Du Pinet paraphrased Meyer but added two further reasons to justify the aptness of the comparison between the apostolic church and a woman. The church was aptly compared to a woman because the church's head is Christ in the same way that a woman's head is her husband (1 Cor. 11.3; Eph. 5.24) and because the church is in mystic union with Christ through faith, just as a woman is joined to her husband.

In 1539, du Pinet insisted on the church's direct dependence on God, and on God only. In 1543, by a not very original recourse to the metaphor of the Christian marriage, he specified the relationship that should obtain between Christ and his church. She should be totally dependent on him, and any power that she has, be it spiritual or physical, must be due to him alone. As well as warning his readers against the papacy, du Pinet thus also aimed to teach them the basic norms of the Christian marriage as he conceived it. The addition had little or nothing to do with the biblical text; du Pinet simply used the text as a springboard for moralizing about the nature of the church and the Christian marriage.

Apc 12.4: *the dragon stood in front of the woman*

In 1539, du Pinet had already basically adopted the exegesis of Bede (PL 93:166), who interpreted *stood* to mean "attempt to put out the faith in Christ which the faithful have in their hearts." Lambert's[28] exegesis took up both the aspects of his interpretation of the woman, as the church *and* as Mary. The dragon, for Lambert, wanted to stifle the word of God, but also, more specifically, he tried to prevent the birth of Jesus or to make sure that he would be killed by Herod after his birth. Meyer took over Bede's exegesis but devoted only one sentence to the interpretation of *stood*. Du Pinet's exegesis of the word in 1539 ran to a paragraph stating that Satan's sole aim was the destruction of Jesus Christ and his Word, and that he brought his aim about in various ways: by tyrannizing the faithful, by making them doubt the Word, and by distracting them. However, whatever persecutions the church has to bear, it will carry on, giving birth to the true faithful with the aid of its ministers, he concluded.

As it stood in 1539, du Pinet's exegesis was no more than a paraphrase of Bede. In 1543, he suppressed this interpretation and wrote a new one,[29] adding to it an interpretation of 12.5: *and the woman gave birth*, which, as we saw, he had included in his comments on 12.4 in 1539.

The basic exegesis remained unaltered. What changed was the tone. In 1543, Satan's threat to the church and its faithful was portrayed in extremely vivid terms, and the church's successful delivery of the "new man" was seen as all the more heroic. Satan tried to "murder and annihilate" the church's offspring. He "stalked" the church, his jaws wide open, making sure that all her fruit—that is, God's Word—was stillborn. If any Word of God came to be announced, Satan would immediately eat it, thus murdering those who were weak in faith. He murdered not only by the sword but also by promise of earthly rewards, such as benefices, bishoprics, and so on. Du Pinet compares Satan to a crocodile that sweeps up with his tail everything he wants to devour, but, more important, he gives Satan an identity: There is no doubt that the dragon of Apc 12 is the papacy of du Pinet's own time. Similarly, the church, whose exact identity had been left open in 1539, was now implicitly defined as the Protestant church. It alone had God's support to fashion Christ in the hearts of the faithful and so to produce the "new man" who could bring about the destruction of the dragon. All in all, du Pinet's comments on Apc 12.4–5 triple in length between 1539 and 1543. Like the addition in Apc 12.1, this one too has very little to do with explaining the text. What du Pinet very consciously set out to do was to apply the biblical text to his own time and religious situation.

Apc 12.10: *Then I heard a voice in heaven*

In 1539, du Pinet had already commented the passage in a way which was very much his own. Lambert and Meyer had both set the great battle at the time of the first martyrs;[30] du Pinet, however, by referring to Col. 1.20 and Rom. 8, implicitly set it at the time of the Crucifixion and Redemption. By 1543, du Pinet obviously realized that this silencing of Satan once and for all in Apc 12.10 did not accord very well with the other polemical passages of his commentary. Furthermore, his comments of 1539 made the text seem very far removed from the situation that he and his flock found themselves in. He therefore added a long passage[31] which included a comment on 12.11 (*they have conquered him*) showing that Satan was so evil that he unashamedly pursued the faithful even after the Redemption, although he was very well aware that God was watching and would punish him. Commenting on *they have conquered him*, du Pinet specified that the only way to conquer the devil was by faith in the Lord. When afflicted in spirit, all the faithful could and needed to do was listen to the word of God. The devil, still according to du Pinet, did not fear holy water, signs of the cross, exorcisms, and "other non-sense" used to procure solace. He would use such things only to distract men from faith and so to subjugate them. In 1543, du Pinet thus situated Apc 12.10–11 in two different periods: at the Redemption, when man's debt to Satan was canceled, and, more pastorally, in his own time, when Satan, although no longer a legitimate debtor, used the trappings of the Roman Catholic Church to undermine the faithful.

Du Pinet was moved by polemical and pastoral considerations, and his interest in the text of the Apocalypse was very scant. He above all wanted to impress on his flock the diabolical nature of the Roman Catholic Church. It was not for nothing that the second edition of du Pinet's *Exposition* coincided with the setting up of the Genevan consistory in 1542. However, the additions, such as those in Apc 12.4–5, were also very useful if the commentary was to be sent as propaganda to France.

Apc 12.14: *But the woman was given two great eagle's wings*

Du Pinet's final major addition in Apc 12 shows the same pastoral concern. In 1539, he followed the exegesis of Primasius and Bede[32] (also adopted by Meyer),[33] emphasizing that the Old Testament and the New Testament arm the church against the ploys of Satan. The congregation of the faithful, he concluded, will always be safe so long as it has recourse to Scripture. In 1543,[34] he added a passage identifying the wings with a God-given, never faltering strength, but he did not specify what link obtained between the two interpretations. The entire passage in its 1543 version could be interpreted to mean that the church has the two wings of the Scripture, which, when imparted to the faithful individually, give them the strength to resist the devil (i.e., it is implied, the Roman church).

In Apc 20, du Pinet added four passages, of which only two have doctrinal significance. The development of his exegesis of Apc 20.7 (*when the thousand years are over*) between 1539 and 1543 is particularly interesting. Du Pinet's exegesis of the final chapters of the Apocalypse was strongly Augustinian.[35] Our commentator counted the *thousand years* of Apc 20.4 as the time between the coming of Christ and the Last Judgment. During that time, Satan was chained up only in so far as Christ reigned in the hearts of the faithful. That exegesis remained unaltered, and it is worth noting that, as we shall see, it went against both Lambert and Meyer. The former opposed the Augustinian exegesis and took the *thousand years* to signify the few years of the Reformation.[36] The latter, on the contrary, placed the millennium in the past and took it to mean the period from the foundation of the church in Acts until the time of the Moslem invasions and the increase of papal power.[37] As for the *thousand years* of Apc 20.7, du Pinet assigned no temporal limits to the end of the *thousand years* in the early version of his commentary. Continuing in the Augustinian vein and closely following Bede's definition of Gog and Magog[38] to mean all the enemies of the Gospel, he concluded, after referring particularly to Ezek. 38, that the faithful must expect Satan to be let loose at any moment, and that their peace is never complete. They can, however, be confident that once Satan is unleashed, he will be destroyed shortly afterward at the Last Judgment. Unlike Augustine (*City of God* 20.11–17), to whom he refers,[39] du Pinet does not dwell on Satan's unleashing lasting three and a half years and so ensures the temporal vagueness of his commentary.

The 1543 addition, although not making any overt reference to time, gave the commentary on Apc 20.7 an eschatological flavor which was absent from the 1539 version. Du Pinet described what would happen upon the unleashing of Satan. There would be war between him and the church; he would raise not just all the tyrants and blasphemers he could muster, but also heretics and hypocrites who would do everything to bring down the kingdom of Christ. Against those, the faithful would pitch their "spiritual camp." Seen in the context of the additions, it is plain that the passage was alluding to du Pinet's own time and that the Reformation's function was to combat the satanic armies in the final battle preceding the Last Judgment. However, as Du Pinet made no explicit temporal reference, the eschatology of the passage remained, so to speak, anchored within a spiritual framework: du Pinet might also have been alluding to an inner struggle going on for an indefinite period of time prior to the Last Judgment, or simply exhorting the faithful to be ready.

Apc 20.12: *And I saw the dead small and great*

The addition here is of a purely didactic order. Du Pinet's comment on the verse in 1539 merely emphasized the omnipotence of God's judgment. In 1543,[40] he added a passage (apparently taken from Chrysostom) stating that the reference to books should not be taken literally—naturally, God does not need any books to judge humankind, seeing as he knows everyone's innermost thoughts. The metaphor is taken from civil proceedings but is no more than a metaphor. Although the added passage is rather long, it does very little to alter the basic exegesis—it simply serves to justify it. The addition is taken neither from Lambert nor from Meyer.

To sum up, du Pinet did not substantially modify his basic exegesis of the Apocalypse in 1543. The basic schema of the seven visions remained unaltered, and the lengthy additions, judging by the sample examined, were of didactic rather than exegetical interest.

The Contents of du Pinet's Commentary

Still taking Apc 12 and 20 as a representative sample, I shall address the problem of the contents of the commentary. It was obviously not a straightforward patchwork, contrary to what its author claimed. In what ways was it derivative, and what exactly were its models? An examination of two particularly derivative passages should prove helpful. I shall then examine two original passages from the commentary and finally attempt to answer the question of why du Pinet relied on his "predecessors" for some parts of his commentary but not for others.

Apc 12.4: *The seven heads of the dragon* (i.e., the devil)

Victorinus of Poetovio took the seven heads of the dragon to symbolize the seven Roman emperors, in other words, the first incarnation of the Antichrist. This exegesis was taken over with some modifications by Primasius, who argued that the seven heads stood for seven kings without any reference to the Antichrist. Bede interpreted the seven heads as all of the devil's kings. Joachim of Fiore took the seven heads to represent "names of seven tyrants who succeeded one another through the ages in persecuting the church." Nicholas of Lyra suggested that six of the seven heads were six kings, subjects of the dragon with himself as the seventh. In his moral exposition, Lyra took the seven heads to represent all the inferior demons.[41]

In the sixteenth century, the commentator who devoted the most attention to interpreting the seven heads of the dragon was François Lambert. Holding to the recapitulation principle, he sees the seven heads as evils revealed upon the breaking of the seven seals, in other words, as universal evils, diversely incarnated in Old Testament and New Testament times, culminating in the ultimate Antichrist, who is still to come and who will make all previous evils pale into insignificance.

According to the former Franciscan, the heads can be described in detail if, and only if, other passages of Scripture are referred to. The first head is thus that of a dragon or a serpent because that is how the devil is described in Gen. 3, Ps. 58, 74, 91, 104, and 140, Wisd. 11, Isa. 27 and 51, Ezek. 29 and 32, Matt. 23, and 2 Cor. 11. The second head is that of a calf, according to Exod. 32 and 2 Kings 12. The third head is that of a lion, according to Ps. 22 and 91, Ezek. 19 and 32, 2 Tim. 4 and 1 Pet. 5. The fourth head is that of a bear (Prov. 28 and Dan. 7); the fifth head is that of a leopard (Dan. 7); and the sixth head is that of a beast which differed from all the other beasts (Dan. 7). The seventh head is that of a man (Prov. 6, Matt. 5, and Luke 6 and 21).The serpent or dragon stands for malice, the calf for idolatry, the lion for pride and rapaciousness, the bear for greed and cruelty, the leopard for inconstancy, and the beast that differs from all the others for excess. The man stands for ungodliness and the wisdom of the flesh.

These evils, according to Lambert, were unleashed by Satan upon the world in sequence. At the beginning of the world, he appeared to Adam and Eve in the form of a serpent and caused God to regret having created man, so He sent the Flood. After the Flood, the devil appeared with the head of a calf—that is, idolatry. This led to the time of the lion's head—that is, the Assyrian kingdom—which was succeeded by the kingdom of the Persians, or the bear's head. Then came the kingdom of the Greeks, or the leopard's head, followed by the Roman Empire and the papacy, the two making up the head of the beast that differed from all the others. It is the man's head that represents the future "summus Antichristus."

As well as manifesting themselves in the history of the world, the devil's seven heads also manifested themselves in concrete events and actions, both in the Old Testament and in the New Testament. The serpent brought about the original sin. The calf's head aspect of the devil was particularly evident in the worship of the golden calf; the lion's head was the pride of those who built the Tower of Babel; the bear's head represented the cruelty of Nimrod and his like toward the pious; and the leopard's head stood for diverse iniquities. The head of the different beast was instantiated by the reign of Antiochus Epiphanes, and the man's head was brought about by the scribes' and the Pharisees' excessive attention to human wisdom.

The seven heads as revealed by the seven seals also manifested themselves in New Testament times: the serpentlike guile of the Jews under the first seal; the calflike nature of the pagans who killed the first Christians under the second seal; the lionlike heretics who rose up under the third seal; the bearlike greed of the clergy under the fourth seal, which marked the rise of Islam and of the papacy; the leopardlike diversity of sects under the fifth seal; and the culmination of the papacy under the fifth and sixth seals, which marked it as the beast that differed from all the others. The seventh head is the ultimate Antichrist, also incarnated by the pope and the Islam. It will shortly unleash such iniquity that all the other iniquities will pale into insignificance.[42]

His identification and interpretation of the seven heads represents an able attempt on Lambert's part to show how the Apocalypse is biblically founded and how it refers to both the past and the future. Although not giving any date for the final onslaught by the seventh head of Satan, it is strongly eschatological in tone.

Du Pinet, as was his wont, abridged and translated this particular passage of Lambert's commentary and also referred to the commentary of Rupert of Deutz. Whereas Lambert was careful to show that the seven heads manifested themselves in the history of the world, but also more specifically in the Old Testament and the New Testament, du Pinet confined himself to listing their manifestations in world history, completely omitting the Old Testament and the New Testament. The result is insipid, all the more so as the eschatology of the passage is reduced to a mere line of what would have been seen as antipapal polemics. However, because of his use of Rupert, du Pinet also effected some interesting transformations. Where Lambert referred the seven seals only to the New Testament manifestations of the seven heads, du Pinet refers them to the history of the world. Where Lambert insisted that the ten horns simply represented the devil's kingdoms and should not be investigated in too great a detail, du Pinet relates them directly to the kingdoms enumerated in the manifestations and insists, like Rupert, that there are ten horns because Greece was split into four.[43] Above all, du Pinet, by ignoring Lambert's triple level of manifestation, reduced the impact of the passage for his readers. Unlike Lambert's readers, they could not trace the manifestations of Satan through various stages in the history of salvation and feel that they were living at the end of time.

Du Pinet condenses Lambert as follows: The seven heads represent all human wisdom, all the riches and kingdoms of this world, and all the wiles deployed by the devil against Jesus Christ on the opening of the seven seals, against the Ten Commandments. Du Pinet then repeats word for word the ex-Franciscan's biblical justification, complete with references, of the identification of the seven heads as the serpent's, the calf's, the lion's, the bear's, the leopard's, the different beast's, and the man's. However, du Pinet omits Lambert's identification of the different animals with different evils and goes directly on to his exposition of world history:

> With his first head, he deceived Eve and all mankind putting them under his jurisdiction. By his second head, idolatry greatly flourished and reigned. By the third head, the Kingdom of the Assyrians expanded and by the fourth, that of the Persians. By the fifth head, the Kingdom of the Greeks and Macedonians arose and it was divided into four after the death of Alexander. . . . Thus, for seven heads, there are ten kingdoms because of Greece which was divided into four. . . . The sixth head represents the Roman Empire and the seventh the kingdom of the Antichrist, which is symbolized by a man because the Antichrist will be imbued with worldly wisdom. In other words, these seven heads represent all the adversaries revealed by the opening of the seven seals.[44]

In his interpretation of the seven heads of the dragon, du Pinet gives his readers a watered-down version of Lambert, combined with some elements from Rupert of Deutz.

Apc 12.5: She gave birth to a male child who is destined to rule all nations with an iron rod

In the Western exegetical tradition, Victorinus of Poetovio did not comment on the child's gender but automatically identified him with Jesus.[45] Primasius made the same link, while drawing attention to the fact that the virgin birth was painless, so the analogy could not be exact. However, the attack of the red dragon on the male child was exactly analogous to Herod's and the Jews'

attacks that Jesus had to suffer from his birth onward. Primasius also commented that the child had to be a male, "since we know that victory over the
devil could only be accomplished by one of male, superior, sex." Bede was
more specific and dwelt on the child's gender at some length. The child was
indeed Jesus, born not of Mary but of the church, against all the wiles of
Satan. Bede referred *he should rule all nations with a rod of iron* to Ps. 2.8–9
and explained the insistence on the child's gender (all sons are male by definition) by the author's wish to show that this particular son would conquer
the devil, who had conquered a woman. Joachim of Fiore identified the "male
son" with all the just, to whom the church gives birth just as Mary had given
birth to Jesus. This exegesis enabled him to settle especially the question of
the birth pangs, left up in the air by Primasius. Nicholas of Lyra, in his moral
exposition, interpreted the "male son" to mean Jesus and took the church,
represented by the woman, to be his spiritual mother. In his literal exposition, Lyra interpreted the child as the Byzantine emperor Heraclius, born of
the woman, that is the church.[46]

Bede's and Primasius' exegeses were extremely popular with the early
Protestant commentators, who also show themselves indebted, directly or
indirectly, to Joachim of Fiore in that they tend to interpret the "male son"
as both Jesus and the just. Given that Lambert's and Meyer's comments on
this passage are fairly brief and given that du Pinet copies from both, we shall
cite them here in extenso.

Lambert, 204v.–205v.:

It is obvious from what has been said that this woman is the church, and
it has also been made plain how this birth should be understood. As she
struggles to give birth to her son (Christ), as she tries with all her might
and neglects nothing, the dragon stands in front of her trying to take
Christ, that is, his Word, away from the faithful by making it ineffectual.
For to devour the son means to remove the true faith in his name. And
indeed, Satan literally did all he could so that Christ born of Mary would
be killed by Herod. When he noticed that that plan did not work, he did
not rest until Jesus was killed by the Jews. After Christ rose from the dead,
he [Satan] stopped at nothing to suppress the faith in his Resurrection
and so render Christ useless to us. When the holy apostles and other fathers taught this faith with total sincerity, thus giving birth to Christ in
others, he and his own tried to take it away from the elect and are still
trying to this day by every kind of subterfuge. Every time the church gave
birth, the dragon tried to eat the offspring . . . what was it she gave birth
to? A male son. Why add *male*? Is it not every son a male? Male is the
symbol of courage and strength. . . . So when he adds *male* it is as if he
were saying: This son will not be weak like the others. . . . His strength
is shown by the following sentence: *who will govern*, etc. Christ's iron
rod is his unconquered Word. With this rod he was going to govern,
together with his ministers, all his nations, as he had been told by the
Father in Psalm 2: *you shall break them with a rod of iron*.[47]

Meyer, 46r.:

Not only did the church give birth, she gave birth to a male son, that is, to one who is strong and mighty in battle. *Who would govern all nations,* that is, would give them the heart and the spirit to observe the Law . . . *With a rod of iron.* That is, with inflexible justice. Psalm 2: you *shall break them with a rod of iron,* and Psalm 45: *your royal rod, a rod of righteousness.* In Hebrew, *rod* means *royal sceptre.* And the devil did not cease until he turned against Christ Judas the traitor and the Jewish high priests and chieftains so that they crucified him. And it was then that he thought he would eat him, but he was wrong. . . . [49r.:] *and she gave birth to a male son.* Either she gave birth to Christ in the hearts of the elect . . . whom he calls rightly *male,* as one who will put an end to the doings of the dragon and will finally crush his head and kill him. Or else this refers to another excellent man to whom Satan will have to yield with his false prophets. Such were in former times Stephen, Paul, Apollo, and their like. Also Athanasius, John Chrysostom, Ambrose, Augustine, and John Hus and in our time Oecolampadius. . . . Note therefore that it did not seem enough for John to say *son,* without adding *male.* As if he were saying: however sharp Satan's attacks, the church continues to give birth with the help of Christ. And she does not give birth to just anyone, but to a male son, robust, swift, and who will fight the dragon.[48]

Whereas Lambert's exegesis combined elements of Primasius (Herod's attack on Jesus) and Bede (reference to Ps. 2, Jesus being born of the church), while giving it a classically reformed slant by identifying Jesus primarily with God's Word, Meyer added to it an adaptation of Joachim of Fiore's exegesis of Jesus as all the just and even went so far as to give historical examples of all the just. Both took over the classic Western ambivalence in their interpretation of the "male son": He was both the historical Jesus and the consequences of his birth, that is, his Word and his heritage on earth, from the apostles onward. Both emphasized the strength and vigor of the "male son," but neither took up Primasius' recapitulation theory that only a *male* could conquer Satan, who had defeated a *female.*

Du Pinet's exegesis was a tepid mixture of Lambert and Meyer. It left out Meyer's list of good Christians and the ambiguity between the birth of the historical Jesus and its consequences for the church that all previous commentators had brought out with great subtlety. On the other hand, probably due to his circumstances, du Pinet did insist on the efficacy of Christ's preached Word much more strongly than did any of his predecessors:

Du Pinet, 230–1:

Whatever the unpleasantness or seduction invented by Satan, the church with God's help gives birth to and fashions Christ in the hearts of the faithful, in other words, a new man who is created in justice, saintliness, and truth. He is male and virtuous so that he can crush the serpent's head, seeing as he is conceived, fashioned, engendered, nourished, and governed by the Spirit of Christ, the Spirit of strength and counsel, who cannot be vanquished by Satan. *A male Son to govern all nations with a rod of iron*, that is, Jesus Christ, strong and robust, having the power in heaven and on earth, was, despite the Devil, fashioned by the preaching of the Word in men's hearts, so much so that the faithful, true to his nature, are male and strong in true and living faith. They govern by virtue of the invincible Word all the unfaithful, announcing that the judgment of God will come upon them because of their incredulity.[49]

Du Pinet took from Meyer the idea of a strong Jesus in men's hearts crushing the serpent's head and the idea that the church continually gives birth to the faithful. He took from Lambert the idea that the church faces opposition every day, and the insistence on the strength of Christ. However, his exegesis is oriented by moral and polemical concerns which give his commentary a strongly homiletic tone. His emphasis on Christ's strength transmitting itself to the faithful so that they can then announce God's judgment on the reprobate was very much du Pinet's own; it was dictated by the needs of his situation. Exegetically, however, his work was not only derivative, it was flat.

Original Passages

Apc 20.1: *Then I saw an angel*

Apc 20.3: *and chained him up for a thousand years*

Victorinus of Poetovio declined to comment on *angel* in Apc 1 and, as is well known, gave a literal interpretation of the millennium. Bede took the angel to be Christ himself and the tying up of Satan to refer to the period since the Incarnation. This was also the exegesis adopted by Primasius. Both Bede and Primasius thus took a *thousand years* to mean what remained of the thousand years of the sixth age in which Jesus was born, presupposing Jesus to have been born in the year 5199 since the creation of the world (although Primasius also admitted that *thousand* could simply refer to "the fullness of time."). This was also the view of Rupert of Deutz and Joachim of Fiore, whereas Nicholas of Lyra referred the angel either to Pope Calixtus II, who "chained up" the secular power of the emperor Henry V for a certain number of years, expressed symbolically by the figure *thousand*, or to Pope Innocent III, who protected the Franciscan order, thus restraining the powers of darkness.[50]

François Lambert took the angel of Apc 20.1 to mean simply ministers of Christ, a *corpus angelicum* as opposed to a *corpus diaboli*. He vigorously opposed the traditional (Bede's) exegesis of a *thousand years* as the period from the Redemption until the Last Judgment and suggested that the phrase should be taken figuratively. He argued that Satan was tied up not from the

Redemption but from the beginning of time, so he could only perform such evil actions as Christ permitted. The *thousand years* therefore could only refer to a short period when Satan would be prevented from provoking the unbelievers to act against pious Christians. Lambert left open the question of when that should happen.[51]

Meyer's interpretation of the passage was completely different. Citing Augustine's *De ciuitate Dei* 20.7, he took the angel to mean Christ himself and then went through all known interpretations of a *thousand years* before giving his own. He began with the chiliastic interpretations, according to which the Antichrist would perish six thousand years after the creation of the world; the seventh millennium would be the reign of Christ on earth, which would be followed by a temporary release of Satan just before the Last Judgment. Without being at all harsh, Meyer considered that this interpretation had been thoroughly discredited by the Fathers. However, contrary to what might be expected, he did not adopt the interpretation of Augustine and Bede, although he recounted it in some detail: Taking as a basic presupposition that Christ was born in the year 5199 from the creation of the world, the *thousand years* was a symbolic expression for 801 years, the period between Christ's birth and the end. During that time, the devil was held captive by the church, prior to being released for a short while just before the Last Judgment.

Meyer dwelt in even greater detail on the exegesis of the Dominican Giovanni Nanni (Annius of Viterbo, 1432–1502), whose *Glosa super Apocalypsim* was first published in Genoa in 1480; Meyer found the Italian's interpretation absurd. According to Annius, victory over the Moslems, followed by a reformation of all the churches and their total obedience to the pope, would last a *thousand years*. Then Satan would be unleashed again and the remnants of the Moslems would rise up, together with Gog and Magog. The Dominican situated the victory over the Moslems in 1481, which meant that the churches' total obedience to Rome should last until 2481. Naturally, Meyer found this (rightly) to be no more and no less than a false prophecy. Admittedly, the Turks were chased out of Otranto in 1481, but what followed was neither a period of peace from their menace nor the universal submission of all the churches to Rome! It is interesting to note, however, that Meyer, although angry with the contents of Annius' prophecy, did not question his method of relating the symbols of the Apocalypse to events of his own time. No more did he question the method of Nicholas of Lyra, whose prophecy he also found risible.

Indeed, Meyer's own interpretation of a *thousand years* is also prophetic. He takes as its beginning the spreading of the Gospel by the apostles. It came to an end when the Turks and the papacy began to wage war upon the Gospel, and that, according to Meyer, happened five hundred years previously.[52] In other words, he is living at a time when Satan is unleashed. The obvious step for Meyer to make at this stage would have been to qualify the literal meaning of all numbers in the Apocalypse. However, he had already committed himself to a historical interpretation, which meant the five hundred years of Satanic freedom needed to be explained. As we noted elsewhere, Meyer at this point in his commentary gives a long summary of chapter 62 of the *Onus ecclesiae* usually attributed to Berthold Pürstinger (1465–1543), bishop of Chiemsee.[53] Written in 1519, the work was vehemently opposed to the Reformation. Pürstinger called for a general penance as the sole means of saving the church from its imminent end. According to him, Luther with his theological disputes only made the situation worse. In a word, Pürstinger was the last author one would expect Meyer to take at all seriously. However, the bishop of Chiemsee did offer a solution to Meyer's rather hopeless description of the Reformation as an event occurring during the unleashing of Satan, after the millennium. For Pürstinger put forward the hypothesis of a triple advent of Christ: The first was the Incarnation at the beginning of the sixth age. The second advent, still to come, was due to happen at the end of the sixth age, when Christ would descend to judge the Antichrist; the third advent would be the Last Judgment at the end of the seventh (final) age. Pürstinger considered that Christ's Second Coming would be accompanied by a period of peace which would last until Judgment Day. Meyer found the hypothesis very tempting, as it allowed him to place the Reformation in a more optimistic context: It was a sign of Christ's Second Coming and not just another event in the five-hundred-year period of the unleashing of Satan. However, after considering Pürstinger's option, Meyer was forced somewhat regretfully to abandon it, as it contradicted Dan. 12 with its clear description of the time of delivery being accompanied by a time of unparalleled distress.[54]

After experimenting, somewhat tentatively, with the moderate millenarian position, "the Bernese preacher" found it untenable. His exegesis of Apc 20.2 is, however, eschatological. Meyer lived near the end of time; the Reformation was a sign of the imminence of the final delivery. His interpretation of the *thousand years* directly influenced Bullinger's interpretation of the same passage in his *Sermons* on the Apocalypse, published in 1557.

Du Pinet, needless to say, took up neither Lambert's implicit identification of the Reformation with the *thousand years* of Satan's imprisonment, nor Meyer's identification of it with the time of unparalleled distress immediately preceding the Last Judgment. As might be expected, the Genevan pastor's exegesis is spiritual and as atemporal as it can be, given that the text to be commented concerns a definite period of time.

He gives a double interpretation of *angel* as *either* all the faithful who come in the name of Christ and by spreading his word "put out the darkness of Satan," thus preventing all the false prophets from spreading their doctrines, *or* as Jesus Christ. By his passion and Resurrection, Jesus has tied up Satan by making him powerless to persecute the faithful and to remove faith from the world. Du Pinet has thus combined Bede's and Lambert's interpretations. His interpretation of a *thousand years*, however, is resolutely Bedean, although he dispenses with Bede's insistence on the real length of *thousand* being 801, the number of years left between Christ's birth and the brief unleashing of Satan prior to the Last Judgment. Although du Pinet's exegesis of this passage remained unaltered from 1539 onward, and although in 1539 he stated overtly in his preface (which he subsequently removed) that he saw himself as living in the sixth age when the faithful Christians would give battle to the Antichrist, he obviously did not wish to develop this idea in the body of the commentary. Had he done so, he would have had to comment on Bede's "remnant of a *thousand years* of the sixth age" which would have involved him in some highly embarrassing eschatological calculations. If Christ died in the year 5199 from the creation of the world, that meant that Bede was living in the year 5899 from the creation of the world, at the very end of the sixth age. Were du Pinet to follow that line of reasoning, he would have had either to alter the calculations or to find that *he*, living as he was some 800 years after Bede, was already living in the seventh age.

It is not surprising that du Pinet opted for a purely symbolic interpretation of a *thousand years*. It was simply an expression equivalent in meaning to *half an hour* in Apc 8.1, that is to say, all the time from the Incarnation until the end of the world, or the Second Coming. That time is called *half an hour* because it seems brief compared to eternal life. However, it is also called a *thousand years* because a *thousand*, repeats our commentator after Primasius,[55] is a perfect number, the sum of *ten* multiplied several times by itself. It can therefore be used to symbolize eternity, and Christ (since his Resurrection) reigns for an eternity in the hearts of the faithful.

The number *thousand* has thus lost nearly all its temporal connotations. Only Christ's first coming fixes its starting point; its duration and end are completely unclear and irrelevant.

Du Pinet ends his exposition of the verse with a lengthy rebuttal of ante-Nicene millenarianism, of which he considers the prime exponent to have been Lactantius.

If we read du Pinet's exegesis of this verse together with his exposition of Apc 20.7, which, as we have seen, was given a slight eschatological twist in 1543, it is obvious that, after reading carefully all the available commentaries, du Pinet made his own choice on doctrinal grounds: In the period between Christ's first coming and his Second Coming, the powers of darkness were rendered sufficiently impotent for the true faithful to spread the word. The duration of the period, and indeed the function of the Reformation in it, were not matters for speculation, given that true faith would win in any case. By combining the two exegeses of *angel*, du Pinet also gave his commentary a strong pastoral flavor: The real ministers were those who were sent by Christ to tie up the devil and his representatives, such as the pope,[56] whom he had already identified as the Antichrist, stripped of most of the latter's traditional, eschatological connotations.

Du Pinet's commentary is a curious production that combines much pla-
giarism (or, rather, the unfortunate adaptation of earlier commentaries) with
his own exegesis. The latter is admittedly not very original. It does, however, have the merit of putting forward a clear doctrinal line on Apc 20. It
seems as if du Pinet did far less word-for-word copying than he claimed in
his preface. He did constantly refer to Lambert and Meyer, but he only took
from them and from other commentators the elements that fitted into his
resolutely antipapist and spiritual framework. There was no sense in which
his faithful could feel that they were living at any special time. They could,
however, after reading his commentary, feel that Christ had always been and
would always be on their side and against the satanic powers of Rome.

3

AUGUSTIN MARLORAT AND NICOLAS COLLADON

Augustin Marlorat

Marlorat is a little-studied figure; the fullest account of his life is still to be found in Eugène and Emile Haag's *La France Protestante*.[1] Born at Bar-le-Duc in 1506, he was orphaned at the age of eight and placed in an Augustinian monastery, where he took his vows in 1524. He acquired a good knowledge of the Fathers and of scholastic theology and was soon famous as preacher. He converted to the Reformation while he was prior at Bourges and was called to preach the new doctrines at Bourges, Poitiers, and Angers. Fleeing persecution, he went first to Geneva, then to Lausanne, where he was put in charge of the parish of Crissier in 1549. Ten years later, when he was pastor at Vevey, he was called back by the Genevan consistory and sent to Paris. In 1560, he presided over the provincial synod of Dieppe while pastor at Rouen and attended the colloquy of Poissy. He died in the same year, a victim of the Roman Catholic authorities, who ordered his hanging in front of the church of Notre-Dame at Rouen on 30 October 1561. He is the author of several exegetical works, most of them compilations, some of which were published after his death, such as the *Catholica Expositio ecclesiastica*, in which his commentary on the Apocalypse appeared; *Genesis*, 1562; *Expositio in 150 Psalmos*, 1562; and *Esaiae prophetia*, 1564. Among his other works are *Remonstrance à la royne mère*, 1561, and the *Traité de Bertram, prestre, Du corps et du sang de notre Seigneur, Jesus-Christ*, 1558, a French translation of *De corpore et sanguine Domini* by Ratramnus of Corbie, which found great favor with the Protestants because it denied a change in the substance of the consecrated bread and wine (and had in fact been condemned by Pope Leo IX at the Synod of Vercelli on 1 September 1050).

Expositio in Apocalypsin

As we noted in chapter 1, Marlorat's *Expositio in Apocalypsin* was also an expression of hope for the speedy end of the reign of the popish Antichrist, which would be followed immediately by Christ's descent for the Last Judgment. Reading the Apocalypse as a persecuted Christian, the French minister was a priori unlikely to adopt a spiritual interpretation of the text. Before examining his exegesis in detail, a word about his method. All of Marlorat's *Expositiones* are literally compilations, put together on the same model. Each chapter and verse is commented by selected passages or phrases from identifiable commentators, some ancient but most contemporary. The passages are identified by initials, to which Marlorat himself provides the key. The following key is given for the Apocalypse:

Bullinger = B	Pierre Viret = V
Primasius = P	Antoine du Pinet (Pignetius) = G
Sebastian Meyer = S	Marlorat = A
François Lambert = L	

Neither the key nor Marlorat's identification of the authors turns out to be very reliable. A very cursory inspection of Apc 12 and 20 shows that Sebastian Meyer's commentary is denoted by M as well as by S and that, as we shall see, Meyer is by far the most often cited commentator. However, M does not invariably refer to Meyer and is occasionally used to denote authorial interventions by Marlorat himself. Bearing this in mind, we shall now look at representative samples from Apc 12 and 20 of the *Expositio* in an attempt to examine the specific nature of his exegesis. Why is Meyer the main source? Which passages from him and other commentators are selected? In what manner and to what end does Marlorat himself intervene?

Unlike most Protestant commentaries of the period, the *Expositio* is not divided into seven sections or seven visions; the text is simply commented on chapter by chapter. Marlorat introduces every chapter with his own summary, thus providing a doctrinal framework. In Apc 12, the introduction is particularly unclear, as the first sentence is preceded by the initial A (Marlorat), and the next paragraph, identified by the initial M, is not traceable to any commentary used by the French minister and therefore can be safely assumed to stem from his own pen. The first sentence is a one-line summary of the whole chapter: According to Marlorat, it treats of the struggle between the church and Satan, with the church obtaining the final victory. Contrary to what he said in his preface, Marlorat wants to avoid giving an impression of referring that struggle (and the church's final victory) to his own period. He therefore specifies how *church* is to be understood. According to the "holy doctors" (he does not say which), the term has a triple meaning: (1) All the Christians, regardless of whether they are good or bad (in contradistinction to *synagogue*); (2) any one congregation of the faithful, regardless of whether it is good or bad; and (3) the total number of those who are predestined to salvation. The church in the latter sense is the only true Catholic Church, and it is the church that Satan is continually attempting to turn away from her spouse, Jesus Christ, as described in Apc 12.[2] At this point, Marlorat gives every appearance of adopting the Tyconian interpretation of the church as the entirety of the true faithful in a timeless struggle against the forces of evil. In the body of the compilation on verse 1, however, it becomes obvious that he is using Meyer (and for one or two isolated phrases, du Pinet) to show the continuity between the struggle of the apostolic church and the Protestant church of his own times. The apparently timeless struggle is simply a struggle that has remained unaltered since apostolic times.

Marlorat goes about obtaining the desired effect in very deliberate fashion. It is worth remembering here that Meyer interpreted the first verse as follows:

WOMAN: The church of the faithful.

SUN: Having put on Christ or the Gospel as a robe. The apostolic church is compared to a woman who is weak by nature but strong and fecund due to Christ, giving birth to many faithful.

MOON: Administering temporal goods in conformity with divine commands, and not being subservient to them; *or* the access of even the lowliest members of the church to some divine light, albeit not in its strongest form; *or* the Law as compared to the Sun of the Gospel.

TWELVE STARS: The twelve patriarchs *or* the twelve apostles, more likely the latter. Moreover, twelve being a number denoting perfection and universality, it can also denote all those who teach Christ in pure faith.[3]

Marlorat cites in extenso Meyer's interpretation of the apostolic church as the small weak woman made strong by Christ. He adds to it one line from du Pinet on the church as the bride of Christ. He then quotes Meyer's interpretation of the sun which represents the light of the Gospel and follows it with his own injunction to his readers, composed of two biblical quotations:

Be such that no one can complain about you, sincere sons of God, blameless in the midst of a crooked and depraved generation in which you shine like stars in the world and proffer the word of life, Phil. 2.15. And also: all you who are baptized, have put on Christ as a garment, Gal. 3.27. Indeed the church which has put on Christ as garment in her conversation and doctrine is lit up by the Spirit much more brightly than air by the sun.[4]

Is Marlorat's message addressed to the apostolic church? Or is he exhorting the true faithful of his own time to battle against Satan? The ambiguity seems deliberate at this stage in the commentary. Even the use of the second person does not give the injunction all the immediacy it should have, seeing as it is already to be found in Paul.

Marlorat's use of Meyer is equally deliberate. He emphasizes even more than the Bernese preacher the female qualities of the church, a weakling until she has put on the light of the Gospel supplied by the male Christ, whose bride she is. By comparing, with reference to Paul, members of the true church to stars in the dark world, Marlorat hints at their elect status, and by insisting on the luminous nature of a church that has put on Christ as a garment, he leaves the image of the woman completely behind and transfers his readers' attention from the text to its allegorical interpretation.

In the rest of the commentary on the verse, Marlorat intervenes more extensively and his intentions become more and more clear. He discards tacitly Meyer's interpretations of the moon representing either the Law as opposed to the Gospel or the inferior divine light accessible to even the lowliest members of the church. He does, however, maintain and indeed elaborate upon his interpretation of the moon as representing temporal goods which should be kept in an inferior position. To Marlorat, the moon, because of its changeable nature, is the perfect symbol of the inconstancy of worldly affairs. Those who have dedicated themselves to Christ tread underfoot all earthly things and look only to his glory.

The exegesis becomes thus more strongly focused on Christ so as to counterbalance the ecclesiological exegesis of *sun*. Christ and the church emerge as the two main actors of the opening verses of Apc 12. Having defined the nature of the union between them—she is weak and helpless, whereas he is the bridegroom, the garment, the focus, and all earthly things are unstable and dimly lit comparing to him—Marlorat has to define the function of the crown. Again, he uses Meyer as source. Although he ignores the option of the twelve patriarchs, he elaborates considerably upon the transfer of the power of the twelve apostles to all true ministers of God's Word. It is thus that he establishes perfect continuity between the struggles of the apostolic church and those of the Protestant church of his own times:

> Even though the twelve apostles of the early church are no longer among us, their doctrine has been, as it were, handed down to us so that the church of Christ is not deprived of that splendid ornament that John attributed to it. For those things which the Scripture teaches about the apostles should not be restricted just to them; they apply to all those who are true successors of the apostles, that is, those who announce the one crucified Christ to others.[5]

It is interesting to note that these remarks, although manifestly Marlorat's own, are not preceded by any initial and blend in with the quotation from Meyer. A curt refutation of the Marial exegesis of the chapter (as practiced by Rupert of Deutz and later by Hugh of St. Cher) closes Marlorat's very complex interpretation of the first verse. By ably adapting Meyer's interpretation and by interspersing it with his own remarks, he avoids the danger of presenting his church as the church of the elect waging a time-defined war against Satan.

The eschatological element, present in Meyer's exegesis, does not disappear completely; it is, however, tempered with the much more explicit reference to the Protestant church's apostolic antecedents and with the notion of the real church as an ahistorical body of the elect.

Chapter Twenty

However, as will be seen from his exegesis of Apc 20, Marlorat, like Meyer, feels that he is living at the time of the final unleashing of Satan, just before the end. Meyer is practically his sole source here. Yet, it is important to note that, whereas the *ecclesiasta Bernensis* appended to his commentary on Apc 20.6 a series of propositions intended to show that the pope could not possibly be a priest of Christ,[6] Marlorat barely refers to the papacy (via Meyer) in his *Expositio* of Apc 20. Meyer's eschatology and its insistence on identifying the papacy with the Antichrist is thus weakened considerably. The question that remains is in what sense does Marlorat feel that he lives at the time of the final unleashing of Satan. His own comments on the first verse of Apc 20 suggest a tension in his conception of the last days. He could very well have followed Primasius or Bede and interpreted the angel to mean Christ, who stopped the devil from attacking mankind by the power of his inscrutable [= abyss] judgments for a *thousand years*, that is, as long as the world lasts.[7] In his summary of Apc 20, Marlorat does not preclude an atemporal exposition, according to which the imminence or nonimminence of the Last Judgment is of secondary importance:

> The closer the Day of Judgment will draw, the more savagely will Satan attack the Christian Church in an effort to subjugate it. However, Christ, the bridegroom of the church and the supreme king of all, will free it completely on the day of the resurrection and will avenge himself horribly on his enemies, as John teaches us in this chapter. This angel is Christ the strong warrior of whom Luke 11.22 says: "When someone stronger comes upon him and overpowers him, he carries off the arms and armor on which the man had relied. . . ."[8]

Unlike Primasius, Bede, and du Pinet, Marlorat concentrates on the future. His basic concern is to show fellow Protestants who are persecuted for their faith that the true church will be rescued by Christ at the Last Judgment. The imminence of this rescue is difficult to judge, and Marlorat's use of Meyer's exegesis of verses 2 and 3 does nothing to make it more specific.

As we said in chapter 2,[9] Meyer's interpretation of a *thousand years* in verses 2 and 3 was prophetic. According to him, the millennium had begun with the spreading of the Gospel and had come to an end around the year 1000 when the papacy and the Turks began to wage war upon the true church. Resisting the temptation to adopt Pürstinger's schema (which he cited at great length), which would have enabled him to interpret the Reformation as a period of peace attendant upon Christ's second coming, Meyer was regretfully forced to admit that he was living in the five-hundred-year-long period of the final unleashing of Satan. Marlorat omits the detailed quotation from Pürstinger. He does, however, reproduce word for word Meyer's comments on verse 2, complete with Meyer's rejection of chiliasm, his refutation of Giovanni Nanni, and his dating of the millennium, long since come to an end.

Marlorat's eschatology is thus the same as Meyer's, with one notable exception: The French pastor is much more concerned with consoling his faithful than was his Bernese counterpart; by insisting on the ultimate victory of Christ in his summary and by downplaying the Satanic nature of the papacy, he gives them hope for a better future, which Meyer fails to do.

Marlorat's *Expositio* is not just a compilation, and it would be a mistake to use it to reconstruct Meyer's commentary because, although it is practically the sole source of the *Expositio* on the Apocalypse, selections made by Marlorat do not constitute a faithful representation of the source. Thus in Apc 12, only those excerpts from Meyer are maintained that emphasize the relationship between Christ and the church. Interpretations to do with the relationship between Law and Gospel are completely discarded. The church is defined much more clearly than in Meyer's commentary as a body of the true faithful originating with the apostolic church and continuing in a more or less visible form through the Reformation. In Apc 20, Meyer is followed more faithfully. However, Marlorat takes great care not to include the long extract from Pürstinger, as it was likely to mislead. He also omits Meyer's seventeen propositions that identify the papacy with the Antichrist. Moreover, he very deliberately adds a brief preface consoling the faithful. Although, like Meyer's faithful, they are living during the final unleashing of Satan, they are members of the true apostolic church and, as such, should have faith in the final victory of Christ at the Resurrection.

Nicolas Colladon

Nicolas Colladon is known to historians first and foremost as coauthor, with Theodore Beza, of the famous *Life* of Calvin published in 1565. Indeed the *Life*, together with *Iesus Nazareus, siue Explicatio loci Euangelii Matth. 2.22* (1565, 1577), and the *Methodus facilima* [!] *ad explicationem Apocalypseωs Iohannis* constitute the sum total of his literary production. The *Methodus* is of particular significance as a commentary on the Apocalypse composed by a theologian who was a close associate of Calvin's at a time when the reformer was at the height of his power.

A native of Bourges, Colladon became pastor at Vandoeuvres in 1553 and, as minister, was granted the *bourgeoisie* of Geneva on 22 July 1557. From 1560, he was a city minister, and in 1564 he became rector of the Academy, then, two years later, second professor of theology. Favoring a decrease in the church's dependence on the State, he came into conflict with the Genevan magistrates over a financial matter in 1571. On 26 August of that year, he attacked the government from the pulpit, and the council feared that he might incite the populace to mutiny. He was disavowed by the Company of Pastors and lost his job. After a short stay in Heidelberg, Colladon settled in Lausanne, where he taught at the Academy from 1572 onward. Shortly afterward, his former colleagues in Geneva asked him to send back the Register of the Company of Pastors which he had kept during the years 1561–1571. After the intervention of the Berne Council, Colladon finally sent back the Register, which, it turned out, was extremely skimpy and full of gaps. During his ten years as secretary, Colladon had done no more than take brief notes on loose leaves of paper, very many of which got lost. He died in Lausanne in 1586.[10]

It is difficult to say whether his commentary on the Apocalypse went through two or three editions in his lifetime. The first edition, extremely rare nowadays,[11] appeared in 1581 under the title *Methodus facilima ad explicationem sacrosanctae Apocalypseos Ioannis theologi ex ipso libro desumpta. Authore N. Colladone Biturige, sacrarum literarum professore in Schola Lausannensi. 2 Thessal. 2 vers. 5. An non meministis me cum adhuc essem apud vos, haec dixisse vobis? Nunc vero quid obstet nostis vt is suo tempore retegatur etc.* The printer was Jean Le Preux at Morges.[12] There is no trace of the second edition, but several copies exist of the third edition, also printed by Le Preux. The title of the third edition is identical to that of the first, with the exception of the following addition after *Lausannensi: Tertia editio multis partibus auctior prorsus quam praecedens. Priuilegium Romani pontificis est in fine epistolae.* The content and method of the actual commentary remained unaltered between 1581 and 1584. Colladon did, however, add some overtly satirical and polemical pieces against Rome, which we shall discuss. The pope's privilege is in fact an extract from the canon law. We shall now examine Colladon's preface to the Bernese Council, found only in the 1581 edition, his other prefatory material, his exegetical method, and his comments on Apc 12 and 20.

Preface to the Bernese Council, 1581

In 1577, Colladon published the second edition of his *Iesus Nazareus, siue Explicatio loci Euangelii Matt. 2.22*, his only extant work apart from the *Methodus* and the *Life* of Calvin. As he makes clear in the preface to the

Bernese Council, the *Methodus* was intended as a sequel to *Iesus Nazareus*, "teaching the Roman Antichrist just as the first work had taught Christ."[13] Given that his relations with civil authorities were not always very good, Colladon's attempts to ingratiate himself with the Bernese Council come as something of a surprise. Moreover, his preface tells us little about his real motives for writing the commentary. It does, however, make it quite plain that the *Methodus* is to be considered a work of anti-Roman polemics rather than a biblical commentary *stricto sensu*.

He begins by explaining to the council why he had not kept his word and had not published any manuals for Lausanne theology students since the *Iesus Nazareus*. The silence was apparently due to various misfortunes that had affected the printing house and made it stop work.[14] However, the moment the printer started working again, Colladon insisted on publishing his commentary on the Apocalypse. His choice of that particular biblical book was quite deliberate and dictated by several considerations. First, he found it to be of great consolation. Second, by reading and rereading it, he found he had reached a particularly good understanding of it. Third, and most important, he found it a book full of praise for the truly Christian kings, magistrates, and princes—in other words, for all those battling against the Roman Antichrist and the whore of Babylon, as depicted in Apc 17. Colladon cites the names of several truly Christian rulers, starting with Elizabeth I of England and finishing with the authorities of the Swiss Protestant cantons and of Geneva.

There is no doubt that the principal object of the *Methodus* is to instil hate of the papacy into the Protestant rulers. Colladon repeats several times that he is praying for God to give them strength to resist the Antichrist.[15] He also paints a particularly gruesome picture of the Roman pontiffs, taking Sixtus IV and Julius II as representative examples. He then seeks the approval of the council for his *Methodus*, which, he hopes, will be useful to young people entering the ministry.

He says very little about his method of working, confining his comments on this to stressing that he aimed for total simplicity. In Colladon's view, simplicity has always been the hallmark of the wisest commentators, both ancient and more recent. It is interesting to note that Colladon quotes two first-generation reformers—Oecolampadius and Luther—in support of this view. The (unidentified) excerpt from Oecolampadius makes a sharp distinction between the study of sacred and of profane writings, exhorting students and teachers of the former to be more pious and more attentive to God's word; the passage from Luther is an attack on preachers who are too learned and who add to the basic Christian doctrine in an attempt to appear clever. Colladon's use of Luther and Oecolampadius shows that they had assumed a status analogous to that of the church Fathers: They constituted the ultimate court of appeal in matters of biblical exegesis.

However, as he himself admits, Colladon makes no mention of the past commentators of the Apocalypse that he used as models and as a source of inspiration. He assures his readers that this omission is quite deliberate and due neither to forgetfulness nor to pride and ingratitude. The reasons given, however, are extremely unconvincing. First, Colladon felt that their works commend their authors sufficiently. Second, he did not want to give the appearance of favoring some commentators at the expense of others. Third, he did not want to be accused of attempting to curry favor with those commentators who were still living. The preface is dated 27 January 1581. What were the real reasons for the Lausanne preacher's reticence about other commentaries on the Apocalypse? Colladon probably wanted to avoid being put in a school of exegesis. It went without saying that Primasius' and Bede's commentaries were generally considered respectable, but, given Colladon's former links with Calvin, he would have been reticent to mention Joachim of Fiore for fear of being branded a disciple. As for the moderns, they were not much safer. Lambert's views on the Reformation as a short and blessed period before the Last Judgment were reminiscent of chiliasm. Meyer was too eschatological and too dependent on "dubious" writers such as Pürstinger. Marlorat's *Expositio* was a compilation; du Pinet's commentary was mediocre, and its author had fallen out with the Genevan establishment. The commentaries of the Zurich reformers constituted a much safer bet, but Colladon, despite all that had happened, was still attached to the memory of Calvin and would not have wished to make it seem as if he was favoring the Zurich reformers. Indeed, his exegesis often opposes Bullinger. On the other occasions, however, he shows a preference for Bullinger's theology as opposed to Calvin's. Only Beza was still alive, and any mention of him would indeed have looked like deliberately currying favor after the Registers incident, although his annotations on the Apocalypse were sufficiently reputable to be referred to explicitly.

Although the 1581 preface to the council was never reprinted, its polemical tone was taken up by other prefatory material in Colladon's *Methodus*. Colladon dispensed with eschatology. His commentary was first and foremost a treatise of anti-Roman polemics, as was made plain by the preface and the postface added in 1584.

Privilegium Romani Pontificis siue *Alpha et Omega Papae*

The prefatory "privilege of the Roman pontiff or the papal alpha and Omega" is extracted from the paragraph of canon law entitled *Si Papa*.

> *Decreti,* 1a pars, dist. 40, c.6: If it is discovered that the Pope neglects his salvation and that of his brethren, that he is ineffectual and remiss in his duties and that he is averse to doing good but rather detrimental to himself and everyone else, he will nonetheless lead countless hoards of people with him to hell as his subjects, and once there will eternally whip himself and others. No mortal here has the right to accuse him of his faults

because he himself will judge everyone but is to be judged by no one, unless it is discovered that he has deviated from the true faith.[16]

Anyone opening Colladon's work would thus be in no doubt about its antipapal orientation.

The Appendix: Colladon to the Christian Reader and "The Hunt," a Poem by "Cardinal Adrian"

In his comments on Apc 18.14, the Lausanne pastor promises his readers to print a poem by "cardinal Adrian" entitled *The Hunt*, as it constitutes a particularly apt description of the debauched pleasures of Babylon. He therefore encloses it in an appendix to his commentary. "Let our mother, the Roman church, read it and rejoice that its monstrous Romanity is becoming better and better known to the world."[17] The poem shows "severity of life, austerity, temperance and the wondrous concern of the cardinals for their church" as instantiated by cardinal Ascanius, to whom it is dedicated. Colladon assures his readers that the poem recounts events that really took place, as the writer was after all a cardinal. His ironic tone might suggest that it was Colladon himself who composed *The Hunt*, satirizing thus the clerical poetasters in the curia of Sixtus IV. However, the poem is authentic, and Colladon shows an excellent knowledge of Sixtus' entourage and its mores. He suspects, he says, that "Ascanius" is the son of Girolamo Riario (count of Imola)[18] and that Catherine is the illegitimate daughter of the prince of Insubria. Girolamo Riario was of course the nephew of the notorious Pietro Riario (d. 1474), cardinal "S. Sisto," who in his lifetime surrounded himself with poets, most of whom composed licentious verses. As the nephew of Sixtus IV, Pietro Riario rose to power instantaneously. His generosity to his protégés was legendary, and he died leaving a debt of 95,000 ducats, which was paid off by his nephew, Girolamo.[19]

Colladon is aware of Riario's excesses and asserts that his grand-nephew Ascanius was as prodigal as the great uncle if not more so. Unfortunately, Colladon does not reveal his sources. Whatever they were, they provided him with a very sound knowledge of the most decadent period in the history of the Roman curia. He could use that knowledge to good effect by actually citing a frivolous poem written by a descendant of the infamous Riario and showing the full decadence of Rome. In order to convince his readers that he is not hostile to pagan poetry as such, Colladon cites some lines from Lucan condemning luxury.[20]

The poem, dedicated by Adrian to Ascanius, stretches over fifteen pages (455–470) and is of the utmost banality, although not overtly obscene (it would hardly have been appropriate in a biblical commentary). It is interspersed with brief comments by Colladon, all intended to show the iniquity of the Roman curia. Some of the remarks are specifically anchored in the context of the Revelation, which allows Colladon to transpose Babylon into papal Rome and vice-versa. Others are Gospel based, so as to show his reader that Rome, as depicted by the poem, is acting against the message of Christ. One example of each type of remark will suffice here.

Commenting on the lines "Diana half-sits on the couch / virgin resplendent with shining jewels," Colladon refers the reader to Apc 18.16—"alas for the great city that was clothed in fine linen and purple and scarlet, bedizened with gold and jewels and pearls!"—which tells of the downfall of Babylon or Rome.[21] Somewhat further on in the poem, the lines "This small jar is brimming over with the best Greek wine / This golden water container (metreta) is full of must / This bowl contains the sweetest mead" give rise to the following comment on his part: "The festive wedding at Cana, where our Lord was present with his mother Mary and his disciples, did not flow with such a variety of wines. But the cardinal Ascanius with his Diana and his bright curly-haired youths cares nothing for this."[22]

The contrast between the humble figures of Jesus, Mary, and the disciples on the one hand and Ascanius, the pagan goddess of hunting, and the decadent youths on the other is brought out very ably. Colladon also notes ironically that the Rome of the Renaissance popes (which he extends into his own period) had a variety of wines which exceeded that of the miracle of Cana. Colladon's attack on Rome is severe and unbridled.

Colladon's Relationship to Calvin and His Exegetical Method

However, Colladon was well aware that Rome could be attacked by means other than a commentary on the Apocalypse. Indeed, commenting on the last book of the Bible was a particularly delicate matter for one who considered himself a faithful disciple of John Calvin, whose silence on the Apocalypse and eschatology in general was a well-known fact. Calvin's insistence on the spiritual presence of Christ in every aspect of the life of the church ostensibly left little room for speculations about what would happen between Christ's first coming and his Second Coming, the chief concern of the book of Revelation.[23] In a recent study, Eric de Boer put forward the hypothesis that Calvin intended to preach and lecture on the Old Testament prophets as a preparation for commenting on the Apocalypse. It was death that stopped him from finishing his *praelectiones* on Ezekiel, and had he not died in 1564, he would have probably commented on the Book of Revelation too.[24] De Boer's hypothesis suffers from the vast assumption that the Apocalypse can be reduced to the status of "sequel to Old Testament prophecies," without any attention being paid to the way that John uses not only Old Testament prophecies but also the Gospels and indeed astral cults to explain the absence of the Lamb, his in-between function in heaven and on earth, and his imminent return. However, de Boer's hypothesis with its underlying assumption had already been put forward by Colladon. Unlike Beza, who never went much further than defending the canonicity of the book, Colladon produced a commentary and therefore felt the need to convince his readers that he was not betraying his master. He therefore claimed privileged knowledge of Calvin's real attitude to the Apocalypse:

> Some good and erudite men of excellent doctrine are of the opinion that it was indeed Calvin who said correctly and wisely (following I know not what rumor) about the book of Revelation and its author, that he had no idea what it meant and that its author was not only unclear but that scholars were uncertain about who he actually was. I, on the other hand, remember very well and recall fully, how sometimes Calvin happened to come across the text, and some friends at his home, including myself, would discuss it. His opinion about this most holy book was quite different to what some have rumored after his death. I do not deny that, when asked by some brethren to read upon the Apocalypse either at school or in the church to all the congregation, he replied that he could not understand it all. In the same way, he left the final chapters of Ezekiel untouched in his holy lectures on that book. However, I do not doubt . . . that had he had more leisure or had it been granted to him to live until today . . . we would have some very useful reflections on the Apocalypse, on the final chapters of Ezekiel, and on certain other books of the Scripture set down by this excellent servant of God.[25]

It is difficult to know whether by "sacrae conciones in Ezechielem" Colladon means Calvin's (so far unpublished) sermons on Ezekiel delivered in 1554 with their very summary treatment of the final chapters (notably Ezek. 38, much used by the author of Revelation) or Calvin's lectures on Ezekiel, which were interrupted by the reformer's death in 1564.[26] It is more likely the latter that are meant, as Colladon could not claim that the final chapters of Ezekiel were untouched (*intacta*) in Calvin's sermons. They were treated, although only very briefly. Be that as it may, Colladon does suggest that Calvin had real difficulties with the Apocalypse which he likely would have overcome in the end.

Calladon's own commentary is thus to be seen as a fulfillment of Calvin's very long-term project. Writing some twenty years after the reformer's death, Colladon could simply be rewriting history. This, however, is unlikely given his generally good understanding of Calvin and also the fact that many of Calvin's contemporaries (e.g., Beza!) were still alive and could have easily contradicted him. Furthermore, Beza's own vigorous defense of the canonicity and apostolic authorship of the book in Calvin's lifetime (1556) would suggest that an anti-Erasmian consensus had formed in Calvin's circles fairly early on. However, there is no firsthand evidence for Calvin's attitude to the book of Revelation, and Colladon's assertions are probably partly motivated by apologetic concerns. Indeed, that is not his sole mention of Calvin in the commentary. Commenting on Apc 17.13–14 (*For they have but a single purpose among them and will confer their power and authority upon the beast. They will wage war upon the Lamb, but the Lamb will defeat them, for he is Lord of lords and King of kings, and his victory will be shared by his followers, called and chosen and faithful*), Colladon cites extensively from Calvin's poem *Epinicion Christo cantatum*. Composed of sixty-one distychs (on the metrical model of Ovid's *Fasti*), the *Epinicion*, as its name suggests, celebrates the victory of Christ and also makes some damning remarks about Christ's enemies such as Eck, Cochlaeus, and other Roman Catholic controversialists. It contains no references to the Apocalypse. It was written by Calvin during the colloquy of Worms in 1541 and circulated in manuscript until 1544, when it was condemned and put on the Index by the inquisitor Vidal de Bécanis. Only subsequent to this condemnation was it published in Geneva in 1544 by Jean Girard.[27]

Colladon cites forty-two lines from the *Epinicion* in support of his own exegesis of Apc 17.13–14.[28] According to him, verse 14 can be interpreted in two ways: Either the called, the chosen, and the faithful will be in some sense kings of kings and lords of lords with the Lamb, or they will join with the Lamb in gaining victory over the ten kings. If the latter interpretation is adopted, the phrase *for he is Lord of lords and King of kings* is to be taken parenthetically.

Although he does not say so in so many words, it is obvious that Colladon prefers the second interpretation, in that he sees the prophecies of the Apocalypse fulfilling themselves in the confessional struggles of his own time The original purpose of the colloquy of Worms, which attempted to reunite Catholics and Protestants, seems completely lost on him! He notes that the sharing of the royal authority with the beast (17.13), the great whore sitting on the ocean (17.15), and the general uprising against the Lamb (17.14) have been accurately explained by the passage of *Epinicion* (*inc.* Est aliquid fateor, quod salus robore regni; *des.* Sanguine nunc passim tingit, vt ante manus) in which Calvin condemns the papacy for its temporal ambitions and the power it exercises over monarchs. Similarly, notes Colladon, the second part of verse 14 (the Lamb's victory) and also Apc 11.7–11 (the defeat and resurrection of the two witnesses and the terror of their adversaries) are explained by a longer passage of the *Epinicion* (*inc.* Sed quia mors vita est et crux victoria Christi; *des.* Inuideat tanto laurea serta duci?), which he cites in extenso. In this passage, Calvin stresses that Christ's victory is one obtained through the cross and not through the use of ordinary weapons. Colladon obviously wanted to show his readers that although Calvin did not write a commentary on the Apocalypse, he did leave some writings that could perform the function of a commentary, and that he, Colladon, was simply drawing upon what was available without departing in any way from Calvin's original intention.

However, there was no commentary by Calvin, and Colladon had to work out his own exegetical method. He explains his hermeneutic in a long section entitled *Libri partitio et argumentum*, which follows upon the extract from canon law on the "privilege of the pope."

Colladon had a very good understanding of the dynamics of the text, and his commentary would have been first-rate had his exegesis not been overridden by his desire to show that the visions of the Apocalypse concerned solely the excesses and the ultimate downfall of the papacy. As he admitted himself, his main purpose in writing the commentary was the conversion of the pope and of the Roman Catholic clergy, which was why he used the text of the Vulgate (although, as we shall see, he did also pay attention to the Greek text).[29]

The great merit of Colladon's commentary thus lies in his explanation of the structure of the text—which resembles the explanation given in modern commentaries. It is usual nowadays to divide the Apocalypse into three parts: Apc 1, vision of the Son of Man, who gives John the order to see and write down what he saw; Apc 2 and 3, letters to the seven churches; and Apc 4–22, vision of the throne of God and the heavenly liturgy and the presentation of the sealed scroll, which is then opened by the Lamb, that is, the crucified Christ. The opening of the scroll sets in motion events which culminate in the defeat of the forces of evil, the Last Judgment, and the replacement of the world as we know it by the heavenly city.[30]

Colladon also divides the Apocalypse into three parts. According to him, the first part consists of Apc 1–3; the second, of Apc 4–20; and the third, of Apc 21 and 22. This division is at least partly due to Colladon's concern to show that Apc 21 and 22 take place in a different dimension and that his readers should not expect the heavenly Jerusalem to descend upon the earth. He insists on recapitulation and states clearly that several visions are repeated, that the sequence is not linear, and that the book contains interludes.[31] Given those caveats, he attempts to present the text in as schematized a way as possible.

First part. Although he takes the first part to include Apc 1–3, Colladon does draw attention to the title and the vision of the Son of man as constituting a separate section. Naturally, that section was of special importance to Colladon, as it showed that in some sense it was Jesus Christ himself who was the author of the much contested book. The rest of the first part contains admonitions, consolations, threats, and so on addressed to the church universal, past, present and future, symbolized by the seven churches of Asia.

Second part. Colladon's explanation of the second (longest) part suffers from tensions between his feeling for the text and his polemical concerns. The whole of that section is, according to him, devoted to showing the abomination of the Roman papacy.[32] However, there is nothing in his subdivision of the seventeen chapters into eight sections that would suggest that it is motivated by antipapal feelings! Thus, the first section (or the divine liturgy) is seen, rightly, as preparation for the opening of the seven seals which follows in Apc 6 and 7. The third section consists of Apc 8.1–6 (silence and what follows) and constitutes a preparation for the blowing of the seven trumpets, which occupies Apc 8–11 (fourth section). This division enables Colladon to see Apc 12, 13, and 14 as the fifth section, constituted of visions which are in some sense dependent on the seven seals, seven trumpets, and seven bowls. The sixth section, Apc 15, is a preparation for the pouring out of the seven bowls, and the seventh section is the pouring out as recounted in Apc 16. The eighth section consists of Apc 17–20, which contains visions that support and confirm everything that had been said so far. To this point, it could be said that Colladon has sketched out a perfectly viable structure for the Apocalypse: The bulk of the text is composed of the recapitulation of seven seals, seven trumpets and seven bowls, with other visions intervening and supporting the main sevenfold revelation, which, it is important to note, has nothing to do with the traditional (Bede's) division of the book into seven visions or parts.

Third part. Apc 21 and 22 constitute a description of the total joy and blessedness of the true faithful, who inhabit heaven after the end of the world and the Last Judgment.

Colladon's Hermeneutic and Its Application

In the body of his commentary, Colladon sets out in parallel columns the first, second, third, et cetera seal, trumpet, and bowl. Then, in commenting on the assemblage, he shows how the material from the other visions is to be integrated into the basic tripartite structure.

The first series of three are the three preparations.[33] Apc 4 and 5 is the preparation of the opening of the seven seals, Apc 8.1–5 is the preparation of the sounding of the seven trumpets, and Apc 15.1–8 is the preparation of the pouring out of the seven bowls. Apc 4 and 5 show the sovereign power of God and of his Lamb, Jesus Christ. The four animals represent the animal kingdom, and the twenty-four elders are the church universal. All are subject to God and the Lamb. The same reverence for the sovereign power of God is to be found in half an hour's silence (and the prayers of the saints) in Apc 8.1–5 and in the prologue to Apc 15, in which, according to Colladon, the elect—those who have conquered the beast—are portrayed standing on a sea of glass singing the hymn of Moses to show that there is only one God of the Old Testament and the New Testament. Furthermore, the sanctuary being barred until the completion of the seven plagues means that there will be no resurrection until the Last Judgment. The three preparations, in Colladon's view, are symbolic representations of God's and Christ's power over the church, over all creation, and over life and death.

In treating of the threesome—first seal (Apc 6.1–2), first trumpet (Apc 8.6–7), and first bowl (Apc 16.1–2)[34]—Colladon insists that all three symbolize victory. The rider of Apc 8 is Jesus Christ (who is also he who opens the seals), and the victory celebrated by the first trumpet and the first bowl is also his. The second seal (Apc 6.3–4), the second trumpet (Apc 8.8–9), and the second bowl (Apc 16.3)[35] all describe in varying detail God's wrath and vengeance. The third seal (Apc 6.5–6), the third trumpet (Apc 8.10–11), and the third bowl (Apc 16.4–7) are meant to put men off trusting in earthly goods and make them trust in Christ and fear God.[36] Colladon adds an excursus insisting that the period covered by the Apocalypse stretches only from the creation of the papacy until the Last Judgment. The book does not cover the period of the persecutions by the Roman Empire and does not allude to any of the early heretics, such as Marcion, Carpocrates, Cerinthus, and so on. Calvin's biographer admits that they did a certain amount of harm to the church, "but there were also God's ministers in the churches, energetic shepherds of the flock and industrious overseers of sheep who refuted their pernicious errors."[37] It was only after the establishment of the "papal Antichrist" that everything degenerated. John's revelation is thus simply a revelation of the diverse misfortunes that God inflicts on humankind to punish it for worshiping the beast.

With the content of the Apocalypse thus reduced to its bare, polemical minimum, Colladon has to harmonize the fourth seal (Apc 6.7–8), the fourth trumpet (Apc 8.12–13), and the fourth bowl (Apc 16.8–9) so that they constitute a triple catastrophe.[38] The bowl poured on the sun causes general drying out, sterility, and death. A similar catastrophe is depicted the fourth trumpet, and the fourth seal reveals the power of death.

Establishing a parallel between the fifth seal (Apc 6.9–11),[39] the fifth trumpet (Apc 9.1–11), and the fifth bowl (Apc 16.10–11), Colladon notes that the fifth seal describes the souls of those slaughtered for the sake of the word of God and shows that still more will be killed. The fifth trumpet describes the authors of the persecutions in which the souls will perish. The fifth bowl expresses the same message more concisely but also more clearly: As the kingdom of the Antichrist grows stronger, God will retaliate by sending darkness down on the throne of the beast. Colladon makes the *thousand years* of Apc 20.3–5 dependent on the fifth trumpet. The "chaining up of Satan" had taken place prior to the establishment of the papacy, which means his release "for a short while," that is, for the duration of the papacy. The very souls that cry to the Lord in Apc 6.9 are seen by John as sitting in judgment and reigning for a *thousand years* (i.e., "eternally," according to Colladon) with Christ in Apc 20.4. In other words, it is the redemption of the elect that in Colladon's view is portrayed by both Apc 6.9 and Apc 20.3. The elect (i.e., those who reject the papacy) can thus be sure that they will reach the kingdom of heaven regardless of any woes they endure.

The sixth parallel, according to Colladon, is an anticipation of the Last Judgment, which is expressed only very briefly by the seventh seal, the seventh trumpet, and the seventh bowl. It was his sensitivity to the structure of the text that made Colladon see Apc 10 and 11 as part of the events encompassed by the sixth trumpet. The content of his commentary, however, as we already noted, is anything but sophisticated. Virulently antipapal, it situates the Apocalypse, with the exception of the first three chapters, in the reign of the papal Antichrist, which gets more and more violent as it draws to an end. Although Colladon makes sure that he keeps the elect somewhat apart from the main woes, plagues, and punishments, his division of the book and his insistence on the struggle between the forces of darkness and the forces of light inevitably means that he bypasses or ignores other less polemical and more peaceful aspects of the text.

Given this basic framework, it is legitimate to ask two questions of Colladon's commentary. First, How does he portray the church as depicted in Apc 12? Second, given that, as we saw, his millennium is situated in the past, How does Colladon interpret Apc 20? Is he, like Meyer, living at the end of time?

Apocalypse 12

Colladon sees Apc 12 as fulfilling the function of an interlude between the various visions of disaster. However, he stresses that the events depicted there are not to be seen as coming sequentially after Apc 11 (the two witnesses) but simply as a clearer description of what has already been said elsewhere in the book,[40] especially as regards the celestial orientation of the true church and its struggles with the satanic powers. Apc 12 is thus, in his view, a recapitulation of ideas and images scattered throughout the first eleven chapters.

Like Meyer, du Pinet, and most other commentators, Colladon takes the woman to symbolize not the Virgin Mary but the church. However, unlike all preceding commentators, he avoids as much as possible commenting on details such as "seven heads," which makes his exegesis far more spiritual than those of du Pinet, Meyer, and, as we shall see, Bullinger. Although no less polemical than the rest of his commentary, Colladon's exegesis once again has the merit of following the dynamic of the text to very great effect. He thus makes a point of saying that the woman's flight into the desert in verse 13 is no more than a repetition and an elaboration of the same flight described in verse 6, and he notes that as Satan is supposed to have fallen from heaven, a problem is posed by his appearance there with the woman. Colladon solves the problem by saying that just as the woman (i.e., the church) is on earth and yet looks toward heaven as her true location, so conversely Satan was an angel in heaven before his downfall in verse 7. It is therefore right to depict the struggle between the two as taking place simultaneously in heaven and on earth.[41] Colladon's reading of the text is quite correct, although his solution to the problem may be seen as overly schematized. The vision of Apc 12 in fact does take place in heaven and on earth and is characterized by an imperceptible shifting of levels at which the various battles occur.

In a long paragraph devoted to Apc 12.7 (*and there was a great battle in heaven*), Colladon insists (against Meyer and Bullinger) that *Michael* here does not refer to Christ but to the archangel Michael. This means that he avoids the rather unfortunate interpretation of having Satan climb up to heaven in order to combat Christ. Indeed, Christ is practically absent from Colladon's interpretation of Apc 12, when we consider that it is supposed to be an account of his birth and Ascension. Unlike nearly all the earlier commentators, Colladon does not even suggest that a double interpretation—church / Mary-Jesus / the just—might be possible, let alone advisable. The woman is thus the church robed with the sun, that is, with Christ. The moon under her feet stands for all things that are changeable and that belong to this world and for which she has no regard. The crown of twelve stars on her head is the doctrine of the twelve apostles that she preaches, and she is pregnant not with Christ (he is her robe) but with all the true faithful, past, present, and future.[42]

Thus far, there seems to be nothing to distinguish Colladon's exegesis from that of the spiritual commentators such as Primasius, or, more particularly, Bede. However, as is shown by his comments on verses 3–7, he follows the text more carefully than did his predecessors, and so he thinks to ask whether the dragon that appears in heaven in verse 3 appears there at the same time as does the woman. Colladon's answer is no: All prophecies depict sequentially or contemporaneously events that are in fact very far removed from one another, and John's is no exception. Verse 3 thus refers to events immediately prior to the fall of Satan and therefore prior to the appearance of the woman. Yet both are portrayed in the present. This piece of textual subtlety on the part of our commentator is immediately counterbalanced by a piece of fairly clumsy moral exegesis: It is in our interest, claims Colladon, to have Satan depicted thus so that we can meditate daily on his fall from heaven. Moreover, Satan "stands before"—that is, threatens—the church in the present (every day), and she gives birth to the "male son" every day as more and more faithful are born.

"The giving of birth to the male son" in verse 5 is conceived solely in terms of the relationship between the church and the faithful. The faithful come from any period of history whatsoever (this includes presumably the Old Testament times, although Colladon does not say so). They are symbolized by only one son because there is only one true faith. The woman's flight to the desert is interpreted as a reduced state in which the church on earth is often to be found. In contrast to Lambert, Meyer, and du Pinet, Colladon does not give any interpretation at all of the phrase *rod of iron* but insists that the "son being snatched up to God" simply means "the sons of the church who die and migrate to heaven."[43]

All in all, Colladon interprets Apc 12 as the timeless struggle between the church and Satan, which has a *terminus a quo*, Satan's fall from heaven, but no *terminus ad quem*. He is completely uninterested in details such as the meaning of *seven heads, ten horns, rod of iron*, or indeed *the wings of a great eagle*. Indeed, he is one of the very rare Protestant commentators not to take the *two wings* given to the woman in verse 14 as allegorical representations of the Old Testament and the New Testament (after Primasius).

The dogmatic message of the chapter is made very clear, as Colladon omits comment on all phrases that might be construed as ambiguous and that are not seen by him as an essential part of the message he wishes the chapter to convey. It is not for nothing that he explains the significance of the woman's clothing in verse 1: The sun, the moon, and the twelve stars are all intended to make the church, who would otherwise have remained a rather vague, female figure, more tangible. However, the clumsy dogmatic message is made more palatable to the modern reader by Colladon's un-doubted flair for the dynamics of the text. He is the only Protestant com-mentator to draw his reader's attention to the fact that of the various battles depicted in Apc 12, some take place in heaven and some on earth, and that the chronology of the visions in verses 1 and 3 should be reversed.

Colladon and the Millennium

We saw that the early Protestant commentators were rather uncertain of their ground when it came to interpreting *thousand years* in Apc 20.2–4. Lam-bert saw it as a brief period of time when Satan would be prevented from provoking persecutions of pious Christians by the unbelievers. Meyer situ-ated the millennium as beginning with the spreading of the Gospel by the apostles and coming to an end around 1039, when the Turks and the papacy began to wage war upon the Gospel. Du Pinet gave a spiritual interpreta-tion of the millennium as a state in which the true faithful find themselves between Christ's first coming and his Second Coming. The angel in verse 1 was also variously interpreted: Lambert and Meyer took it to mean Christ himself, and du Pinet gave it a double meaning: Christ and the faithful who come in his name.

Colladon was obviously familiar with chiliastic authors such as Irenaeus and Lactantius and also with all the other schools of exegesis that either rele-gated the millennium to the past or gave it a purely spiritual interpreta-tion. However, true to his method and principles, he refers to no other commentary on the passage, although he devotes two separate sections to Apc 20 in his commentary, one in the prefatory exposition (pp. 19–22) and one in the commentary itself (pp. 431–42). In the prefatory exposition, Apc 20 is discussed verse by verse in terms which suggest that he sees the approach of the Last Judgment. In the body of the commentary, however, his view of history comes across as much more optimistic, and Colladon envisages a future. Why the apparent contradiction, and what sort of future does he envisage for the church? I would like to argue that the difference between the two accounts is simply one of emphasis. In the summary, Colladon is more interested in the history of the visible church, whereas in the commentary itself he concentrates on the spiritual significance of the millennium on the one hand, and on antipapal polemics on the other hand. His message thus turns out to be basically optimistic and as dogmatic as the rest of his commentary: The true church will always be saved, regardless of any persecutions it has to endure.

In the summary, he analyzes the chapter briefly, verse by verse. The first three verses (the chaining up of Satan by the angel) are, according to him, a description of the "happier time in the life of the church of Christ when truth was not yet completely extinguished and when some appearance of the holy ministry of the church remained."[44] The millennium is thus relegated to the time of the early church, which, although not completely free of heresy and persecution, could nonetheless be said to live a *thousand years* of happiness in so far as the papacy had not yet asserted its power. It is important to note that the exact date and duration of this period are of no interest to Colladon. As we saw, he had established a parallel between Apc 6.9 and Apc 20.4, emphasizing the redemption of the souls of the elect. In his summary of Apc 20, however, he emphasizes not their redemption but the persecutions they have had to endure at the hands of the papacy. Their eternal reign with Christ (Apc 20.5 and 6) is mentioned only very briefly.[45] Verses 7, 8, and 9 (the unleashing of Satan and the hosts of Gog and Magog) refer to the invasions *still to come* of the Judeo-Christian church by the Turks. These invasions, according to Colladon, will happen at the end of time ("sub finem saeculi"); he gives no further details as to their imminence. Moreover, he assures his readers that the heathen invaders will be wiped out by the hand of God. Verse 10 describes that punishment in detail, he concludes, and verses 11–15 follow naturally with a description of the Last Judgment.[46]

Thus the millennium is in the past, the true faithful since the institution of the papacy have suffered nothing but persecution, and all that the future holds is the promise of invasions by heathen hoards which will be wiped out at the Last Judgment. Colladon's vision of the fate of the visible church on earth is grim indeed!

This pessimism, however, is only apparent when we examine Colladon's actual commentary on the chapter. Unlike the earlier commentators, Calvin's biographer is of the opinion that the *angel* in Apc 20.1 is not Christ but God himself, who chained up Satan "by his power through the preaching of the Gospel which he rendered most effective by the Holy Spirit."[47] He says nothing about the nature and the duration of the *thousand years*, so it can be assumed that the period is still to be situated in the beginning of the church prior to the rise of the papacy. Colladon then confronts the problem of the unleashing of Satan, which, as we saw, was left unresolved by the earlier Protestant commentators. If the unleashing of Satan is coterminous with the papacy, how can it be said to last only *a little while*?[48] Colladon's answer is calculated to inspire optimism in the hearts of the true faithful: The time during which Satan is unleashed, although long in historical terms, is short when "compared with the infinite eternity of the ages of the reign of Christ."[49] It is in his explanation of Apc 20.4–6, which, as we saw, he treated only briefly in the summary, that the full complexity of Colladon's concept of the *millennium* is brought out. For him, the period of a *thousand years* of chaining up of Satan (Apc 20.3 and 7) has nothing to do with the *thousand years* during which the saints reign with Christ (Apc 20.4 and 6). This differentiation of *millennium*, already partly adopted by Bullinger in 1557, as we shall see later, means that the papacy can be identified with the unleashing of Satan (without causing any undue problems of how to interpret *a short while*), and at the same time the true faithful can be given hope of their millennium. The latter, however, as Colladon makes quite clear, is not a period in history. The celestial peace of the souls of the faithful is a condition, not a period, and it is given to all the true faithful dead for Christ at *any* period in history. Colladon paraphrases Apc 20.4–6 thus:

> Just as the faithful who take part in the first resurrection [= faith in the Gospel in this life] lived and reigned with Christ for a thousand years, that is all their time on this earth, so after the first death (that of the body, natural or external) . . . they will reign with Christ for a thousand years, that is for all the time to come.[50]

Although, as we saw, Colladon protested in his preface that he based his commentary solely on the text of the Vulgate, he frequently, as here, uses the Greek text to support a point of exegesis. He insists that the aorist καὶ ἔζησαν καὶ ἐβασίλευσαν in Apc 20.4 should be translated by the past and not by the prophetic future tense and that the expression should be attached to the preceding phrase, thus giving the sense "those who had not worshipped the beast and its image or received its mark on the forehead or the hand came to life again and reigned with Christ for a thousand years." It is interesting that Colladon deliberately adopts a different interpretation from that of his contemporaries. Both Bullinger in his *Sermons* and Beza in his *Annotations* suggested the interpretation "those who had not worshipped the beast . . . will come to life again and will reign with Christ for a thousand years."[51] However, Colladon sees no reason to translate the aorist by the future in Apc 20.4, given that the same verbs are used in the future tense in Apc 20.6. If the tenses in the original vary, they must vary for a reason, and that reason happens to be theological: The true faithful who have faith in the Gospel and do not worship the pope are mortal, but as some die, others are born, so that the true church, however diminished, lives and reigns with Christ on this earth for a *thousand years* (i.e., a very long time). Now, the aorist shows that the time of each true member of Christ on this earth is finite. However, once in heaven, all will reign with Christ until the Last Judgment, or for an infinity of time. "For whereas John said *a thousand years* in verse 4, he says *thousand years* in verse 6; the first expression with an article denotes a time that will come to an end; the second denotes an infinity of time and ages never ending."[52]

In all, Colladon sees three separate periods of a *thousand years* in Apc 20.1–6; the *thousand years* of the chaining up of Satan, a period in the distant past of the church; the *thousand years* of the spiritual reign of the true church on this earth; and the *thousand years* of heavenly glory of all the true faithful. Colladon refers to Augustine's *City of God* (20, 7–17) those who wish to know more about the expression a *thousand years.*

In contrast to the eschatological and doom-laden message in the summary of Apc 20, the actual commentary ignores the Last Judgment completely and gives the elect hope for their life on this earth and for their life after death. There is also no mention of the final end in Colladon's comments on Apc 20.8, although he maintains, as he did in his summary, that Gog and Magog refer to the Turkish invasions. However, instead of explaining what exactly he meant by situating the invasions "just before the end of time," Colladon devotes a long excursus to explaining why the Apocalypse does not say more about the Islam. Our commentator does indeed stand out from many of his contemporaries in focusing his attention on the book's undoubted hostility to Rome and extrapolating from it (without any justification) a hostility to the papacy. Other commentators (as we saw) included the Islam in their identification of enemies of Christianity portrayed in the text. Colladon, perhaps under the influence of Bibliander, justifies his indifference to the Islam by arguing that the purpose of the revelation granted to John was to show the churches that the pope was the Antichrist. There was no need, he claims, to put them on guard against the Turk, as he is an obvious and not an insidious enemy. Moreover, he notes, the papacy indirectly supports and encourages the Turk! Obviously feeling that this outrageous statement requires some sort of substantiation, Colladon confines himself to citing the sack of Rome as an example: Had Charles V had the support of princes in 1527, he could have deposed the pope, installed himself in Rome, and devoted his full energies to fighting the Turk. Instead, the princes yielded to Clement VII's cries for help to restore the papacy, and so the opportunity of defeating the Turk once and for all was lost [!].[53] Whatever one may think of Colladon's analysis of the sack of Rome, it has nothing to do with Gog and Magog or with the final assault by the Turks that, he had told the reader, is supposed to be a sign of the impending end. Colladon gives no commentary of Apc 20.11–15.

Despite its very uneven quality, Colladon's *Methodus* when it appeared was intended as a Calvinist statement on the Apocalypse (although perhaps not one that Calvin himself would have made). Given this claim, it is legitimate to ask how Colladon's exegesis compares with equally hidebound Roman exegeses of the same period. Given the absence of Roman Catholic commentators of any reputation in the 1580s, we shall compare Colladon's exegesis of Apc 12 and 20 with that of the ultraconservative Sorbonne theologian of the previous generation, Jean de Gagny, in an attempt to see what is "Calvinist" about the *Methodus.*

Colladon and Jean de Gagny

Jean de Gagny studied theology at the College of Navarre, where he became professor in 1527, lecturing on the *Sentences* of Peter Lombard. He was made rector of the University of Paris in 1531 and became doctor of theology a year later. In 1533, he was asked by the Paris theology faculty to examine the case of the reformist preacher Gérard Roussel, judged dangerous, and to pronounce himself on heterodox-seeming passages in Cajetan's commentaries on the New Testament and the Psalms. In that same year, Gagny published his own commentary on Romans, which earned him a call to the court of Francis I, where he became royal counselor, then chaplain and preacher, gaining access to the royal collections of books and manuscripts in the process. He was often called to defend the privileges of the University of Paris. Among his friends were Marcello Cervini (the future pope Marcellus II), Sixtus of Siena, and Possevino. His most notable enemy was Robert Estienne, whose Bibles were condemned by the Paris theology faculty at Gagny's instigation.[54] The Paris theologian published his brief scholia on the Apocalypse in 1543, adding them somewhat reluctantly to his scholia on the Pauline corpus and on the Catholic Epistles. The second edition appeared in 1550, shortly after Gagny's death.[55] Thus, although not of the same generation as Colladon, Gagny was certainly familiar with Calvin's doctrines, which he strove to combat. One would therefore expect his scholia on the Apocalypse to take the form of an anti-Calvinist manifesto, and indeed there is a very strong polemical flavor to them. However, as we shall see, Gagny's exegesis is not substantially different from Colladon's.

Like Colladon, Gagny found the Apocalypse to be fundamentally an obscure text, but unlike Colladon, he did not conceal his reliance on earlier commentaries—all of which, incidentally, he found wanting. Overwhelmed by the obscurity of the book and the contradictions in its exegesis, he initially had no intention of commenting on the book himself. However, he explains in his preface, he finally yielded to his friends who insisted that all commentators of the New Testament should comment on its last book, and he has decided to elucidate the grammar of certain passages and to select some existing interpretations that seemed to him closest to the meaning of the text.[56]

Gagny refers to the authority of the church and more particularly to Gregory of Nazianzus for claiming that the book is canonical and the work of the apostle John. Although he is familiar with the doubts cast upon the book by the third- and fourth-century Greek Fathers, he does not explore them.

Despite his claims not to go beyond summarizing the exegeses of others, Gagny does include his own polemical comments. Thus, Apc 1.10 (on *the Lord's day*) means to him that John had a prophetic vision of Sunday as the Lord's day, and—he reminds the reader—"the Sabbath was abolished and replaced by Sunday solely on the authority of the apostles without any support from the Scripture and even in contradiction of the Scripture, in case there are people who think that we should believe only those things which are to be found in the Scripture."[57] In a similar vein, he takes the measuring of the Temple in Apc 11.1 to mean adapting divine teaching to the public and not translating the Bible into the vernacular to make it accessible to laypeople.[58]

As regards his exegesis of Apc 12,[59] Gagny shows no understanding of the dynamics of the text and only the absence of any comment on Apc 12.6 would suggest that he sees the flight of the woman described there as simply an anticipation of the flight in Apc 12.13. As for the symbolic meaning of the woman, Gagny prefers her to stand for the church, but he does include a second exegesis (printed in smaller characters, 277r.–278r.), with the woman as the Virgin Mary, who gives birth to Christ, who is then persecuted by Herod, or the dragon.

His main, "ecclesiastical" interpretation of the chapter naturally has certain details in common with Colladon. Thus both take *robed with the sun* to mean "having put on Christ" (Gagny specifies [274r.] "through baptism"), and both interpret *the moon at her feet* to mean "having no regard for earthly things" (Gagny adds Rupert of Deutz's exegesis of the moon standing for "heretical doctrines," also put forward as a possibility by Sebastian Meyer). However, Gagny does not explain why the dragon appeared in heaven with the woman and has no interest in the sequential order of the visions or indeed in the theory of recapitulation. He gives two interpretations of the birth of the male son in Apc 20.5, neither of them incompatible with Colladon's interpretation: the birth of Christ in the hearts of the faithful, or simply the birth of the faithful. Writing from the standpoint of the established Roman Catholic Church, Gagny is under no pressure to define the true church and takes it implicitly to be the church he serves. The woman's flight to the desert is interpreted as a search for a contemplative life (after Joachim of Fiore), and the two wings are taken to stand for the two Testaments (after Primasius). Like Colladon, Gagny takes *Michael* in Apc 20.7 to mean archangel Michael (and not Christ). The struggle between him and Satan is seen as a timeless struggle, the archangel being the emissary of the church in her fight against evil. Gagny comments on several details of the text that Colladon deliberately omitted, such as the *seven heads* (interpreted as the seven deadly sins). However, what really distinguishes the two commentators is, first, Colladon's grasp of the dynamics of the text, completely absent from Gagny's *Scholia*, and, second, the two theologians' conceptions of the church. To Colladon, the church is all the faithful from any era in history; to Gagny, the church is something that can be taken for granted—it is the Roman church universally recognized as true and apostolic.

Gagny's exegesis of the *thousand years* in Apc 20.3[60] appears at first sight similar to Colladon's. The Paris theologian takes it to stretch from the Passion until the arrival of the Antichrist. However, neither the identity of the Antichrist nor the time of his arrival is stated; what is made plain is that Gagny, unlike his Calvinist counterpart, is still living in the *millennium* during which Satan is chained up "until the Antichrist will come." Satan will then be unleashed for three and a half years, that is, for the duration of the Antichrist's reign.[61] It is obvious that Gagny did not see the Reformation as the beginning of the reign of the Antichrist, and, in contrast to Colladon, did not feel the need to identify the Antichrist as his religious adversaries.

The presence of the papal Antichrist and the firm conviction that the elect had a future—those were the distinguishing features that marked Colladon's commentary as representative of Genevan Calvinism. Indeed, his *Methodus* can be seen as an attempt to combine a "scientific" interpretation of the Apocalypse with the principal tenets of the Calvinist doctrines of the church, election and reprobation. It is to be regretted that polemical concerns so outweighed Colladon's undoubted interest in and gift for explaining the biblical text.

4

THE APOCALYPSE AND THE
ZURICH REFORMERS

Leo Jud and His *Paraphrase of the Apocalypse*, 1542

Leo Jud was born at Gemar in Alsace, southwest of Strasbourg and attended the Latin School at Sélestat at the same time as Martin Bucer. In 1499, he matriculated at the University of Basel, where he met and became friends with Ulrich Zwingli. He intended to study medicine but soon turned to theology under the influence of Thomas Wyttenbach. Jud was ordained a priest in Rome in 1507. From 1507 until 1512, he was deacon at Saint Theodore's in Basel, and from 1512 to 1518, he was preacher at Saint Hippolyte in Alsace. In 1519, he succeeded Zwingli at Einsiedeln, while becoming increasingly favorable to the Reformation. In 1522, he was chosen, on Zwingli's recommendation, to become pastor of Saint Peter's in Zurich, where he took up his duties on 2 February 1523. He was at Zwingli's side during the Second Zurich Disputation (26–28 October 1523) and during the confrontation with the radical Anabaptists in 1525. He was a judge (one of the two clergymen together with four laymen) of the marriage court from its inception in 1525.

Although Zwingli's closest associate, Jud seems to have had an interest in spirituality which was completely absent from Zwingli's own theology. As he was relatively unproductive as an original writer, this interest manifested itself in translations Jud undertook of authors such as Thomas à Kempis and Erasmus. His 1542 German translation of Erasmus' *Paraphrases*, entitled *Paraphrasis oder Postille teütsch* (Zurich, C. Froschouer), was very obviously an attempt to provide the new faithful with some basic reading. The inclusion of the Apocalypse, which Erasmus had resolutely refused to paraphrase, would suggest either an interest in eschatology or, more likely, a concern with providing his congregation with a consolatory text. Which of the two motives was uppermost in Jud's mind will become clear in the rest of this chapter.

In general Jud's talent as a translator was undoubted. Together with Konrad Pelikan and Theodore Bibliander, he took part in the translation of the Zurich Bible into dialect between 1525 and 1529. After Zwingli's death, it was Jud who nominated Bullinger leader of the Zurich church. After the quarrel over the separation, which Jud advocated, of civil and ecclesiastical jurisdiction in 1532, he worked closely with Bullinger and devoted the final years of his life to the translation of the Bible and of Erasmus' *Paraphrases*, which appeared in the year of his death.[1]

Leo Jud's *Paraphrase of the Apocalypse*, entitled by him simply *Die Offenbarung Sant Johanns des Theologi*, although the first to appear, was not an isolated effort among Zurich reformers. A couple of years later, Theodore Bibliander gave lectures on the book which were attended by Heinrich Bullinger, whose extremely popular *Hundred Sermons* were written in 1554 and published in 1557. The three commentaries were very different from one another and attempted to answer different needs: Jud was addressing the faithful of his own canton and city, Bibliander wrote for the learned community, and Bullinger addressed all those who were persecuted for their religious beliefs and who therefore had to seek refuge in foreign lands.[2]

Leo Jud and the Apocalypse

Jud's paraphrase is in fact a commentary which, unlike many sixteenth-century commentaries, ignores the division of the book into seven sections or visions and closely follows the fabric of the text. Its author seems to combine the spiritual and the historico-prophetic approach in such a way as to make it clear to his public that the message of the Apocalypse, while timeless, is of particular relevance to their time.

He has no doubts about the apostolic authorship of the book or about its canonicity. It was dictated by Christ himself to John, Christ in his human nature having been given the power to reveal via chosen servants "the future of the Christian condition until the Last Judgment." In his eyes, thus, John is not merely an unfolder of the contents of the Scripture, a function made possible by Christ's Passion, he is also a prophet of what will happen to the church in the time between the Incarnation and the Parousia.[3] Through the seven churches of Asia Minor, the message, according to Jud, spreads to the church universal.

A characteristic feature of the spiritual approach to the Apocalypse was the interpretation of the seven seals not as a sequence of events but as a once and for all unsealing of the mysteries of the Scripture, made possible by the Passion of Christ. This interpretation, going back to Victorinus of Poetovio,[4] was taken up by Primasius, the Venerable Bede, and all "spiritual" commentators.

Leo Jud adopts a dual interpretation of the seven seals in Apc 6. The first interpretation is that of Victorinus: The seven main articles of Christian faith can be unsealed in the Old Testament thanks to the action of the Holy Spirit attendant upon Christ's first coming (Jud refers here to Erasmus' interpretation of Luke 24.27, in which Christ points out to his disciples the Old Testament passages that predict his coming).[5]

His second interpretation, however, is historical. It is the seven ages of the church that unfold with each of the seals. Thus, the first seal and the white horse it reveals stand for the apostolic times "gantz rein, unschuldig und heilig." The second seal and the red horse stand for the time of the martyrs, from Stephen until the conversion of Constantine, with the color red symbolizing the blood of the faithful and the sword representing the violence of the era. Jud's chronology is not perfect, nor does he intend it to be, given that he interprets the third seal and the black horse as the famine under Trajan, which preceded the conversion of Constantine by more than two hundred years. What is more interesting, he includes both heathens and Jews in his historical interpretation. He notes that the Jews were decimated in seal two and that Jews, pagans, and Christians suffered the famine in seal three. Seal four symbolizes the time of heresies. With seal five, Jud reverts to a double interpretation, spiritual and historical: The souls under the altar are the souls of all the true faithful at all periods in history who cry for an increase in God's righteousness. However, they are also the souls of the dead faithful, who wait in heaven for the Last Judgment "welche zeyt und zal dem Herren allein zewüssen ist." The sixth seal stands for the time of the Antichrist, who is personified by Mahomet in the East and by what Jud considers to be the most superstitious aspects of popery in the West: image worship, monastic life, purgatory, temporal claims, and papal wealth.[6] The silence after the seventh seal is also interpreted by a reference to history, albeit in a very wide sense: There have been many periods in history when, through God's grace, some peace was given to the church. However, the forces of evil being what they are, that peace was always of limited duration.[7] It is interesting to note that Jud refers all brief periods of peace that the church might have enjoyed to the past, thus carefully avoiding the temptation to give any prophetic meaning to the Reformation. The similarity between his exegesis of the seven seals and that of Nicholas of Lyra is only apparent, seeing as Lyra relates each seal to specific persons and events in the history of the church.

The specificity of Jud's interpretation is brought out even more clearly if we compare it to those of Rupert of Deutz and Joachim of Fiore. For Rupert, seals one through six symbolize the period stretching from the Incarnation to the *vocatio gentium*, with the seventh seal standing for the Last Judgment. Given that, for Rupert, the Apocalypse recounts the history of the church up until the Council of Nicea in 325, with the Last Judgment constituting a future event which is not to be dated, the half an hour's silence in heaven necessarily denotes the future rest of the saints after the Last Judgment.

For Joachim of Fiore, the first seal denotes the primitive church, the second seal stands for the Roman Empire, the third seal symbolizes Arius, the fourth seal denotes Mahomet, and the fifth seal represents the four spiritual orders. Joachim sees his own time as the end of the fifth seal. It will be followed by the battle of the martyrs, with the silence of the seventh seal denoting the silence of the contemplative life which will characterize the Age of the Holy Spirit due to take place on this earth. Jud was obviously influenced by joachite exegesis in his identification of the sixth seal with the time of the Antichrist and in his interpretation of the half an hour's silence as a time of earthly peace. However, Jud makes very certain that he does not follow Joachim in establishing anything resembling a spiritual age on earth. The half an hour's silence is a sporadic event confined to the past.

In all, with his dual interpretation of Apc 6, Jud aims to impose as wide a meaning as possible on the Apocalypse to make it relevant to the largest number of faithful who would draw spiritual nourishment and consolation from it.

What of his interpretation of Apc 12? Like Lambert, he begins Apc 12 not with the appearance of he woman but with the laying open of God's temple in Apc 11.19 as a "preparation for the new and splendid vision"[8] of Apc 12. He introduces it by voicing an implicit disagreement with Luther in his assessment of Old Testament and New Testament prophecies.

According to Jud, the earlier prophecies in the Old Testament (e.g., those of Isaiah and Jeremiah) are much clearer than the later prophecies such as those of Daniel and Ezekiel. In the Apocalypse, however, which Jud sees as the sole prophetic book of the New Testament, the prophecies nearer the end of the book are clearer than the ones at the beginning. Thus for Jud (as for Colladon in 1581!), the vision of Apc 12 constitutes a recapitulation, or even an exegesis ("ausslegung"), of the previous visions in Apc 1–11.[9] The female figure, however, receives a highly original interpretation. She appears in heaven, which is the kingdom of heaven, the church triumphant, and the seat of all true faithful who have ever existed from the beginning of the world. She looks toward the sun. However, she represents neither the church militant nor the Virgin Mary but the Word of God, "clear and strong." The moon that is under her feet is human reason completely subjugated to the Word of God. The Word of God is pregnant with Christ in the sense of ardently desiring him, as all prophets have done. In other words, according to Jud, the Word of God, or the Gospel, engenders faith in or ardent desire of Christ.

By thus shifting the points of comparison, Jud has transposed Apc 12 into the realm of the pastoral, immediately accessible to his readers.

However, having temporarily consoled his readers, Jud wants to show them that God's Word is not heard without opposition. The second portent is thus, predictably enough, Lucifer himself with his seven heads and ten horns, who represent his henchmen, who have always done everything to harm true faith. Commenting on Apc 12.4–7, Jud notes that Satan, who "stood in front of the woman," initially tried to stop the progress of the word of God through the disobedience of Israel. As Jerusalem was destroyed, the holy word of God became adulterated by human reason. However, God's goodness prevailed over Satan's power, and Christ was incarnated and born of the Virgin Mary.

Although Jud thus overtly refers to Christ's virgin birth, it is important to note that his basic exegetical framework has not undergone any shift. The female figure of the Apocalypse at no stage becomes identified with the Virgin Mary. Jud simply says:

> Then the child was born; God's word became man, truth was victorious, falsehood was laid low, the devil's trick was found out by God in his wisdom and made known to the world. This child, Christ, the eternal word of God become man in the sacred bosom of the virgin Mary, was accepted by God the Father in his mercy for all the sins of the world.[10]

Thus the divine Word of God, which was female, became a man and was born of another woman, the Virgin Mary. Jud's intention was certainly not to give a gendered exegesis of Apc 12. He does, however, constitute an exception among mediaeval and Renaissance commentators in the importance he accords to the female element of the chapter. Although in contradistinction to, for example, Joachim of Fiore, Jud considers the Incarnation the crucial event in the history of salvation and insists on its central nature throughout the chapter, he also specifies, after Augustine, that it did not stop the devil's onslaughts completely. However, the devil's onslaughts are not concentrated in the papacy. Unlike Colladon, Bullinger, and many other Protestant theologians of the period, Jud does not explicitly identify the papacy with the Antichrist. Just as he took the half an hour's silence to denote several brief periods of peace throughout the history of the church, so here Jud simply notes that Satan has tried to attack true faith in various ways at various stages in history—sometimes through false apostles, sometimes through heathens, sometimes through the Roman emperor, and at other times through "prelates and monks."[11] In this framework, Jud cannot but identify the 1,260 days with 1,260 years since Constantine's time during which the church has been protected by civil authorities. After thus implicitly paying tribute to the Zurich magistrates, Jud adopts the spiritual approach again in his comments on the war in heaven, which he sees as the timeless struggle between the forces of Satan and the true believers, who will be ultimately victorious. Equally spiritual is his interpretation of the woman's flight into the desert in Apc 12.14. Without considering whether the flight in Apc 12.14 is the same as the one in Apc 12.6, Jud maintains his interpretation of the woman as the Word of God (giving birth to Christ in the hearts of the faithful), constantly attacked by Satan. Ignoring the traditional Primasian exegesis of the two wings as the two Testaments, he prefers to see the two wings as the consolation imparted to every faithful soul by the Holy Spirit. However, the Holy Spirit guides the soul not to solid faith but to "a place in the wilds," one of spiritual refuge entailing "contempt of this world, love of the next world, the solitude of a peaceful conscience contemplating the cross of Christ, and trust in God's Word." Those are the things that, according to Jud, help the Christian soul to flee the snares of Satan.[12] Although it may seem as if the Word of God has metamorphosed into a Christian soul in the course of Jud's interpretation of the final verses of the chapter, this in fact is not the case: He has simply moved from the objective to the subjective description of it. The female Word of God who imparts Christ has become the (female) Christian soul receiving the Word of God. Jud's emphasis on solitude and the contemplation of Christ's cross is, it should be noted, very uncharacteristic of Zwinglian theology. There is no doubt that Jud aimed to give his readers spiritual guidance which they could not find in Zwingli's and Bullinger's writings.

This does not mean that Jud's work is completely devoid of polemics, as is shown by his interpretation of the "number of the beast" in Apc 13. He sees Apc 13.15–18 as referring to idolatrous image worship, the source of the greatest abuses in recent years. It is plain that Jud uses the passage to vindicate iconoclasm, which was a classic feature of the Zurich Reformation.[13] To Zwingli's associate, images are the most flagrant symbol of papacy. Those who want to live in earthly peace, to "buy and sell," as the text would have it, without being disturbed, can and will carry on worshiping images. However, Jud stresses, God's will is that the beast (i.e., the papacy) with its images is to be destroyed. Ignoring all standard or classic interpretations of the number, Jud suggests that if one subtracts 666 from 1520 (the year which marked the beginning of the Reformation in Zurich), the remainder is 854, the year which he wrongly associates (if the marginal remark "Ludovicus Pius 856" is anything to go by) with the reign of Louis I and the beginnings of the papal state. Although Jud's historical knowledge is weak, his evangelical message is absolutely clear: Read correctly, the passage means that the "number of the beast," in other words, the papacy with its image worship, is about to come to an end. The semimonastic spirituality he advocated in Apc 12 is possible only in the context of the Reformation.[14]

Thus the Reformation denoted to Jud the end of the papacy. Did he see himself as living at the end of history? His very careful interpretation of

Apc 20 suggests that this was not the case. Indeed, Zwingli's associate is very careful to adopt with some slight changes the standard Augustinian interpretation of the *thousand years* in Apc 20.2–3. He considers Apc 20 a recapitulation ("abred und widerholung") of all the prophecies in the book that describe the majesty of God and the saving power of Jesus. It is interesting to note here that Jud implies that Jesus is a recapitulation of Adam and that his redemption was promised to the first man when he sinned in the Garden of Eden, an idea which goes back to Irenaeus' *Aduersus haereses* (5.1.2). Thus Christ is seen to have chained up Satan when he died on the cross, redeeming the fault of Adam and Eve.[15] Although, with this interpretation, Jud clearly situates the *thousand years* in the past, he refuses to interpret it with any precision and will not commit himself to a period longer than "a long time." Unlike Augustine in *De ciuitate Dei*, Jud admits that the millennium did in some sense start before the Incarnation, in that all the true faithful, including those of the Old Testament, did to a certain extent limit Satan's power, thus contributing to his chaining up.

However, the Old Testament faithful do not play any part in Jud's interpretation of Apc 20.4–6, in which the judges are paraphrased as the apostles and the Christian martyrs. The first resurrection takes place in heaven and on this earth—in heaven for the true faithful who died, on earth for those who are physically still alive and who experience a spiritual renewal through Christ. It is to be noted that Jud does not repeat Lambert's mistake of identifying the Reformation with a period of blessed peace on earth prior to the Last Judgment. Although, as his comments on Apc 13 show, the Reformation does mean the end of the papacy, it has no particular eschatological significance. In fact, it could be said that Jud does his best to minimize the impact on the reader of the phrase *thousand years*: After paraphrasing it in Apc 20.2, he resolutely refuses to refer to it in his paraphrase of Apc 20.4 and 7.

In all, Jud uses the Apocalypse to great effect as a vehicle for expounding his own theology and manages to fit into the text spiritual exhortations, praise of the Zurich magistrates, approval of iconoclasm, and condemnation of the papacy, while showing himself to be a true disciple of Zwingli in his deliberate dismissal of the *thousand years*. Unlike Bullinger, Jud does not see himself at the end of history. Although he does see the final unleashing of Satan as taking place in the real future and not in an atemporal framework,[16] nothing in his paraphrase of Apc 20.7–10 suggests that this future is anything but remote. What interests Jud above all is Christ's final victory and the final defeat of Satan.

With its insistence on some of the essential points of the Zurich Reformation, its exhortations to devotion, and its simple theology, Jud's *Paraphrase* effectively neutralized all potentially dangerous aspects of the Apocalypse and made it useful reading for the wider mass of the faithful. Theodore Bibliander's commentary, first published only three years later, was written from a very different standpoint.

Theodore Bibliander and the *Relatio Fidelis*

Known chiefly for his edition of the Koran[17] published in Basel in 1543, Bibliander (or Buchmann) did not undertake the Apocalypse lightly. Although he admitted in a letter to Myconius written in the summer of 1543 that he found the book extremely exciting in that it put together the Old Testament and the Gospel to show how both could be used for building up the church, he nonetheless had serious doubts about his competence and, more to the point, about his reading of the last book of the Bible. Having read the commentaries of contemporaries such as Sebastian Meyer and Oswald Bär, and those of ancient theologians such as Bede, Augustine, and several other Greek and Latin Fathers, Bibliander was aware that his interpretation of the Apocalypse was very different from theirs.[18] In spite of his hesitations, he started lecturing on the Apocalypse in Zurich on 10 December 1543. The lectures were written up and published in shortened form in the *Relatio fidelis* in 1545. There, Bibliander devotes pages 114–161 to questions to do with the book's status and hermeneutics. As we noted in chapter 1, Bibliander's criteria for the canonicity of the Apocalypse were very much his own: It was known as canonical to all those who knew the apostle John, and, added to that, its contents conformed to the contents of other canonical texts. The issue of the book's clarity, while of great interest to Bibliander, did not impinge on the problem of canonicity. Faced with such unusual criteria for the book's canonicity, the reader might thus expect the Zurich reformer's hermeneutic to be equally idiosyncratic.

Although one of Bibliander's chief arguments for wanting to tackle the Apocalypse was the underlying conviction that his own era—characterized by wars against the Turks, the calling of the Council of Trent, schisms, sects, and the identification by some of the pope with the Antichrist—was the object of John's prophetic visions,[19] his account of the book is quite untainted by any eschatological fears or expectations.

Bibliander's division of the book shows a very subtle appreciation of the text. He divides it into four parts: Apc 1–3 constitutes the first part, Apc 4–11 the second, Apc 12–16 the third, and Apc 17–22 the fourth. The third part is then further divided into four (Apc 12, 13, 14, 15–16), thus making seven parts in all. It is to be noted that although Bibliander thus arrives at the traditional figure of seven visions, his seven do not in any way correspond to Bede's seven. Moreover, the Zurich reformer does not elaborate on the subdivision of the fourth part.

There is no doubt that his division of the text is dictated by his interpretation of it. Bibliander concurs with what was to become the opinion of modern scholarship in dating the Apocalypse in the sixty-fourth year after the Ascension, that is, 96/97 A.D., the era of the emperor Domitian.[20] However, like nearly all sixteenth-century theologians (with the exception of Erasmus) and unlike modern scholars, he unhesitatingly attributes the text to John the Evangelist. The Apocalypse contains the divine account of the history of the true Christians from the creation of the world until the Last Judgment, the date of which is left undetermined. Although Bibliander admits that all the best theologians agree that the Apocalypse is a prophecy of Christ, the church, and the church's enemies, covering the period from the last days of Domitian until the Last Judgment,[21] he very deliberately makes John into a historian, as well as into a prophet of the imminent demise of the papacy (identified with the second beast of Apc 13).

Bibliander is the only sixteenth-century commentator to bring out the full significance of the prologue (Apc 1.1–3) and the epilogue (Apc 22.18–21). Although obviously not aware of apocalyptics as a literary genre, the Zurich reformer picked out two of its most salient features: first, the authentification of the divine origin of the revelation and its transmission to the "seer" by the divine messenger in the prologue, and second, the appeal to God's justice and omnipotence contained in the epilogue.

The specificity of Bibliander's dual conception of the seer as both prophet and historian, taken together with the circumstances in which he wrote the commentary, made his account of the Apocalypse, as Bousset noted,[22] a curious mixture of stock and highly original interpretations. We shall now analyze Bibliander's interpretation in an attempt to show how the commonplace and the original come together. We shall then address the question of his possible sources.

The prologue is included in the first part (Apc 1–3), whose purpose it is to show that Christ is the sole head of the church; the seven letters to the seven churches constitute the symbol of his relationship to it. They serve to show what Christ approves of and disapproves of; he uses them to admonish, to blame, and to encourage.[23] Bibliander has thus left the Christian community in Asia Minor. It is the dogmatic issue of Christ as the sole head of the church, a commonplace since the disputations of Baden and Berne, that interests him in Apc 2 and 3.

Bibliander's summary of Apc 4 and 5 appears equally stereotyped and Reform-oriented; these chapters, for him, constitute the section "that explains the workings of divine providence and shows which men enter eternal life and which are damned and for what reason."[24] However, his demonstration of the workings of divine providence is anything but commonplace. Indeed, he is the only exegete to claim that the Lamb, on breaking the seals, reveals the course of universal history from the creation of the world until the end of time.[25] There is nothing unusual, he admits, in dividing the history of the world into seven parts.

His division, however, is different from all the others, including that of Leo Jud. To Bibliander, the first seal represents the first age, from the Creation until the Flood. It was in his view the most innocent age, as thereafter the world became steadily worse. The second age (the second seal) stretches from the Flood until Moses, the third from Moses until Christ, and the fourth from the Incarnation until the preaching of the Gospel and the peace of Constantine. The fifth seal covers the period from Constantine until the appearance of the "fully mature Antichrist." In contrast to most Protestant commentaries, the Antichrist is, interestingly enough, symbolized not by the reign of Hildebrand but by that of Pepin the Short, who won back for the papacy the exarchate of Ravenna and the rights and territories of the Roman republic prior to making the famous "donation of Pepin" to Pope Paul I. The sixth seal covers the period from the reign of Pepin until the destruction of Babylon and the revelation of the Antichrist, in other words, until the Council of Constance. The sixth seal is followed by the seventh, which will last until the end of the world and the Last Judgment.[26] It is plain that Bibliander lives during the time of the seventh seal. However, given that the period covered by each seal is at least seven hundred years, and given that barely a hundred years have elapsed since the Council of Constance, the Zurich reformer does not feel the Last Judgment to be imminent. The periods revealed by the seven trumpets are found to correspond exactly to those of the seven seals. Bibliander, rather like Colladon, works on two levels. His very great sensitivity to the structure of the Apocalypse is neutralized by his desire to use it as the text that ultimately condemns the papacy and identifies it as the Antichrist.

The first chapter of the third part, Apc 12, is firmly situated in the time of John himself, and the persecutions endured by the church, represented by the woman, are the persecutions that the church had to endure in John's own time—that is, shortly after the Ascension. Satan persecuted the church first of all via the Jews, asserts Bibliander, then via the gentiles, as is shown by the Acts of the Apostles and by Apc 2 (the letter to the church of Smyrna). However, he notes, commenting on Apc 12.14, the church will find a place among the gentiles at some time *future* to that of the writing of the Apocalypse. It will be sustained there until the Last Judgment, a time span denoted by the cryptic phrase *ad tempus et tempora et dimidium temporis*, God deliberately not wishing to reveal the date of the end.[27]

Along with Jud, Bibliander is one of the rare commentators to completely abandon Primasius' exegesis of the woman's two wings as a symbol of the Old Testament and the New Testament, and to propose his own interpretation instead. To him, the two wings represent, respectively, God's hidden help and God's open help for the church. As an example of this help, Bibliander cites intervention by the Romans in Jewish persecutions of Christians before Nero's time. All in all, the Zurich commentator devotes very little attention to Apc 12, seen by many Western commentators as the central vision of the Apocalypse. To him, Apc 12 and 13 are to be read together as a history of the persecutions endured by the church from the birth of Christ until the pontificate of Martin V. In fact, Apc 13 assumes a greater importance than Apc 12, as Bibliander uses it as a springboard for the history of the church from Nero's time until 1429, which he had already briefly out-

lined in his interpretation of the fifth and the sixth seals. His account of
Apc 13 is extremely detailed but touches on the text only occasionally, while
outlining with some subtlety the transition from the first to the second beast.
His scheme of history enables Bibliander to stand as forerunner of modern
biblical exegesis, in that he identifies the first beast of Apc 13 with the Roman
Empire. The rest of his commentary on the chapter, however, follows a typi-
cally sixteenth-century Protestant pattern: Bibliander is intent first and foremost on showing the links between the iniquities of the Roman Empire and
those of the papacy.

The wounded head of the beast is the death of Nero. The wound, however, was soon healed by Vespasian, who attributed his success in capturing
Jerusalem to the help of heathen gods and who, together with his succes-
sors, considered the Christian religion an offshoot of Judaism. Throughout
his commentary, Bibliander refers at great length to the corresponding passages of Daniel, and it is plain that he sees the capture of Jerusalem by
Vespasian as a mirror image of its capture by Antiochus Epiphanes, mentioned (he claims) in the eighth chapter of Daniel. Finally, he concludes,
the Lord ordered "the first beast," or the "old" Roman Empire, to be destroyed by the Goths.

However, no sooner was the first empire gone than the second Roman
Empire, that of the papacy, began to rise, at the same time as the Islam. The
Islam, according to Bibliander, "exercising its anti-Christian tyranny outside the church, would show up the Antichrist raging in the entrails of the
church and of the people of God."[28] It is interesting to note that Bibliander,
unlike du Pinet, does not see the Islam as one of the manifestations of the
Antichrist, preferring to interpret it as something that was concomitant upon
the rise of the Antichrist and that would serve to point it up. This view enables him to give an ideological justification for his own edition of the
Koran, while unequivocally identifying the Antichrist with the papacy, also
represented by the second beast of Apc 13. The number of the beast, 666, is
interpreted historically. According to Bibliander, 666 added to 97, the year
when the Apocalypse was written, gives "the year of the fully-grown Antichrist, victorious over three kings, dreaded by civil rulers and worshiped by
ignorant Christians."[29] It is the time of the fifth seal and the alliance between
the papacy and the Carolingian kings. Consistent with his earlier interpretation of the seals, Bibliander adds another 666 years to the year 763, thus
obtaining a total of 1429, the end of the pontificate of Martin V, and the
year "when you can see the Antichrist with protruding horns and very long
ears, exposed, with his mask off and fully revealed by the light of the word
of God."[30] Bibliander cites Horace *Ep.* 1.17.62 as an appropriate illustration
of the fate of the Antichrist in 1429. It is interesting to note that no particular pope is the Antichrist: neither Stephen II nor Paul I nor Martin V are
personally identified with an eschatological anti-God. However, the Antichrist is closely linked with the papacy, and his power is directly proportional

to the power exercised by any given pope. Secondly, it is important to note that the Zurich reformer sees the conciliar era as the beginning of the propagation of the word of God. Admittedly, Martin V strengthened the papacy, but the damage had been done, and Bibliander knows full well that Martin V was finally unable to curb the Hussites.

Passing over Apc 14 as containing a *doctrina saluberrima*, he devotes great care and attention to commenting the last two chapters of his third part, which are situated in the seventh seal, Bibliander's own era. It is no surprise to learn that at this stage Bibliander's commentary becomes even more polemical and virulently anti-Roman. Indeed, the time of the seventh seal, covering Apc 15 and 16, is the most important time in the history of salvation. It is then that Christ punishes the sins of the wicked "etiam in hoc saeculo" by the seven plagues and the seven bowls. The seven plagues, equivalent to the ten plagues that afflicted pharaoh, have been unleashed on the Roman church for over a hundred years. The bowls are commented on in greater detail. The first bowl denotes all the epidemics that have been sent by God (to punish the offspring of the Antichrist) in recent years. The second bowl represents recent wars, nearly all of them instigated by the papacy. The third bowl stands for the sacred doctrine, which turns to blood when received by the wicked. The fourth bowl is poured out over Christ himself, "the sun of righteousness," so that he burns the impious instead of illuminating them. The fifth bowl is God's wrath poured out over the papal throne, as is shown by the general disrespect in which the once dreaded indulgences are held, not to mention all the laws and edicts of the Roman church, now universally mocked. The sixth bowl, poured out into the "river of Babylon," illustrates the use of ecclesiastical riches to feed the poor, and the seventh bowl causes the (already damned) reprobate to commit the sin against the Holy Spirit.[31] There is no doubt that, although, as we shall see, the seventh age is emphatically not the millennium in the ante-Nicene sense of the term, it is nonetheless the best time on earth prior to the Last Judgment, which apparently will not be preceded by any final unleashing of Satan, as he has been unleashed already. Bibliander's fourth part, covering Apc 17–22 devoted to the eschatological future, recounts in detail "the rewards that are in store for the pious worshipers of Christ and conversely the tortures that await the devil and the Antichrist with his disciples and all the wicked."[32]

According to Bibliander, Apc 17 is a description of both ancient and papal Rome. Together with most modern exegetes, he notes that "the seven hills on which the woman sits" could refer only to Rome. However, here, as throughout the commentary, this flash of modernity is completely isolated, and Bibliander goes on to state that the Rome of his day is no more religious than pagan Rome, since over the years it has diverged so much from the apostolic doctrine of Peter and Paul. The entire condemnation of Rome is backed up with references to Dan. 7. Commented only briefly, Apc 19 is God's final judgment, that will be pronounced on Rome and her vassals at some undetermined future date, and Apc 20 recounts the tortures that will be suffered by the damned. Bibliander does not seem at all interested in the first resurrection of Apc 20, generally interpreted as a metaphor for the reward of the just and *not* for the tortures of the damned! One of the most original features of his commentary is his identification of the *angel* of Apc 20.1 with the apostle Paul, whereas most commentators identify him either with Christ himself or with all those who have taught the true Christian doctrine. Bibliander's identification is quite unequivocal, as indeed is his relegation of the *thousand years* to the past.

> For the light of the preached word of the Gospel came to the whole world through the apostles, but most of all through that teacher of the gentiles and that chosen instrument of God, Paul. Called from heaven by Christ himself to the office of the Gospel, he received it neither from men nor through men, and that is why he was more efficacious than the other apostles. Therefore, he is depicted most aptly by the angel descending from heaven. However, men preferred darkness to light so that a thousand years after the demise of the Jews and the affirmation of Christ's kingdom on earth, Satan ruled the world just as he did before Christ was announced.[33]

We saw that for Bibliander the fourth seal covered the period from the Incarnation until the peace of Constantine and the fifth seal represented the period from Constantine until the appearance of the fully mature Antichrist in the eighth century. Here, Bibliander proposes a slightly different chronology which complements rather than contradicts his earlier one. Assuming that by *consummatio Iudaeorum* he means the destruction of Jerusalem in 70, the *thousand years* during which Satan was chained up cover the period between 70 and 1070. What is important, however, is not that those years represent any kind of golden age (as we saw, the Antichrist was fully mature in the reign of Pope Paul I), but that Satan is unleashed with full force once they are over. The signal of the unleashing of Satan was in Bibliander's eyes the First Crusade, in which all the participants distinguished themselves by their barbaric cruelty and were accordingly punished by God. Bibliander's negative assessment of the First Crusade is largely motivated by its Roman inspiration. Be that as it may, our exegete is no millenarian. The *thousand years* of the chaining up of Satan by Paul is a period in the past covering some of the fourth and some of the fifth seal. Satan, far from being unleashed "for a little while," has been unleashed since 1070 and the time of the First Crusade. It is only since 1429 and the end of the Great Schism that his dominion has been curtailed (Bibliander implies) by the seven bowls. However much the Zurich reformer announces his intention of commenting on the eschatological future, he always returns to the past. It is obvious that he is convinced of the nonimminence of the Last Judgment and that he finds the Apocalypse of interest as a book of history which shows his own era to be especially important. In a word, the Apocalypse in Bibliander's eyes is a perfect apology for the historical importance of the Reformation. Not surprisingly, Apc 21 and 22 are dealt with very briefly; he interprets both to refer to celestial bliss in the hereafter.

Bibliander's Originality

The preceding analysis shows that the Zurich commentator did not directly rely on any of the sources that were available to him and that the hesitations he expressed in his letter to Myconius dated from 30 August 1543[34] were perfectly genuine. He really had read the commentaries of Oswald Bär, Sebastian Meyer, Bede, [pseudo-]Augustine, and many others and found that he disagreed with them. Although of some help in establishing the canonicity of the book, the existing commentaries were of little or no use in providing its exegetical framework. It is obvious that Bibliander, unlike most exegetes, did not find Apc 20 and the passage on the millennium crucial to the interpretation of the book and that he was not convinced by the spiritual exegesis of it, represented notably by Primasius and Bede, which took the *thousand years* of Apc 20 to represent the inner state of the faithful from the Incarnation until the end of time. Bibliander's millennium is, as we saw, a real period in history, stretching from the beginning of Pauline ministry until the time of the First Crusade. However, it is by no means a period of earthly bliss, and it has nothing whatsoever to do with the Second Coming. Both in terms of length and in terms of intensity, it is equivalent to the period of the unleashing of Satan, which includes Bibliander's own era and which is superior to the millennium in several respects, not least the full revelation of the iniquity of the papal Antichrist. The key to the interpretation of the Apocalypse is, so far as Bibliander is concerned, the opening of the seven seals, each seal representing one of the seven ages of the world from the Creation until the end of time, the Reformation itself falling within the final period, that of the seventh seal. Bibliander is obviously an advocate of the historico-prophetic exegesis of the Apocalypse, but the historical schema that he imposes on the text is very much his own. It is interesting to note that the very originality of his exegesis most likely prevented the Zurich reformer from ever publishing a conventional commentary on the Apocalypse. Despite the support notably of Bullinger and Myconius[35] (Bullinger even made a copy of Bibliander's lectures on the Apocalypse), the editor of the Koran preferred to conceal his exegesis within a treatise addressed to the Christian princes, whose object was to show that "it is only from the word and the Son of God that we should seek exact knowledge of times present and future and of the Antichrist himself (the greatest scourge in all the world), and also the right and the best way of governing a state and the whole Christian existence."[36] To Bibliander, Christ himself was the only authoritative historian, one able to point to the Antichrist.

Bibliander's Lecture Notes: The Relatio Fidelis *and the Antichrist*

Bibliander finished lecturing on the Apocalypse on 15 February 1544, having started in December 1543. Significantly, his notes are entitled *De revelatione diuinissima et die nostri Iesu Christi commentarius*. Infinitely more copious and more repetitive than the *Relatio fidelis*,[37] they reveal much more fully than the *Relatio* the thoroughness of his reading of the text and of the existent commentaries—both Greek and Latin—and would certainly merit a critical edition. In the context of the present work, they help to answer the question of why Bibliander identifies the papacy with the Antichrist without drawing the traditional eschatological conclusions. The Zurich manuscript Car I 91 contains a passage entitled *Antichristi Imago* which obviously formed a part of his lectures and which was not included in the *Relatio fidelis*.

Bibliander's conception of the Antichrist is much more traditional than his exegesis of the Apocalypse. According to him, the Antichrist is announced by the Holy Scripture as one who will come and "wreak much evil," and therefore it is fitting to attempt to describe him so that all true Christians can be warned and avoid him. However, he continues, the Antichrist is not just one person, for first, as is shown by 1 John 2.18, all those who are opposed to Christ and who will not serve him are Antichrists. In this category, Bibliander includes all the pagans and even more so the Jews "who had the light more than the gentiles via the Scriptures and through other means, but they did not accept the light and persecuted it more harshly than the gentiles."[38] He then narrows the definition of the Antichrist even further: Just as Christ is the head of all good and true Christians, so the wicked and the false Christians must also have a head, which will be the contrary of Christ in every respect "and worse than which cannot be imagined."[39] It is interesting to note that Bibliander does not include the time of the Antichrist's appearance (shortly before the end) in his definition: The Antichrist is not an eschatological anti-God; he is simply everything that Christ is not, the leader of the forces of evil just as Christ is the leader of the forces of good. Referring to 2 Thess. 2.8 and the passage following, Bibliander notes that the Antichrist is supposed to be a man, not a demon, although he is to be driven by Satan. Moreover, he is a Christian and, as is shown by Paul in 2 Thess. 2.4, a priest.

However, Bibliander is well aware that one man in the course of a relatively short life would not be able to do enough evil to count as the Antichrist. There must be several Antichrists, all succeeding one another and all called by the same name, just as all kings of Egypt were called pharaoh.[40] The stage is thus set for the portrayal of the papacy as the Antichrist, which occupies the rest of the text. Christ as God took on the form of a servant, whereas the pope, being human, claims to be a god; Christ was born of the Virgin, having been conceived by the Holy Spirit, whereas the pope is elected by a thoroughly corrupt conclave. Christ fled the golden crown, preferring one of thorns, whereas the pope, not content with one crown, wears three coronets on his headdress. The catalogue of contrasts is long and is aimed at showing that the papacy is anti-Christian in the sense of being against Christ. Bibliander's portrayal of the Antichrist has nothing to do with eschatological hopes; it is motivated primarily by confessional polemics. In tone, it is slightly reminiscent of certain chapters of Thomas à Kempis' *Imitatio Christi*, except that its purpose is to convince Bibliander's students *not* to imitate the papacy or anything to do with it.

Heinrich Bullinger and His *Hundred Sermons*

There are no obvious signs of Bibliander's influence on Bullinger's *Hundred Sermons*. The literary form is very different: Bullinger's exegesis is as detailed as Bibliander's was sparse. More importantly, however, the *antistes* does not take the opening of the seven seals to stand for the Lord's revelation of the history of the world, from the Creation until the Last Judgment, but for the unfolding of the workings of divine providence. Before discussing Bullinger's interpretation of Apc 6–8, 12, and 20, a brief reminder of the nature and context of his *Hundred Sermons* is in order.[41]

It was on the arrival in Zurich of the Marian exiles in 1554 that Bullinger composed his *Sermons*, which were first published in Latin, in 1557, in Basel.[42] As I have argued elsewhere, the *Sermons* obviously filled an important gap in the market of Protestant apocalyptics, for they were translated into French and printed in Geneva less than a year later.[43] The publisher, Jean Crespin, obviously intended them to supplant du Pinet's commentary published by his competitor Jean Girard. He was not unsuccessful, as the French printing of Bullinger's *Sermons* came out in Geneva in 1565 from the presses of Bonnefoy and Fournet, whereas nothing more was heard of du Pinet's commentary (which had undergone five editions between 1539 and 1557) after its publication with Beza's preface in 1557. However, Bullinger's interpretation was very much his own and had little to do with du Pinet's traditional, spiritualist approach. It was not for nothing that Bullinger's preface was openly addressed "to those who are banished from France, from England, from Italy, and from other kingdoms or nations, in the name of the Lord, and scattered throughout Germany and throughout the land of the Swiss, and also to all the faithful, wherever they are, awaiting the coming of Jesus Christ, Judge and Lord of all."[44]

Bullinger's preface and Bibliander

The preface occupies more than fifty in octavo pages. Before discussing its salient points and its (limited) affinity with Bibliander's *Relatio fidelis*, it is important to assign a status to Bullinger's *Sermons*. The very word *sermons* would suggest that the *antistes* actually preached on the Apocalypse. On the other hand, the publication of the sermons in Latin and the large number of allusions to works of history, theology, and exegesis by ancient and medieval authors make it a priori unlikely that Bullinger actually published what he preached. The answer to the puzzle is provided in the preface. Yes, Bullinger did preach on the Apocalypse in Zurich, but he adapted his sermons for publication so that the finished product would perform the function of a blueprint for sermons. This is how Bullinger himself describes his endeavors:

> I divided my exposition into Sermons not only because I publicly preached on this book in the true church of Jesus Christ which I serve—I gave sermons on this book to the people in 1555 and 1556 in a practically identical form to that found here—but also because, on being asked, I wanted to provide a model for those who wish to preach upon or explain this same book to the churches which have been entrusted to them.[45]

Bullinger insists that the *Sermons* should not be recited word for word by the preachers who decide to use them. They contain several passages which were not preached and, conversely, the sermons when delivered contained material "according to time and place of delivery" that Bullinger judged unfit for the printed version.[46] In a word, his *Sermons on the Apocalypse*, albeit formalized, show a strong pastoral concern which was completely absent from Bibliander's *Relatio fidelis*. They are correspondingly much more Christocentric: To Bullinger, the Apocalypse is an account by Christ himself, who is sitting at God's right hand, of all the misfortunes that the church will have to endure from the time of the Ascension until the Last Judgment, which, as we shall show later, is drawing near for Bullinger, in complete contrast to Bibliander's view. However, although implicitly rejecting Bibliander's eschatology and, more importantly, his view of the Apocalypse as a revelation of history of mankind from the Creation until the Last Judgment, Bullinger does take over his colleague's interpretation of Apc 13 as the transition from the Roman Empire, represented by the first beast, to the papacy, represented by the second beast. In his preface, Bullinger insists that this transition and the emergence of the papal Antichrist is a key to the book.[47] Once Rome was destroyed by the Goths, he notes, there was no Roman emperor for 320 years, until the reign of Charlemagne. However, during that time, the bishop of Rome began to set up his own empire. Bullinger cites testimonies of Tertullian and Jerome that purportedly show that the Antichrist would not come until after the destruction of the ancient Roman Empire. The second beast of Apc 13 corroborates this; his two horns represent, according to the *antistes*, the two realms of papal authority, temporal and spiritual. Interestingly, Bullinger only partly adopts Bibliander's explanation of the number 666, both in the preface and in the body of the commentary. Like the man whose lectures on the Apocalypse he so much admired,[48]

Bullinger adds 666 to the date of the book's composition (97). The total (763) represents the reign of Pepin the Short and the subjugation of the temporal powers to the papacy. However, unlike Bibliander, Bullinger does not then repeat the operation, which would bring him up to the pontificate of Martin V and the revelation of the full iniquity of the Antichrist. Living near the end of time, Bullinger does not single out his own era as having an obvious importance in the course of history. Much more important is the unleashing of the Antichrist, which he sees, like Bibliander, as having gone on for more than five hundred years. Unlike Erasmus, Beza, and many others, Bullinger considers the Apocalypse to be a perfectly simple and clear book, worthy of being preached on. Not claiming to say anything new, he sees himself as one in the long line of commentators, and, to prove this, he carefully lists his authorities: Bibliander, Arethas, Augustine, Primasius, Thomas Aquinas, the *Glossa ordinaria*, Meyer, Lambert, Luther, Erasmus, and Valla.[49]

Valla's annotations on the Apocalypse were scant enough to imply scepticism, and young Luther's and Erasmus' hostility to the book was well known by the time Bullinger was writing. What is interesting is that the Zurich reformer had obviously read Luther, Erasmus, and Valla and found that they could be put to some use by one who thought the Apocalypse was both apostolic and clear. Their hostility was thus neutralized, and they were recruited in the common cause of identifying the papacy as the Antichrist. Unlike his Roman Catholic contemporary Jean de Gagny, Bullinger found it only natural to comment on the Apocalypse after commenting on the rest of the New Testament. His friends' encouragement served only to confirm him in his initial resolution.[50] Given that the *Sermons* are very largely given over to the condemnation of the papal Antichrist, the *antistes* finishes his preface with another list of authorities, ancient and modern, who asserted that the pope was the Antichrist. The list includes Tertullian, Jerome, Gregory I, Bernard of Clairvaux, Joachim of Fiore, Petrarch, Luther, Marsiglio of Padua, Lorenzo Valla, Savonarola, and the Franciscan Michael Cesenas.

Thus, Bibliander was an important influence on Bullinger only in so far as the *Relatio fidelis* showed better than most other commentaries how the transition from the first to the second beast was made and so provided a biblical justification for the view that the papacy was the Antichrist. Bullinger also took from Bibliander the idea that the Antichrist had been unleashed for more than five hundred years. However, his primarily pastoral concerns meant that Bullinger's *Sermons*, by their very nature, were much more practically oriented than the *Relatio fidelis*. Bullinger's eschatology was also very much his own.

Bullinger's Views on the Structure of the Book

Having devoted his preface to the general considerations of the book's content and his own attitude to it, Bullinger uses the first sermon (one of those that were almost certainly never preached but were added subsequently for publication) to discuss questions that would have preoccupied the very clergy for whom he intended his work. The title of the sermon is "Of the author of this book, of its parts, and finally of its diverse uses and of its very salutary usefulness."[51] After insisting on the book's apostolic origin, its canonicity, and its use in the early church (Bullinger relies particularly on the testimony of the ante-Nicene Fathers, willfully ignoring their chiliasm), he sketches out two interpretative schemas of the book: (1) the "historical" division into six parts, and (2) the "spiritual" division into seven sections or visions. The first schema divides the book as follows: the prologue, in Apc 1.1–8; Christ's reign in glory on the right hand of the Father and his influence on the church via the Spirit, in Apc 1–4; and Christ's warning to the church of all the evils that will befall it, in Apc 4–12. The struggle of the church against *old* dragon and the *old* and the *new* beasts, representing respectively the old and the new tyranny of Rome, is described in Apc 12–15, which also contains an accurate description of the Antichrist. In Apc 15–22 are a description of the pains and torments that the Antichrist and his vassals will have to endure. Those same chapters describe the Last Judgment and the happiness of the true faithful. The final (sixth) part is composed of the epilogue, in Apc 22.[52]

The second schema that Bullinger recommends to his pastors is the traditional division into seven parts going back to the Venerable Bede. Thus, Apc 1–3 are seen as representing Christ reigning in glory and governing his church. The second vision is the opening of the seven seals and includes Apc 4.1–8.1. The third vision (Apc 8.2–11.9) contains the seven trumpets. The fourth vision occupies Apc 12–14. It depicts, according to Bullinger, the struggle between the woman and the dragon, the *old* beast with seven heads (the Roman Empire), the *new* beast with two horns (the papacy), and the Antichrist. The fifth vision depicts the seven bowls (Apc 15–17); the sixth, the condemnation of Babylon; and the seventh, the glory of all the true faithful in the heavenly Jerusalem.[53]

Bullinger's intentions are quite plain: When preaching and commenting on the Apocalypse, the clergy can use either schema, because the transition from the "first" to the "second beast" and the destruction of the Antichrist constitute the focal point of both.

The Seven Seals

Bullinger's interpretation of the seven seals shows that he totally rejected Bibliander's interpretation of them. Although he makes no reference to Bibliander in his exposition of Apc 6–8, it is plain that the *antistes* deliberately does not interpret the opening of the seals as the unveiling of the history of mankind from Creation until the Last Judgment, and that he prefers to see the first seal as symbolic of early Christianity. Addressing his *Sermons* to religious refugees on the one hand and to Protestant clergymen on the other hand, he wants to concentrate on the fate of the Christian church so as to increase the immediate, practical applicability of his work. The first seal (and the white horse) thus stands for fruitful preaching of the Gospel. It shows that there will always be a church and that the truth will always be taught. However, continues Bullinger, men refuse the peace of the Gospel and the Lord sends wars upon them, which are symbolized by the red horse: Rome was destroyed by the Goths because the Roman emperors refused the peace of the Gospel. The bloodshed of the First Crusade was a living illustration of a similar refusal on the part of the pope. The third seal and the black horse stand for misfortune, famine, and high prices: If men reject the truth of the Gospel with its spiritual benefits, it is only natural that God should make it difficult for them to obtain the bare necessities of life. Momentarily forgetting his decision not to stretch the seals further back than the Incarnation (or perhaps simply wishing to make his point more strongly), Bullinger then gives a list of famines from Old Testament times until 1529. In a similar moralizing spirit, he then asserts that the fourth seal stands for plagues and other mortal illnesses with which God punishes those who refuse his Word. Bullinger's interpretation of the fifth seal (souls under the altar) is overtly anti-Roman. Taking the souls to stand for true faithful killed in persecutions since Nero's time, he insists that the worst persecutions have taken place over the past five hundred years, the era of the Antichrist, or the unleashing of the "papist Satan." He also uses the passage to note that, because the souls of the martyrs have to wait and pray for God's vengeance (Apc 6.10), they obviously have no power to intercede for those on earth. The sixth seal, according to Bullinger, stands for the corruption of doctrine and includes all the ancient heresies (which find their culmination in the Islam), especially the sophistry and corrupt teaching of the Antichrist and his ministers. The earthquake accompanying the sixth seal symbolizes chaos, darkness, and disorder that result from corruption of the true doctrine. The half an hour's silence on the opening of the seventh seal is to Bullinger simply a sign to the congregation to pay particular attention, as the popish doctrine is about to be more fully condemned by the trumpets.[54]

Bullinger's interpretation of the seven seals reveals all his major preoccupations, both theological and pastoral. Although he frequently refers to Orosius, Eusebius, Josephus, and other historians, they are of interest to him only in so far as they bear out his theology. What primarily interests him is the imminent destruction of the popish Antichrist, the salvation of the true faithful, the condemnation of the wicked, and the salutary value of divine punishments. His chief historical interest (which he inherits, as we saw, from Bibliander) is to show that the Roman Empire and the papacy are represented, respectively, by the first and second beasts of Apc 13. In accord with their author's intention, Bullinger's *Sermons* dispense much practical and moral advice for the use of preachers on issues such as seeing famine and war as a just punishment, finding consolation in misfortune, condemning the cult

of the saints, and listening attentively in church. In commenting on the
Apocalypse, the *antistes* reveals in a very immediate way not only his theological and moral concerns but also his daily preoccupations.

Bullinger and Apocalypse 12

Bullinger devotes three short sermons (52, 53, and 54) to Apc 12, which he
considers, as we saw, as the beginning of either the third or the fourth vision. His exegesis of the chapter is for the most part profoundly unoriginal
and resembles nothing so much as a patchwork of interpretations drawn from
earlier Western commentators.

Aware of both the dominant interpretation which takes the woman to be
the church and of the less well-known interpretation of her as Mary, Bullinger
naturally prefers the former and cites several passages from other books of the
Scripture (Eph. 5, Gen. 2, etc.) in which a woman embodies the church.
However, as we shall see, he does not discard the Marial exegesis altogether
but weaves it skillfully into the "ecclesiastical" interpretation. Following Bede
and François Lambert in particular, Bullinger takes the sun to represent Christ,
"the sun of righteousness." His interpretation of the moon under the woman's
feet is, however, very much his own. He agrees with Bede, Lambert, and others
that the church tramples underfoot the moon, which stands for all things cor-
ruptible and changeable.[55] However, he also takes the passage to refer to the
light of the church's righteousness, which waxes and wanes in a similar fashion to the moon, as it is subject to the influence of the flesh.[56] Such flashes of
individuality are isolated, and it is obvious that Bullinger is very much influenced by Victorinus of Poetovio as well as by Primasius, Bede, and Lambert,
seeing as he interprets the stars in the woman's crown as standing for patriarchs, prophets, *and* apostles.[57] However, like Lambert, he insists that it is the
doctrine of the ministry that is being expounded.

Who or what is the woman pregnant with? We saw that according to
Bede she was pregnant with the true faithful (to whom the church constantly
gives birth), whereas for Lambert she was pregnant with Christ in the sense
of "pregnant with the message of Christ." Bullinger adopts neither interpretation wholeheartedly, although he inclines toward Lambert's. Like the
Wittenberg commentator, he notes that Christ is born in the faithful whenever they are reborn by his faith, and, again like Lambert, he cites Gal. 4.19
in support of this.[58] However, not wishing to do away with the Marial exegesis, he also insists that the church can be pregnant with Christ in the sense
of wanting Christ to be born of the Virgin. He does, however, admit, after
Primasius, that the woman herself cannot represent the Virgin, seeing as she
suffers from birth pangs, which are not possible in a virgin birth.[59]

A detailed description of the dragon, closely modeled on François
Lambert's with the notable exception of the identification of each head with
a specific kingdom (Bullinger obviously does not wish to be drawn into a

prophetic explanation), is followed by a rather insipid description of the battle between the church and the dragon (with the archangel Michael representing Christ) which ends with the dragon being expelled from heaven. It is Bullinger's very unwillingness to dwell upon the interpretation of certain details of Apc 12 and his insistence upon the moral importance of the struggle which make his sermons on Apc 12 valuable for pastoral purposes.

Bullinger and the Millennium

Bullinger, as he admitted himself,[60] attached a great deal of importance to the Last Judgment, and he accordingly devoted some attention to the questions of the millennium and of the end of time. His knowledge of ante-Nicene millenarianism was no better and no worse than that of his contemporaries. He would have had access to the incomplete Irenaeus without the millenarian ending, possibly Justin's *Dialogue with Trypho*, Victorinus without the millenarian ending, Lactantius, and various hostile testimonies, particularly those of Eusebius' *Ecclesiastical History*. His condemnation of ante-Nicene chiliasm is correspondingly diffident:

> I know that the heresy of chiliasts or millenarians has had its origins in this passage [Apc 20.2], of which heresy Papias was the author, as Eusebius tells us in book 3 of his *History* [H.e. 3.39]. Personally, I have no intention of refuting the opinions of others, especially as this would be a lengthy and laborious process, and, what is more, it would not greatly profit the readers.[61]

Millenarianism in its literal sense is of no interest and no particular relevance to Bullinger, who orders his exegesis of Apc 20.2–4 as follows: the description of the angel, the angel's work, the explanation of *thousand years*.

The angel in Apc 20 stands not for Christ himself, as most commentators would have it, but for "the order of the apostles, among whom St. Paul stands out so excellently as the teacher of the gentiles."[62] Bullinger explains that the word *angel* is to be taken here in its original sense of "messenger." The apostles, he explains, were chosen by the Son of God on his Incarnation and were sent by him to preach the Gospel throughout the world. From him, they received the keys of the kingdom of heaven and the power to forbid and to allow [Matt. 16.19]. The chain with which they bound Satan is the Gospel. In other words, Satan was chained up for a *thousand years* at the very moment when the Gospel began to be preached. Writing in the mid-1550s, Bullinger sees the millennium as belonging firmly in the past. Using Cardinal Benno's *Vita Hildebrandi*[63] and other *Lives* of the popes, he puts forward three alternative chronologies of the millennium before finally deciding that the third alternative is probably the most exact. The three periods that he feels worthy of being called millennia are chronologically very close to one another. Each begins with a significant event in the apostolic church and ends with an equally significant event that shows an immoderate increase in the power of the papacy. Although Bullinger insists that he does not wish to be overscrupulous in his calculations of the beginning of the millennium, the very fact of suggesting three alternative chronologies shows that he had put some thought into the matter and that he had a fully developed conception of the history of Christianity.

The first likely millennium stretches from the Ascension in 34 A.D. and the ministry of St. Paul to the Gentiles ("whereby he began to oppress Satan") until the election of Benedict IX as pope in 1034. Referring to *Vita Hildebrandi*, Bullinger notes that Benedict IX acceded to the papal throne due to black magic and after concluding a pact with the devil. However, it was in 1045 and not in 1034 that he committed the most iniquitous act, selling the papal throne to Gregory VI.[64] Although there is no doubt in Bullinger's mind that it was around the time of Benedict IX that Satan emerged to seduce the nations via the popes, he suggests a second chronology of the millennium which turns out to be not very different from the first. Starting with Paul's imprisonment in Rome in 60 A.D.,[65] Bullinger takes the *thousand years* up to the papacy of Nicholas II, who committed the crime of condemning the heresy of Berengarius and who thus brought in the iniquitous reign of Gregory VII, who definitively condemned Berengarius, among his other misdeeds.[66]

While admitting that Gregory VII's biographer, Cardinal Benno, calculates his millennium from Christ's nativity until the reign of Pope Sylvester II (d. 1003), Bullinger finally seems to opt for his own chronology, which he puts forward as the third likely time span for the millennium. Beginning with the year 73 A.D. and the fall of Jerusalem, and apparently ignoring the fact that Jerusalem fell in 70 A.D., he takes the *thousand years* up to 1073 and the papacy of Gregory VII. Bullinger's millennium thus finally stretches from the conversion of the gentiles until the flowering of the papacy during the reign of Gregory VII,[67] marked by the investitures controversy and the submission of the Holy Roman emperor, Henry IV, to ecclesiastical powers.[68]

Not only is Bullinger's millennium in the past, it is also a period which had little or nothing to do with the Golden Age of the ante-Nicene Fathers. Through his reading of church histories, Bullinger knows that the doctrine of justification by works, the worship of saints and relics, the dominance of the bishop of Rome, and the Turkish invasions go back to long before the year 1073.[69] This leads him to answer his own rhetorical question: In what sense can the devil be said to have been chained up during the period 73–1073?

He provides an answer by a reference to John 12.31, in which Jesus says: "Now is the hour of Judgment for his world; now shall the prince of this world be driven out." Adopting the standard Augustinian interpretation of the passage, Bullinger takes it that on Christ's Ascension Satan was going to be driven out of the hearts of all those who had followed the Lord but that he was not going to be done away with completely.[70] Bullinger then explains at great length that Jesus broke Satan's power but only for the true faithful. In a word, the millennium for Bullinger amounts to the first *thousand years* of the church, which suggests that Satan has been unleashed not for "a little while," as Apc 20.3 would have it, but for nearly five hundred years—Satan being here the papacy. The entire history of Christianity thus becomes a period of waxing and waning of Satan's power. Referring to Lactantius' *Institutiones diuinae* 7.15 and apparently ignoring their author's chiliasm,[71] Bullinger notes that his own era is the "age of lead," comparing it to the golden age of the early church, and that the closer the Last Judgment approaches, the more iniquity will flourish, so much so that his own age will appear a golden age by the time the Last Judgment has come.

This relativistic approach to history enables Bullinger to interpret the "little while" of Apc 20.3 without resorting to allegory. While admitting that the devil has, according to his calculations, been released for five hundred years, Bullinger can affirm that he has been fully released for a short while only. Papal domination was, he claims, fairly rapidly curbed by the Waldensians, princes such as Ludwig of Bavaria and preachers such as John Wyclif, John Hus, and Jerome of Prague.[72] The veritable unleashing of Satan thus only lasted from 1070 until about 1170.

Given Bullinger's constant appeal to the approaching Last Judgment, the obvious question that arises with regard to his commentary is, When does he expect the final end? Although the *Sermons* contains no explicit reply, some clues to the date of the Last Judgment are provided by this interpretation of the number 666 as the figure of the Antichrist.

As we have seen, Bullinger's interpretation of 666 is the submission to the papacy by Pepin the Short. Like Bibliander, he adds 666 to the date of the book's composition, thus obtaining 763, the approximate date of the donations of Pepin and Constantine. However, the rise of the second beast is not seen by Bullinger as an isolated historical event, for he reads it in the light of Irenaeus' assertion that the rise of the second beast is a recapitulation of all iniquity.[73] Bullinger takes Irenaeus' statement to be prophetic, referring to the papacy in general. Thus the second beast, once risen in or around 763, will recapitulate its iniquity in the successive popes. All that is left to the faithful, concludes Bullinger, is to pray that the Lord comes swiftly and delivers them from this oppression.[74]

A wish for a swift end does not constitute a calculation, and the reader has to turn back to Bullinger's interpretation of Apc 20.3 to get some idea of when the Last Judgment is at all likely to come, although what Bullinger says can at best be considered an intimation:

> Saint John has assigned a certain number of years to the Antichrist, that is
> to say 666, so that we can thereby recognize the name of the Antichrist,
> but it does not follow that the devil has therefore been unleashed completely
> or that the light of truth has been put out.[75]

Here, Bullinger seems to put forward a slightly different interpretation of 666, suggesting that papal iniquity, released in 1073, would recapitulate itself over a period of 666 years before the Last Judgment in 1739. However, it is important to stress that at no stage does he take the speculations any further and at no stage does he mention either 1739 or any other specific date for the final end. Given that his millennium was in the past and that his own period was that of the unleashing of Satan, his fellow Protestants might well have reproached Bullinger with not attributing any particular importance to the Reformation. It was perhaps to anticipate this criticism that the *antistes* put forward a spiritual interpretation of Apc 20.4–5 in his explanation of the first and the second resurrection.

Invoking Arethas and also Augustine's *City of God* 20.7–8, Bullinger takes the first resurrection to be the spiritual event for the faithful who receive Christ and the second to be the general resurrection of the flesh. To reign with Christ for a *thousand years* in the first resurrection is thus to reign with him forever in the sense of being regenerated by him.[76] The passage is to Bullinger a proof against the Anabaptists that the souls of the dead faithful live with Christ in heaven until the Last Judgment, while their bodies wait for the resurrection of the flesh.[77] By implicitly identifying the true faithful with those who would have adopted the doctrines of the Reformation, in the sense of those who at various times in history have attempted to curb the power of the papal Antichrist, Bullinger carries out his initial intention of giving his faithful hope and consolation. Those who are persecuted for their religion are to understand that they are part of the true church and that the Last Judgment approaches and with it the demise of Romish Satan.

As is shown by Jud's *Paraphrase*, Bibliander's *Relatio fidelis* and lectures, and Bullinger's *Sermons*, the Apocalypse was adapted for daily use by the Zurich reformers in ways in which it apparently never was in Geneva. Leo Jud, while not identifying the pope with the Antichrist, tried to make the text mirror various aspects of the Zurich Reformation. Written in German, his *Paraphrase* was an educational text, teaching the faithful not very much about eschatology but a lot about which aspects of religious practice to adopt. Bibliander was more influential than Jud and extremely radical in his interpretation of the text. His major contribution consisted in making the Apocalypse into a history of the Old Testament and the New Testament and, most important, in identifying the first and second beasts in Apc 13 with the Roman Empire and the papacy, respectively. Although living in the time of the seventh seal, Bibliander felt that he had a future, and he was not particularly interested in the Last Judgment. The importance of the Reformation for him was its chronological situation in the seventh seal, the very time when God punished the reprobate by the seven bowls.

Bullinger was the only major reformer of the second generation who devoted a full-length work to the Apocalypse. Whereas Bibliander finally never published his lectures but rather hid his exegesis of the Apocalypse within a treatise addressed (ostensibly at least) to the Christian princes, Bullinger produced no more and no less than model sermons that could be adapted by preachers throughout the reformed churches of Europe. Heavily indebted to Bibliander in some important respects, such as linking the Roman Empire and the papacy and sharing an obsession with the papal Antichrist, Bullinger was nonetheless much more interested in the pastoral aspect of the book and did his best to bring out its discussion of issues such as famine, saint worship, and listening attentively in church which would have been of direct concern to his readers and listeners.

None of the three commentators were driven by any eschatological fears in their interpretation of the book. Bullinger, who lived closer to the Last Judgment than either Jud or Bibliander, cannot be said to fear it but rather to hope for it, as it is only then that the papal Antichrist will finally be condemned.

5

THE LUTHERAN COUNTERPOINT

David Chytraeus and Nikolaus Selnecker

David Chytraeus

Although scholars have recently devoted some attention to David Chytraeus,[1] he remains a little-known figure and his biblical commentaries have remained unstudied to this day. Before discussing his *Explicatio Apocalypsis*, a few words about the author and his contribution to the spread of Lutheranism are thus necessary.

Born in 1530 in Ingelfingen, Chytraeus matriculated under his German name, Kochhaf, at the University of Tübingen on 22 June 1539, where he came under the influence of Joachim Camerarius and Erhard Schnepf, and the theology of Johannes Brenz, without ever being his pupil. After obtaining his M.A. degree in 1544 at the age of fourteen, he moved to the University of Wittenberg, the center of the Reformation movement in Germany. Although deeply impressed by Luther, Chytraeus was particularly influenced by Melanchthon, in whose household he lodged. Luther's death and the division of the Lutheran camp into Philippists and Gnesio-Lutherans marked the latter half of Chytraeus' career. Perhaps because of his attachment to both Luther and Melanchthon, he was to play the role of intermediary between the two camps. In 1551, the University of Rostock was successful in obtaining his services, together with those of Johannes Aurifaber. In 1563, a *Formula concordiae* between the duke of Saxony and the city of Rostock guaranteed financing for the university, which had fallen into destitution. Chytraeus and Aurifaber managed to gather around them a group of Melanchthon's disciples who had in 1536 already developed a program of reforms for the university. In 1564, Chytraeus elaborated new statutes for the theology faculty, making the *Augsburg Confession* and Melanchthon's *Examen ordinandorum* compulsory reading for theology students and teachers. Moreover, the *Examen* and Melanchthon's *Loci communes* were considered by Chytraeus as the best summary of Lutheran doctrine. Like his teacher, Chytraeus laid great emphasis on the importance of Hebrew, Greek, and Latin, as well as dialectic and rhetoric, for the study of theology. During his time in Rostock, he lectured on several books of the Bible, beginning with Genesis and Matthew in 1553. His method was strongly influenced by Melanchthon: A commentary relating the text to the main points of doctrine was followed by points of grammar and rhetoric, with a refutation of heresies coming at the end. The pattern repeated itself for every chapter of the biblical book commented.

It is important to bear in mind that Chytraeus is chiefly known as a historian and not as a biblical commentator. He began to teach history at Rostock in 1559 and lectured on Herodotus, Thucydides, and Melanchthon's edition of the *Chronicon Carionis*. He won fame notably for his *Historia der Augsburgischen Confession* published in Rostock in 1576 and for his *Chronicon Saxoniae*, first published anonymously in Wittenberg in 1586. His interest in history was obviously very largely responsible for his decision to lecture on the Apocalypse and to present his lectures in published form. Between 1563 and 1597, Chytraeus was five times rector of the University of Rostock, after being made doctor of theology in 1561. He was instrumental in setting up in 1570 the Rostock consistory, which he saw as exercising a largely pedagogical function; he was also active in the Lutheran missions to Austria in 1569 and 1574 after Maximilian II had given in to pressures to tolerate Lutheranism on condition that a *Liber agendorum* be drawn up, defining the nature of church service and organization. It was Chytraeus' task to draw up the *Liber agendorum*, which was finally officially accepted by the emperor in 1571. Having traveled as far as the Turkish border during his first stay in Austria, he developed an interest in the affairs of the Eastern churches. In 1580, he even published the famous correspondence between the Tübingen theologian Martin Crusius and Jeremias II, patriarch of Constantinople. His second journey to Austria in 1574 was mainly taken up with drawing up a church ordinance for Steiermark.

He did not play a leading role in the negotiations leading up to the 1580 Formula of Concord, although he did participate and help, mainly due to his excellent relations with the Tübingen theologians. The last twenty-five years of his life were plagued by illness. He died in 1600 in Rostock.[2]

David Chytraeus' Commentary on the Apocalypse

Chytraeus' *Explicatio* appeared for the first time in 1563[3] and was dedicated to Erik XIV of Sweden.[4] The choice was by no means fortuitous, if we bear in mind that the 1560s saw the early development of the distinctly Swedish Lutheran church. A group of strict Lutheran reformers gathered around Erik, wanting to weed out Catholic ceremonies and practices. They were supported by the Calvinists. The king vacillated for awhile between the orthodox and the Calvinist party but sided with the synod of 1566, which rejected the Calvinist interpretation of the Eucharist. However, he did not abandon the Swedish line of tolerance proclaimed at Västerås in 1527. The Calvinists were allowed freedom of belief so long as they did not cause public offense. Erik stayed anti-Catholic his whole life, finally preferring a Phippist humanistic Lutheranism, of which Chytraeus was a representative.

The commentary Chytraeus offered to Erik was, as he says in the preface, the fruit of lectures he had given on the Apocalypse at the Rostock Academy. He intended it not simply as an expression of general respect but as a way of congratulating the Swedish king on the peace of his kingdom and on the excellent state of the "churches of Christ" which he found to be flourishing in Sweden. Making some allowance for flattery (especially as Erik could not be considered peaceful, having declared war on Denmark, Lübeck, and Poland in 1563!), Chytraeus is presumably making an allusion to the religious events of the 1560s which were centered around Erik when he says:

> I wanted to dedicate and present to your Royal Majesty this very clear description of the kingdom of Christ brought by the apostle John from the bosom of Christ, illustrated by some most pleasing figures and images, and publicly expounded by me at the Rostock Academy by virtue of my position. I wanted to present it to your Majesty with due humility and reverence, not only so as to offer your Majesty a token of my respect, love, and admiration, which are excited in my heart (and in those of many other good men in Germany) by the virtues with which you are more blessed by God than other rulers, but also so that I could be seen to rejoice in the pious tranquillity and the flourishing churches of Christ in your illustrious kingdom. It is to their judgment that I submit this work of mine and others published previously. . . .[5]

The Reasons for Commenting on the Apocalypse

Chytraeus' *Explicatio* is highly repetitive and derivative, full of excursus, and certainly not a work of great genius. The repetitions and the excursus suggest that he wrote up his lecture notes in haste. However, although no landmark in the history of exegesis, the commentary throws an extremely interesting light on the author's historical circumstances and especially on his concept of church history. Chytraeus sees the Apocalypse as an illustration of Christ's predictions in Matt. 24 and elsewhere in the Scripture of the evils that would befall the church after his Ascension. It is both apostolic and especially important as being the sole book devoted to those evils. It shows that they do not come about fortuitously but are governed and ordained by the Lamb and God the Father to strengthen the faithful.[6] Unlike the Genevan and Zurich commentators, Chytraeus feels quite free to speculate on the date of the Last Judgment, which he feels to be very close. We shall be discussing his speculations further on. However, it is not the impending Last Judgment that is of crucial importance to Chytraeus but the value of the Apocalypse as a means of checking off and evaluating events in the history of the church. Although influenced by both Luther and Bullinger, he is not completely indebted to either of them.

His commentary consists of the preface (in the form of a dedicatory epistle), the *argumentum* (which includes the standard division of the book into seven visions), a list of the *loci communes*, a glossary, and the commentary proper. We shall now analyze all the prefatory pieces before studying Chytraeus' method and sources in the commentary. We shall be concentrating on Apc 6–8 (the opening of the seven seals), Apc 12 (the woman and the dragon), and Apc 20 (the Last Judgment).

Chytraeus' preface intends to account for the miserable state of the kingdom of Christ, torn apart by divisions and sects. Its author claims that it is composed of three parts. The first is ostensibly an account of the state of the church just before and just after the Council of Nicea, which Chytraeus sees as a mirror of the church of his own time. In the second part, the author sets out to give reasons for the sad state of the church of his own time, and, in the third part, he wants to show his readers how in such a diversity of opinions and sects they can recognize the truth and separate it from error.[7]

The resulting preface is a jumbled, verbose piece, interesting only because its author sees his own age as parallel to the fourth century and attempts to draw useful lessons from history to quell his own dismay.

He notes that 1,333 years have elapsed since Constantine presided over the Nicene Council. That figure is obviously false: If Chytraeus is writing in 1563, 1,238 years have in fact elapsed since the council.[8] There is apparently nothing to account for our commentator's dating. He then returns to his own era, marked by false doctrines which creep in fortuitously and gain ground because of the rhetorical skills of those who promulgate them, until no section of the Christian community is able to withstand them. Against this, Chytraeus sets the constant presence of faith, maintained at all times by the communion of saints, the true faithful, those who are not and who have never been discouraged by external appearances. Having thus established perfect symmetry between the orthodoxy and heresy of the fourth century and that of his own day, Chytraeus substantiates his theory by drawing some very exact seeming historical parallels,[9] which turn out to be based on dogma rather than on history.

Just before Constantine's era, several Roman emperors went to some trouble to undermine and destroy Christianity. Indeed, the most cruel persecutions occurred just before Constantine's accession and were perpetrated notably by Diocletian, Maximian, Galerius "Maximinus," and Licinius. (This accurate list of emperors who were either Constantine's immediate predecessors or contemporaries contrasts strangely with the completely improbable date of the Nicene Council given by our author!) Once Constantine restored peace and tranquillity to the church by defeating Licinius, the devil became envious and fomented strife among church doctors about "the most important article of Christian faith," Christ's divinity. He (the devil) therefore began by raising up Arius, who taught that the Son of God was merely the most superior creature, not consubstantial with the Father. Soon, all of Christianity was implicated in the strife, much to the delight of nonbelievers. Constantine, wishing to put an end to the quarrel, sent Hosius of Cordoba to negotiate with Alexander and Arius. When all negotiations failed, he convoked the council at which Arius was unanimously condemned by the universal Nicene Creed. However, notes Chytraeus, the peace was by no means definitive. Immediately after the council, the Arian party regrouped, and, although Arius himself died "a gruesome death," the heresy initiated by him spread and caused the rise of many other sects. There follows a long list of Trinitarian heresies, starting with Photinus ("whose heresy was repeated by the Spaniard Michael Servetus, burnt on 27 October 1553 in Geneva, in the Savoy")[10] and moving through Aerius, Eunomius, and Sabellius to Macedonius and "his" Pneumatomachi. Chytraeus' knowledge of Trinitarian heresies can be said to reflect the state of historical knowledge of the time.

How can the fourth century be seen as a parallel to Luther's Reformation? is the question that Chytraeus' reader is asking at this stage. The obvious answer would be that Charles V is a sort of latter-day Constantine, with Luther as the contemporary equivalent of Arius, bringing innumerable sects in his wake. However, that is the very parallel that Chytraeus wishes to avoid. Therefore, without so much as mentioning it, he draws the much more contrived and dogmatic parallel between Constantine's settlement and Luther's Reformation. The devil was so annoyed at both the events that he promptly spawned large numbers of sects—Arian in the case of Constantine, of diverse kind in reaction to Luther. Establishing this parallel, Chytraeus was obviously killing at least two birds with one stone: Not only was he showing the true faithful that history, which was ordained by God, repeats itself, he was also showing the monarch to whom he addressed the commentary that by encouraging *Lutheran* religion (of Melanchthonian coloring) in his kingdom, he would be seen as the sixteenth-century equivalent to Constantine. At the same time, as is shown by his list of heresies sprung up in reaction to Luther's reform, Chytraeus was setting up Lutheranism as the norm of orthodoxy.

The sects that the devil raised up in response to Luther's Reformation correspond to what recent historians have called the "radical reformers." Chytraeus singles out the Anabaptists, founded by "Nicolaus Pelargus Cygneus."[11] Although considering Storch's sect as merely a contemporary equivalent of one of many sects raised by the devil after the Council of Nicea,[12] he is well aware of the exact nature of Storch's errors and gives an accurate list of them: Storch wanted to do away with the magistrate and rejected all human traditions, as well as the preaching of the word and the efficacy of the sacraments, while considering enthusiasm as a sign of man's justification "coram Deo." He was admired by many, notes Chytraeus, but more especially by two men "distinguished for their poor learning and considerable rhetorical skills" (*mediocri doctrina et facundia praestantes*), Thomas Müntzer and Andreas Bodenstein von Karlstadt. The former, according to our author, was responsible for the peasants' revolt; the latter was the first to spread the false doctrine of the Eucharist in Germany. Chytraeus is extremely well informed about the radical reformers of the early sixteenth century, and he considers the rise of their sects much more harmful than the "unfortunate" eucharistic controversy, which he sees as confined to the restricted circle of the learned. The eucharistic controversy, he implies, did nothing to drive the faithful away from the church, whereas the teachings of Karlstadt on the Eucharist did actually deter many potential believers.[13] Maintaining his artificial comparison between Luther and Constantine, Chytraeus concludes the first section of his preface by remarking sadly that the church was united so long as Luther was alive. It was after his death that new quarrels and dissensions arose; Luther's doctrine became adulterated, and many were driven to Epicurean doubt and contempt of the church. Chytraeus concludes the first part of his preface on this note. Despite his very obvious dogmatic concerns, he has achieved one objective: His reader is in no doubt that Luther's Reformation is the modern counterpart to the Constantinian settlement.

Parts 1 and 2 of the preface blend into one another: Explanations of the sad state of the church are followed by advice on how to seek out the truth in such a great variety of false opinions. It is by attempting to answer the former question that Chytraeus begins the second part. Leaving aside the Constantinian era, he invites his readers to go further back and study the history of the church from the beginning until his own era.[14] Indeed, Chytraeus' concept of the history of the church provides a key not only to the curious seeming parallel he establishes between Constantine and Luther but also to his interest in the Apocalypse. According to him, the history of the church shows that, whenever the true doctrine of God began to win the day, the worst dissensions and unrest arose. As well as wishing to show the faithful *that* history repeats itself in a particular way by God's command, he wants to show them *how* it repeats itself—and also to prove that the Apocalypse is a résumé of God's decree of how history should be. He therefore invites his readers to go back as far as the prophets and Christ himself and then move toward his own era through the time of the apostles, Athanasius, Augustine, and the Council of Nicea. The symmetry of history should be seen in the light of Christ's prophecy in Matt. 24 and other passages in the Bible. The Apocalypse, according to Chytraeus, is the sole biblical book devoted to the shape that the history of the church should take. Chytraeus insists on the book's great importance: It is not simply a catalogue of evils, it shows that all dissensions, heresies, corruptions of doctrine, and so forth are ordained by God the Father and Jesus Christ in his great goodness and justice. The Apocalypse, thus interpreted, shows that God in his wisdom allows heresies and dissensions in the church so that the faithful can resist them all the better[15] and not fall into a state of what Chytraeus terms "Epicurean doubt."

Indeed, he notes, someone observing the discrepancy between the peace and prosperity of civil powers and the discord in the church might be tempted to think that God favors civil powers above the Christian religion. As an example of this, Chytraeus cites the prosperity of the Roman republic, which he contrasts with the sad state of the church in Judea. A contemporary example of the same phenomenon is the apparent peace and prosperity of the papal curia, which contrasts with the multiple dissensions in the Protestant churches.[16] The Apocalypse provides divine testimony that Christian truth emerges in its full splendor only when confronted with lies and heresies. This, Chytraeus maintains, has been fully documented by events in the history of Christianity: The correct doctrine of grace, free will, and justification by faith would not have been expounded so clearly by Augustine and Luther had they not been confronted, respectively, by Pelagians and Papists.[17]

Seeing himself as living in the final age of the world just before the Last Judgment, Chytraeus finds it natural that the truth should be particularly tried and put to the test. He sees the aged Christian church as similar to an aged human body which attracts every form of disease.[18] But this is no reason for despair, according to our author, who claims that 5,525 years have elapsed from creation until 1563. There is no reason to think that the Son of God will not preserve the church against sects in the little time that is left until the Last Judgment.[19]

The third part of Chytraeus' preface, which deals with the problem of how to recognize and safeguard the truth, has little to do with the Apocalypse. In fact, it could be said to constitute a short sum of Lutheran theology for the layman, which Erik XIV would have certainly found useful. Chytraeus provides, among other things, basic characteristics of a *false prophet*, to be avoided at all costs, according to Jesus' words in Matt. 7.15. A false prophet, claims Chytraeus, can be recognized, first, by an evident corruption of an article of Christian doctrine, and, second, by open wickedness of life and morals.[20] It is obvious that Chytraeus is using his commentary to induct his reader into the basic articles of Lutheranism and that he is carrying out in writing a mission similar to that which he would carry out physically in Austria a few years later. Working within a didactic framework, he sees very well that there is no need to explain to Erik XIV what constitutes a wicked way of life. The nature of true and false doctrine, however, does call for an explanation, as otherwise his reader will not know when an article of it has been corrupted.

As might be expected, Chytraeus' criteria of the true Christian doctrine are inspired by Melanchthon. To begin with, the aspiring true Christian should pray to God that his heart be opened by the Holy Spirit. He should then read the Scripture daily and study the sum and method of Christian teaching contained in the Epistle to the Romans. For Chytraeus, as for Melanchthon, Romans contains the explanation of all the articles of the Christian faith. However, as the major Trinitarian heresies arose after the apostolic era, the major creeds are also postapostolic. They should still be read, however, as an antidote to heresies, together with Luther's *Catechism* and Melanchthon's *Loci communes*.

Having thus sketched out the basic reading program for the Swedish king and those around him, Chytraeus reiterates Melanchthon's distinction between the Law and the Gospel, both of which are the supreme arbiters in matters of orthodoxy and heresy. Finally, he cites some concrete examples of false teachers, with their most flagrant corruptions of doctrine. A good Christian should beware particularly of Roman Catholics, with their insistence on good works, indulgences, and the monastic way of life. He should also beware of Anabaptists, who trouble civil order, deny original sin in infants, and deny that Christ in his human nature was born of the Virgin Mary like any other child born of a human mother. Furthermore, he should be on guard against Schwenkfeld and his spiritualism and against the Zwinglian doctrine (*Cinglianum dogma*) of the sacraments.

In the third part of his preface, Chytraeus thus gives his readers very firm guidelines of what they should abide by so as to resist the various heresies that the Apocalypse shows God sending upon the church the moment the light of true doctrine begins to shine. Although the logic of the preface leaves much to be desired, the basic guidelines in all three parts of it are simple enough to be followed by lay people and by clergy.

The Argumentum

The *argumentum* which follows the preface focuses on the Apocalypse itself, its role in the Bible as a whole, and its structure. Chytraeus never once refers to Luther's negative view of the Apocalypse, which he obviously does not share. The aim of the *argumentum* is to provide a structural guide to the text, the theological guide having been provided by the preface. As if in doubt about his readers' attention span, Chytraeus devotes the first six pages of the *argumentum* to an almost word-for-word repetition of God's all-determining role in history, which is summarized in the Apocalypse. The visions and the symbols in the book are intended as aids to understanding, analogous to parables in the Gospel.[21] He also notes that the Apocalypse is a New Testament interpretation of Old Testament prophecies, notably those of Daniel, Ezekiel, Isaiah, and Zachariah. What God had revealed to the prophets through visions is interpreted and clarified by John. Although Chytraeus is quite right to draw the reader's attention to the use of prophetic literature and language in the Apocalypse, he is obviously overoptimistic in considering it a clarification of Old Testament prophecies.

Indeed, he does not take up the point again in the *argumentum* but goes on to distinguish four types of revelation (apocalypse) whereby God lays open his will and the future to the church. Although Chytraeus would almost certainly have been familiar with Luther's second preface, in which three types of revelation are sketched out, he does not mirror the reformer's scale of "clear," "half-clear," and "obscure" visions, with the Apocalypse placed squarely in the last category. Chytraeus' division of revelation into four types does not reflect any explicit value judgment.

The first type is direct revelation by the Son of God to Old Testament patriarchs, the obvious example here being Moses' assertion that he saw God face to face.[22] Revelations of that type require, in Chytraeus' view, no further explanation. They are no more and no less than what they seem: God communicating his will to a chosen human or to a group of chosen humans.

The second type of revelation is not given directly by God to a human. Instead, the human, a prophet or an apostle, can prophesy about the coming of Christ, the Antichrist, the Last Judgment, and so on because he is directly inspired by the Holy Spirit, in accordance with 2 Pet. 1.20 ("for it was not through any human whim that men prophesied of old; men they were, but, impelled by the Holy Spirit, they spoke the words of God").

The third type of revelation is given by God to a chosen human via a dream, the most obvious examples here being Joseph's dream in which he is told to take Mary home as his wife (Matt. 1.20). Where Luther graded revelations according to the amount of interpretation they required, Chytraeus simply classifies them. The Apocalypse, according to him, belongs in the fourth class of revelations. It is a *vision*, and, what is more, a particular kind of vision, characterized by God's revealing something to a chosen human not directly, not via the Holy Spirit, not via a dream, but via a metaphoric representation. As the best examples of Scriptural visions, Chytraeus singles out Daniel's vision of the four beasts (7.2–9) as symbolizing the four kingdoms—Assyrian, Persian, Greek, and Roman—and also Ezekiel's vision (1.1–22 and 10.1–19) of the chariot and the four animals, which represent the spreading of the kingdom of Christ throughout the world.[23] It is obvious that Chytraeus has a fully developed theology of biblical revelations and visions and that he feels much more at ease with them than Luther did. Given his optic, the Apocalypse poses no fundamental problems and consists of—Chytraeus follows the traditional division here—seven visions.

However, although he adopts the framework of spiritual atemporal commentaries, he sees the Apocalypse not as a spiritual struggle but, he states repeatedly, as a summary of the full course of the history of the church from the beginning until the approaching Last Judgment. His description of the content of the visions thus has nothing to do with the spiritual hermeneutic

of an author such as the Venerable Bede. Bede, as we said, divided the Apocalypse as follows: (1) address to the seven churches; (2) seven seals (Apc 4.1–
8.1); (3) seven trumpets (Apc 8.2–11); (4) woman and the dragon (Apc 12–14);
(5) seven bowls (Apc 15–17); (6) damnation of Babylon (Apc 18–20); (7) heavenly Jerusalem (Apc 21–22). He saw the text as depicting the timeless struggle
between the faithful and Satan, with the Incarnation as a starting point.
Chytraeus' seven visions, while formally identical to Bede's, reflect a historically oriented, anti-Roman hermeneutic. Thus, the first vision contains an
"excellent description of Christ, the supreme ruler and pontiff of the church
and a model of all church government to be applied in this life."[24] The second vision (Apc 4.1 to 8.1) contains the image of God's kingdom and his
government, predictions about the future sufferings of the church, and a
message of that promises eternal glory for the church.[25] The third vision
(Apc 8.2–11) depicts future heresies and corruptions of doctrine.[26] The fourth
vision (Apc 12–14) depicts the struggle between the church and the dragon,
as well as the church's struggle against "the old and the new Roman Empire." It also contains "an excellent description of the Roman Antichrist."[27]
At this stage, Chytraeus parts company with Bede and all spiritual exegeses
of the Apocalypse in that he declares visions five (Apc 15–16) and 6 (Apc 17–
21) to be no more than a repetition and a commentary of Apc 13 and 14.[28]
Thus, for Chytraeus, history stops with the church's struggle against the "new
Roman Empire," in other words (it is implied), the papacy. Although Roman
Catholicism barely surfaced in the preface as one of the sects that arose just
as the true light of the Gospel was about to spread, it is clear that Chytraeus
sees the defeat of Rome as the focal point of the Apocalypse, and that he
considers it to be the major event due to occur before the Last Judgment.
Thus, the fifth vision is no more than a pouring out of divine wrath onto
those who worship the beast, while the sixth vision takes up the image of the
sickle and the grapes of wrath (Apc 14.19–20) and elaborates upon the punishment of the Babylonian whore, the Roman Antichrist and his worshipers.[29] The seventh and final vision is the celestial peace of true believers after
history has run its course.

The classic division of the book into seven visions is thus adapted by
Chytraeus to convey a strongly historical hermeneutic, with the Reformation seen as the crucial event.

The list of Loci Communes

However, this radical conception of the Apocalypse does not stop Chytraeus
from using it as a sounding board for the basic points of good Christian
doctrine, as his list of commonplaces shows. His readers should be able to
learn many useful things from the book and not concentrate entirely on its
historical and eschatological message. What then is its doctrinal content? Like
Bullinger, Chytraeus is convinced that the Apocalypse contains a perfect

description of Christ as supreme head of the church. Luther's doubts about the value of the book, based on what seemed to the reformer its lack of interest in Christ, are obviously of no interest to second-generation Lutherans. The book also contains excellent teaching on repentance (in Apc 2 and 3) and on the victory of faith over sin and death and eternal life (in Apc 2, 14, and 12). It also tells us about what constitutes real good works and true worship (in Apc 2 and 5); it describes the true Catholic Church, militant (communion of true believers on earth, regardless of geographical or historical situation) and triumphant (the dead faithful) and contains the fullest description there is of the Last Judgment, the resurrection of the flesh, the eternal pains of the damned, and the eternal blessedness of the faithful. Although the chief aim of the book is to predict the history of the church and the tyranny of the Antichrist, this is by no means its sole aim.[30]

The Glossary

Given Chytraeus' clear rejection of Luther's view of the Apocalypse, it is interesting to see that he takes from Luther's second preface several of the definitions of key terms in the book, although he does not acknowledge his source. At the same time, however, Luther's influence should not be exaggerated, seeing as Chytraeus' glossary is much more extensive than that in Luther's preface, and, in one or two cases, Chytraeus' definition bears no resemblance to Luther's.

He agrees with the reformer on the definition of angels as ministers and doctors of the church, regardless of whether they are pious or not.[31] He also takes from Luther the idea that the twenty-four ancients represent all the prophets, the apostles, and the entire heavenly church.[32] For both reformers, the horns signify worldly rule and power,[33] the trumpets stand for heretics,[34] and the two witnesses represent all the pious doctors who will give testimony of the true God against the Antichrist.[35] However, whereas for Luther the woman of Apc 12 is a symbol of the true faithful in adversity, Chytraeus adopts the traditional interpretation, which identifies the woman with the church.[36] There is a similar discrepancy between the two authors' glossaries to Apc 13: Both understand the first beast to signify the ancient Roman Empire. However, whereas Luther takes the second beast to represent the papacy only, Chytraeus is more elaborate: To him, the second beast represents the Antichrist, with the two horns standing for his two main kingdoms, the papacy and the Islam.[37]

Other explanations in Chytraeus' glossary, although not influenced by Luther, show the Rostock theologian's aversion to Roman Catholicism. The locust represent Roman clergy and religious orders, the image of the beast stands for "the new Roman Empire established by the pope," the three unclean spirits stand for papal legates, and the great whore symbolizes the ancient Roman Empire and the papacy.[38]

Chytraeus' Interpretation of the Seven Seals

Given Chytraeus' deep conviction that the Apocalypse was a divinely dictated account of history, the reader would naturally expect him to adopt a historical interpretation of the opening of the seven seals as the unveiling of the history of the world. In fact, although history does play a part in his exegesis of the opening of the fifth seal, the basic exegetical framework is provided by Bullinger's interpretation of the seven seals in his *Sermons*. Thus, the white horse that emerges on the opening of the first seal stands for the fruitful and successful propagation of the Gospel throughout the world.[39] The second, red horse stands for war, which Chytraeus considers a just punishment for the contempt of the Gospel formerly predicted by Luther for Germany[40]—a barely concealed reference to the Schmalcaldic War. On comparing Chytraeus' interpretation of the red horse with Bullinger's, it is interesting to note that Bullinger, while also taking the red horse to stand for war, attempts to explain why God allows wars:

> And yet this passage rightly attributes good to God and evil to the devil. But you will object: If God allows it, then he is responsible for it, because he could prevent it. He does not prevent wars because his justice stops him from doing so and it commands that the wicked be punished and the good tried by wars.[41]

Moreover, Bullinger's point of reference is not the Schmalcaldic War, but the wars against the Turks intended to make the faithful experience the full power of the Antichrist.[42] Obviously, to Chytraeus, war as a means of divine justice requires no further explanation. The third horse, which comes out of the third seal, is famine for both the commentators, and the fourth horse represents death.[43] Similarly, both take the fifth horse to represent martyrdom of the saints and persecutions of the church. However, there is a considerable difference in their conception of martyrdom. We saw that Bullinger used it to make some basic points of reformed theology against Rome and especially against the papacy and the doctrine of intercession of saints. He also reminded his congregation that souls were immortal, spiritual substances and that the time of persecutions was determined by God. While happily admitting that the worst persecutions had taken place under the papacy, Bullinger drew no particular eschatological conclusions from this.[44]

Chytraeus for his part appends a long excursus on Christian martyrdom, showing it as something to be aspired to. The second part of the excursus is taken up with the history of ancient persecutions, based on Orosius and Eutropius, who also provided the source for Bullinger's account of early persecutions. Although many of the details are similar, Chytraeus' account is crucially different from Bullinger's in one respect. Addressing his commentary to the Swedish sovereign, he actually exhorts him and his subjects to martyrdom in the sense of giving testimony to Christ against all opposition.

This means that, unlike Bullinger, Chytraeus has to define martyrdom and then tell his readers how to go about achieving it.

Martyrdom, according to him, comprises the following stages: confession of the true doctrine by the mouth, followed by suffering of the body, and going as far as loss of life because of the steadfast confession of the true doctrine. Examples of those who confessed true doctrine but who did not suffer death are Athanasius, Paphnutius, Macarius, John Frederic, duke of Saxony, and Luther. A true martyr is one who dies for his faith. Chytraeus cites as examples Stephen, Ignatius, and John Hus, and notes that many of his contemporaries suffer death for the sake of the truth. Chytraeus is thus seen to put into practice his own hermeneutic of the Apocalypse: It is a summary of the history of the church which is reaching its end in Chytraeus' own time.[45] The opposite of martyrdom, he concludes, is a denial of or a defection from the true doctrine, either for reasons of Epicurean contempt, such as Julian's apostasy, or for reasons of fear, such as the denial of Christ by Peter and many others. Idolatrous practices, such as the mass or lip service to the Gospel not supported by true belief, also constitute the contrary of martyrdom.

Chytraeus, unlike Bullinger, was working in a context where the dividing line between confessions was not clear. Where Bullinger could simply relegate all persecutions to the popish Antichrist and use that very passage as support for dogmatic points such as the saints' incapacity to intercede, Chytraeus had to be much more careful about telling his readers what did and did not constitute the true Christian doctrine. Thus, true martyrdom could only be for Christ. The cause and the nature of the martyrdom had to be right, founded on right examples. Martyrdom could be partial, if modeled on Luther's, or it could be total, if it followed the pattern laid down by Stephen or Hus.

What of the souls of those who are under the throne in Apc 6.9? Their crying under the altar is to Chytraeus (as it is to Bullinger) a declaration of the wisdom of divine providence. However, whereas Bullinger finds it appropriate at this juncture to warn his readers against inquiring into God's ways, Chytraeus considers the text as having only positive value: The question of *when* God will avenge his martyrs does not even occur to him as something to be refuted. Furthermore, although he denies that the saints can affect either the salvation or the damnation of the dead by their intercession, he does grant them the power to pray effectively for God's vengeance,[46] although even that power is ordained by God.

The sixth seal signifies corruption of doctrine for Chytraeus, who does no more than present Bullinger's comments on this passage in shortened form. Both commentators insist that all the corruptions of doctrine, from the beginning until the Last Judgment, are meant. Again, while Chytraeus stresses that heresies arise with God's express permission, Bullinger feels obliged to explain that Christ, while allowing heresies, cannot be seen as their author.[47]

Both authors take the turning black of the sun to represent the temporary dimming of Christ's doctrine through errors, both interpret the moon turning to blood as the deformation of the church by heresies. Both take the stars falling from the sky to refer to doctors of the church who are led astray by false teaching.[48] Most interestingly, Chytraeus also partly follows Bullinger's rather curious interpretation of the silence attendant upon the opening of the seventh seal as an injunction to the congregation to pay attention in church.[49]

Chapter Twelve

In contrast to his interpretation of the seven seals, Chytraeus' exegesis of Apc 12 is very much his own. He sees the text as expounding both the story of the original sin (after Primasius) and the spiritual struggle that the church undergoes every day because of the original sin. He begins by reminding his reader, after Primasius, that the serpent who seduced Eve was the devil and that Gen. 3.15 contains a prophecy of lasting enmity between the woman's and the serpent's brood, with the woman's brood crushing the serpent's head.

The devil is not confined to the Scripture, warns Chytraeus. Contrary to what some think, it is not an empty name used to frighten people, but a real adversary who chooses as his targets pious people in the church. Not only a commentary on Gen. 3.15, Apc 12 is also a warning to the faithful on how to avoid the snares of the devil.[50]

Chytraeus divides the chapter into three parts: a description of the chief protagonists, that is, the church and the devil; the battle against the devil waged by Michael—that is, Christ—and his victory, which guarantees that the faithful will be victorious in all subsequent battles against the devil; and the devil's incursions against the church.

The orientation of Chytraeus' exegesis is very strongly Christocentric, which means that, although he announces the woman as representing the church, he is finally obliged to also see her as a symbol of the Virgin Mary. His initial interpretation is again reminiscent of Bullinger's: The church is pregnant with Christ in the sense of wanting him to be born.[51] However, the similarity with Bullinger stops here; Chytraeus goes on to say that the devil persecutes the church in various ways, so that it is constantly expelled from various parts of the world. Just as the church once found refuge in the desert among the gentiles, so now it has found refuge for 1,260 days on the islands of the Baltic Sea. The attempt to flatter the king of Sweden is woven very skillfully into the traditional exegesis of the church finding refuge among the gentiles. However, the description of the birth in Apc 12.5 refers not to the church, insists Chytraeus, but to the birth of the human Jesus. The woman in that verse is therefore necessarily the Virgin Mary.

In the second part, however, the woman becomes the church once again. Too weak to combat the devil's onslaughts by herself, she relies for her defense on Christ, who is symbolized by the archangel Gabriel. Part 3 stresses the atemporal nature of the persecutions undergone by the church. The isolated allusion to the Baltic states in part 1 is obviously no more than a compliment and should not be seen as an attempt to "historicize" Apc 12.

Whereas Bullinger stressed the moral aspects of the struggle between the church and the devil, Chytraeus stresses its inevitability, as prophesied by Gen. 3.15. Although, since the birth of Christ, the church has had a defender, the struggle continues.

Unlike Colladon or Bibliander, Chytraeus has little feeling for the dynamics of the text, but he uses it ably to convey a particular message: The true church will always be under attack from the devil and can only defend itself by appealing to Christ, its sole head. It has no human defenders. In the context in which Chytraeus was writing, this message was of great importance.

The Millennium and the Last Judgment

While very much influenced by Bullinger's and Bibliander's idea of the millennium, which he situates very firmly in the past, Chytraeus is even more interested in the Last Judgment than were his Zurich models and has a much more highly developed conception of it, so developed that he actually speculates on its date.

Indeed, he begins his exposition of Apc 20 by stating that the Last Judgment constitutes the focal point not just of the final chapters but of the entire book, which is why he devotes a full-scale eight-part explanation to it.[52] The eight parts are entitled: (1) whether there is a judgment after this life; (2) who is the future judge; (3) who will be the judged, that is, all those who are dead and who will rise again; (4) how they are to be judged; (5) what sentence will be pronounced; (6) time and place of the Last Judgment; (7) of the fiery pit in which the damned will suffer eternal torments; (8) of the city of God, that is, the heavenly church where the pious will experience eternal joy.[53]

Before discussing Chytraeus' part 6, which is what distinguishes his commentary from many others, a few words about his exegesis of Apc 20.1–10 are necessary. The contrast between Chytraeus' lack of enthusiasm for the millennium and his interest in calculating the date of the Last Judgment is indeed very striking. He divides the first ten verses of Apc 20 into the following sections: (1) of the tying up and unleashing of Satan; (2) of the thousand-year reign of Christ and his saints; (3) of the war waged by Gog and Magog against the city or the church of God.[54]

Chytraeus' sources for ante-Nicene millenarianism are Eusebius (H.e. 7.25), Justin's Dialogue with Trypho, and book 7 of Lactantius' Institutiones diuinae. He openly condemns the latter two authors, as well as Papias (known to him via Eusebius) and the Anabaptists, who committed the same error "nostra aetate." Whereas Bullinger's condemnation of millenarianism was half-hearted, to say the least, Chytraeus actually voices a concrete theological objection: Christ never promised an earthly kingdom to his disciples.

The Rostock theologian identifies the angel who chained up Satan with Christ. The Savior chained up the devil on his Resurrection, not by taking his power away but by limiting it. The first resurrection is the true conversion to God, synonymous with belief in Christ as the only head of the church.[55] The exact duration of the millennium is of only marginal interest to Chytraeus, who decides to follow table 13 of Bibliander's *Chronologia*, which takes the spreading of the Gospel in A.D. 73 as the beginning of the millennium and the beginning of the papal reign of Hildebrand in 1073 as its end.[56]

The millennium thus relegated unequivocally to the past, it appears that Chytraeus is living at the time of the unleashing of Satan. He therefore devotes some attention to the exegesis of the armies of Gog and Magog, only to come up with the global identification of them as all the enemies of the church, be they Turks, Saracens, heretics, or cruel tyrants. They will burn with the devil in the sulphurous lake.[57] As this is about to happen, Chytraeus naturally turns to the Last Judgment. While paying lip service to the orthodox doctrine that the date of the Last Judgment is divinely determined and not to be speculated on, he nonetheless indulges in a series of calculations.

Taking the cosmic week as his basic scheme for the duration of the world, he considers the seventh millennium as the eternal Sabbath. He then puts forward two calculations (neither of them his own) of how many years are left until the end of the world. Some—by adding up 1,290 days and 1,335 days in Dan. 12.11—reckon that there are 2,625 years from Daniel's time until the end of the world. Another possibility is to take 2 Pet. 3.5 as a basis and to calculate that there are as many years between Christ's coming and the end of the world as there are between the creation of Adam and the time of the Flood, in other words, 1,565. This hypothesis has the backing of Christ himself, who compares the Flood to the Last Judgment in Luke 17.26. Moreover, notes Chytraeus, this figure corresponds to the number of years between Christ's Incarnation and Resurrection, if we count in terms of Jubilee years. Christ rose from the dead at the age of thirty-three, and he will come back to judge the quick and the dead after thirty-three Jubilee years, in other words, 1,650 calendar years. This means the end of the world is due to take place either in 1684 (according to the calculation of Jubilee years) or in 1695 (going by the calculation based on 2 Pet. 3.5). The further advantage of this hypothesis is that it takes in the forty-two months or three and a half years of the Apocalypse, if one counts three and a half Jubilee years, that is, 175 calendar years, from the revelation of the Antichrist until the Last Judgment. Given that to Chytraeus there is no doubt that the Antichrist was fully revealed in his own century, in the year 1520 (with the publication of the bull *Exsurge Domine*), the world should come to an end in the year 1695.[58]

Thus, although appearing to hide behind the opinions of anonymous "others," Chytraeus ends up fixing the date of the Last Judgment. The Reformation plays a crucial part in world history as the catalyst that brought about the manifestation of the Antichrist. Chytraeus' determination to fix the Last Judgment in history, as well as his view of the Antichrist as any force (including the Roman Catholic Church) that is hostile to Luther's reforms, is what most sets his commentary apart from those of the Zurich school. Although heavily dependent on Bullinger for certain details such as the interpretation of the seven seals, Chytraeus has a fundamentally different hermeneutic, in that he quite clearly sees the Apocalypse as a book written for his own time. It was this that made Chytraeus' commentary "Lutheran" and not "reformed."

Nikolaus Selnecker

A co-drafter of the *Formula of Concord*, Nikolaus Selnecker, whose life and work have received rather little notice from scholars recently,[59] was born in 1530 in Hersbruck near Nurenberg. As a child, he showed an exceptional gift for the organ. He studied at Wittenberg (1549–58), where he was a member of Melanchthon's inner circle. As a court preacher at Dresden (1558–65), he attacked hunting practices of the nobility, which may have played a part in his dismissal. He then taught at Jena (1565–68) until he was ousted by the Gnesio-Lutheran duke Johann Wilhelm and then at Leipzig (1568–86), where he also served as pastor of Saint Thomas and as superintendent. Frequently sent on ecclesiastical diplomatic missions by Elector August of Saxony, he left Leipzig to assist Martin Chemnitz and Jakob Andreae in the reformation of Braunschweig-Wolfenbüttel. Under their influence, he began to move away from Philippist theology, and the three formed the nucleus of the team that worked on the *Formula of Concord* in 1576 and 1577 under the political leadership of Elector August. He played an important role in reorganizing the electoral Saxon church between 1574 and 1586, reversing its earlier crypto-Calvinist tendency.

Together with Chemnitz and Timotheus Kirchner, he composed the *Apologia des Konkordienbuchs* in 1583. When the crypto-Calvinist influence began to make itself felt in the Saxon government, Selnecker was dismissed from office and became superintendent of the church of Hildesheim. Recalled to Leipzig in 1591, he died there before assuming office. He is chiefly known for his numerous hymn tunes and texts, for his *Institutio religionis christianae* (1573, 1579), and for his lectures on Genesis, Psalms, and the New Testament Epistles, published in the late 1560s. His complete works were published in Leipzig between 1584 and 1593.

Selnecker's Commentary on the Apocalypse

Like most sixteenth-century commentaries on the Apocalypse, Selnecker's is practically unknown. Written in German for the use of nonprofessional readers, it was published in 1567, together with his commentary on Daniel, under the title *Der Prophet Daniel und die Offenbarung Johannis*. Nothing either in the title or indeed in Selnecker's biography would lead the reader to suspect that his lectures on the Apocalypse represent some of the worst excesses of the historico-prophetic genre of exegesis. The work as a whole is dedicated to Joseph Benno Teiler, a patron of Selnecker. In the preface, the author explains that he would have liked to honor Teiler by producing a commentary on the whole of Daniel, but, for lack of time and failing health, he has managed only three chapters. He has therefore decided to publish what he has done until God grants him an opportunity to do some more.[60] To compensate for the unsatisfactory work on Daniel, Selnecker decided to have the Apocalypse printed in the same volume "because the two are related and together they point to and combat the popish abominations."[61]

The Apocalypse contains, according to Selnecker, three important messages for him and his contemporaries: First, it tells them not to despair at seeing the godlessness and evil of the pope and all the mighty rulers; second, it tells them to rejoice if they have an opportunity to suffer and shed their blood for the truth; third (and most important), it tells them that the Last Judgment is at hand.[62] Among the sources he used, he mentions an apparently unpublished commentary by Michael Stifel and other contemporary works on the Apocalypse. However, he stresses, he only took from them things that would make the text easier to understand for the common man ("für den gemeinen Man").[63]

The commentary is thus anything but learned. Selnecker dispenses with most of the sophisticated exegetical machinery, including the division into seven sections or visions. Here, we shall simply analyze his exegesis of Apc 12 and 20. As if forgetting that Luther himself had doubts about the apostolic origins of the book, Selnecker makes it represent the Lutheranism of his own day, that is, just before the Last Judgment, the date of which he never specifies, in contrast to Chytraeus.

Thus the woman of Apc 12 is the true Christian church of the last days. The twelve stars in her crown stand not only for the apostles but for all the teachers who, influenced by the apostles, honor the church of the last days.[64] The moon under the woman's feet assumes a negative connotation: The moon, being the light of the night, is to be opposed to the true light (the sun, or Christ) and therefore represents philosophy, human reason, and false doctrine, which the woman does not allow to seduce her. Seeing as Selnecker considers the Apocalypse the book written expressly for his time, there is no question of the woman being pregnant with all the true faithful from all periods in history or indeed with Christ. The male child denotes a powerful teacher of the latter-day church, indeed no less a person than Luther:

> From the true Church of God should come an excellent, highly spiritual teacher, such as Luther has been in our time. He should send out thunder

and lightning and speak like a brave hero. But his beginnings should be difficult, as we saw. . . .[65]

Although simplistic in its efforts to reach "the common man", Selnecker's exegesis is by no means naïve. Thus, he is quite rightly troubled by the presence of the dragon in heaven in verses 3 and 4. As the dragon represents Satan, he cannot be in heaven, as he was expelled from there. Selnecker solves the problem by interpreting "heaven" to mean the kingdom of Christ on earth, that is, the true church. Accordingly, it is only after being thrown out of heaven that the dragon wreaked havoc in the church "by sweeping down a third of the stars," in other words, by giving rise to sects and heresies. A true disciple of Luther, Selnecker thus makes the devil assume his place on earth, where he makes his presence felt.[66]

The dragon placing himself in front of the woman refers not to an aspect of some timeless struggle but to 1517 and the quarrel over indulgences. According to Selnecker, the dragon then placed himself in front of the true church so that Luther as reformer would not be born.[67] Selnecker is extremely critical of all spiritual exegeses of the book and constantly reminds the reader that John was a prophet only and not a historian. Thus, the child being snatched up to God refers simply to God's protection of Luther, especially during his exile in the Wartburg, and the woman's flight to the desert symbolizes the problems that Luther's church had to face after the reformer's death.[68] It does occur to Selnecker to suggest that Apc 12.14 might be a recapitulation of Apc 12.6. However, what interests him most is not the recapitulation theory (he never uses the term) but the meaning of three and half years in Apc 12.14, which is equivalent to 1,260 days in Apc 12.6. Obviously feeling that he is addressing an audience who are not very skilled in mental arithmetic, he gives an extremely detailed breakdown of the figures to show that 1,260 days are indeed equivalent to three and a half years. Having thus satisfied his readers that the same figure is meant, he opts for a literal interpretation: The days are days of twenty-four hours each, and they precede the Last Judgment. Needless to say, the stream of water spewed out by the dragon in his persecution of the woman also assumes a contemporary significance.

As it happens, it signifies the 1548 Interim! If Selnecker is living so near the Last Judgment, one would naturally expect him to refer the *thousand years* of Apc 20 to the past. However, while voicing some very strong criticism of ante-Nicene millenarianism, he does not relegate the millennium to the first thousand years of the church but claims that it is a period which comes to an end just before the Last Judgment. Unlike Bullinger, for example, Selnecker does not allegorize or relativize any aspect of the text, and it is therefore inadmissible to him that a "short while" of the unleashing of Satan should be anything other than a short while. In view of his commentary on Apc 12, it is obvious that Selnecker's *thousand years* (he situates himself

at the end of the period) have nothing whatever to do with any earthly paradise. What then is their importance (whatever the actual length of the period meant)? As Selnecker explains in his exegesis of Apc 20.4–5, the *thousand
years* is the period of the first resurrection, not in any spiritual sense but in
the literal sense of the term. The *thousand years* is the period before the Last
Judgment when the true faithful, once dead, are called to Christ and reign
with him.[69] Calling upon Ambrose of Milan and, notably, Luther as his
authorities, Selnecker points out that this resurrection is a sign that Christ
has always wanted to have his beloved (those not bearing the mark of the
beast) by him in heaven. Moreover, he, Selnecker, is convinced that "der liebe
Lutherus" is one of those who reign with Christ while awaiting the Last
Judgment.[70]

However, the importance of the *thousand years* is not confined to the
afterlife. Satan's imprisonment during that period has also meant, according to Selnecker, that he has been unable to completely wipe out Christianity, either through lack of faith among Christians or through the Turkish
and Muscovite invasions.[71]

Moreover, once released, Satan (according to Luther's translation, which
Selnecker uses as his text of reference) will seduce only the heathen and not
the Christians. In the time of Muhammad, at the beginning of the period of
the *thousand years*, Satan was already beginning to seduce the nations, notably by getting Chosdroes II to invade Syria and to impose his power on
Heraclius (prior to being chained up upon Heraclius' victory over the Persians in 627).[72]

However, given that he considers the papacy one of the guises the devil
takes to seduce the true Christian church of Apc 12, it is plain that Selnecker
cannot conceivably think that the devil's imprisonment has guaranteed a
trouble-free existence for Christianity until Judgment Day! His attempt to
extricate himself from the contradiction is not very convincing, although it
is not lacking in a certain verve:

> The chief Devil has been in prison so that he could not seduce any-
> one for 1,000 years, but the other devils have not been lying in prison but
> have been busy seducing, as can be shown from endless examples, espe-
> cially the papacy, which gave rise to all sorts of errors of faith and all sorts
> of sins and depravities. We know that the names and titles that are given
> to the imprisoned devil in this chapter are also given to him above in chap-
> ter 12, where he is thrown out under the secret name of the red dragon
> from the heaven of Christianity. And this happened during the thousand
> years and the time of his imprisonment.[73]

This passage is of capital importance, for it shows the basic difference
between Selnecker's and most other Lutheran and Calvinist conceptions of
the papacy. Nearly all the reformed commentators, and indeed Chytraeus,
consider the papacy as either the Antichrist or at least as one of the manifestations of the Antichrist. Similarly, all of them relegate the millennium to

the past, as does Chytraeus. Selnecker's interpretation is thus completely idiosyncratic: The millennium (which has nothing strictly millenarian about it) is in his own era, and the papacy is a manifestation of one of the lesser devils who have free run while the chief devil is chained up. Selnecker does not explain why the devil had to be thrown out of the heaven of Christianity by Luther's reformation, if he was already chained up in 1517. However, our commentator's thinking is not completely incoherent, as the devil could have made some sort of attempt at Luther via the lesser devils, even though he himself was in chains.

Incoherences apart, Selnecker's commentary would have certainly convinced the common man that the Apocalypse was a book written for the age of Luther's reforms, that there was little time left until the Last Judgment, and that the papacy was a manifestation of one of the minor devils. Unlike Chytraeus, Selnecker does not allow himself any speculation on the Last Judgment. The closing words of his commentary on Apc 20 summarize his intention thus:

> And at the end of this chapter we would do well to remind ourselves to thank the Lord God for protecting us, his faithful children, from Gog and Magog, the Turk, the Pope, and the Muscovites. And also for allowing us in our time to attain to the full knowledge of his grace in Christ our Lord, the knowledge which he granted us anew through the Lutheran religion. For that was what the devil particularly wanted to destroy.[74]

The Last Judgment, Selnecker implies, can come, for God has already guaranteed the Lutherans a place in heaven. His commentary, although fairly extraordinary according to the standards of critical exegesis, is in fact quite close to the spirit of the original text. Like the author of the Apocalypse, Selnecker wanted to console his community before the Last Judgment and to tell its members that their struggles were not in vain, while frequently referring in a more or less coded language to events such as the Interim that were of particular interest to them but not to the whole of the Christian church. His particular approach also enabled him to fully bring out the eschatological impact of the original text without having recourse to either "spiritualization" or "historicization" of the *thousand years*. What he in fact did was to transpose the hermeneutic of Augustine's *De ciuitate Dei* into his own era, while generously adding some explicit references to contemporary events, a thing Augustine, who adhered to the Tyconian perspective, would have never dreamt of doing. For both Augustine and Selnecker, the true faithful (in Selnecker's case, the Lutherans!) were immune against the final onslaught of the devil, and both felt themselves (Augustine more convincingly than Selnecker) to be a part of a relative millennium. By his rather fanciful adaptation of Augustine and by picking up, probably unconsciously, on some of John's original intentions, Selnecker did indeed succeed in making the Apocalypse comprehensible to the Lutheran common man.

CONCLUSION

There was a great deal of unease in the Protestant commentaries on the Apocalypse between 1539 and 1584, which partly explains their fairly derivative nature. However, although Erasmus' objections to the place of the Apocalypse in the canon could not be answered, it is plain that it was not just respect for the canon that made several commentators try their hand at interpreting what they saw as an extremely awkward book. The Apocalypse fulfilled a set of needs that manifested themselves as the reform movements progressed. What were those needs, and how were they dealt with?

For a commentator like du Pinet, the text mirrored diverse ethical and practical reforms that were being instituted in Geneva and that could serve as a model for France. He therefore used the text as a springboard for moralizing about the role of the church and its relationship to Christ, Christian marriage, and the iniquity of Roman Catholic practices. He saw the papacy as the Antichrist to be combatted. Working within a traditional framework of the seven sections (or visions), he was heavily dependent on the exegeses of Primasius and Bede, and also on Meyer and Lambert, whose interpretations he tended to simplify. The overall result was tepid and confused but doctrinally satisfying for the lay French-speaking public for which it was written. Du Pinet's eschatology was unclear, but he did not see the Apocalypse as the book that predicted the Last Judgment: Its chief aim, in his eyes, was to bear out the Reformation teaching on the church.

For Marlorat, writing in the context of religious persecutions, the Apocalypse was the expression of the hope of the speedy end of the papal Antichrist, which would be followed by the Last Judgment (at some unspecified date). He emphasized the continuity between the struggle of the apostolic church and the church of his own era. The Apocalypse thus became, first and foremost, a book of consolation. While dependent on Meyer, Marlorat's *Expositio* cannot be used to reconstruct Meyer's commentary, as it deliberately omits the most prophetic passages in the Bernese preacher's work.

For Colladon, the Apocalypse furnished a proof of the speedy demise (or conversion) of the papal Antichrist and a support for the belief that the Last Judgment was not at hand. Although initially setting out to instill hate of the papacy into civil rulers, Colladon's commentary is not simply a piece of virulent polemic. Structurally the most complex of the commentaries we have discussed, it shows a great sensitivity to the dynamics of the text and a willingness to engage with it. Like Marlorat, Colladon sees in the text a great source of consolation for the true (i.e., the Calvinist) church but also a biblical support for the Calvinist teaching on the church, election, and reprobation.

In a word, commentators in Calvin's circle chose to play safe and to combine traditional exegesis with polemics against the pope.

In Zurich, the interest in the Apocalypse had a more spiritual and historical orientation. It is not clear whether Leo Jud intended to supply an "Erasmian eschatology" when he wrote his German Paraphrase of the Apocalypse, which was not a paraphrase at all but a straightforward commentary. Unlike many Protestant exegetes, Jud did not specifically identify the papacy with the Antichrist; he also avoided any explicit comment on the messianic period of the *thousand years*. His most original contribution was no doubt to interpret the woman of Apc 12 as the Word of God, clear and strong (and not as the church, small and weak, as Primasius and most of the tradition would have it), which becomes male on Incarnation. Jud also used the text as a springboard for praising solitude and contemplation, which could and should be practiced in the context of the Zurich Reformation and for vindicating iconoclasm.

Bibliander's work on the Apocalypse was no more than a summary of his lectures, which are extant in manuscript at the Zurich Central Library. His vision of the book had little or nothing in common with Jud's and was marked by a strong historical orientation. One of Bibliander's most original contributions was to relate the opening of the seven seals to universal history, with the first seal representing the period from Creation to the Flood. He also established a close link between the Roman Empire and the papal (Roman) dominion by his interpretation of the seven seals. Although more historically oriented than Colladon, he was equally antipapal, seeing the Reformation as the best period in history because it revealed the iniquity of the papal Antichrist. As his lecture notes show, he devoted some time to elaborating the concept of the Antichrist, which he stripped of most of its eschatological connotations. To Bibliander, the Antichrist was simply everything that Christ was not. Bullinger's model sermons owed practically nothing to Jud and little to Bibliander, from whom Bullinger took, notably, the interpretation of the two beasts (the Roman Empire giving rise to the papacy). Interested primarily in the fate of the Christian church, he totally rejected Bibliander's interpretation of the seven seals. Although his condemnation of the ante-Nicene millenarianism was more half-hearted than that of his contemporaries, Bullinger situated the millennium in the past and proposed three alternative dates for it. Although there is a constant interest in the Last Judgment in his work, he does not go so far as to speculate about its date. Numerous remarks on issues such as famine and saint worship would have made his *Sermons* first-rate reading for the clergy.

However, on reading Protestant commentaries on the Apocalypse, we do not get the impression that du Pinet, Colladon, Bullinger, and the others saw the Apocalypse fundamentally as a book written for their era. Only the papal Antichrist struck an immediate chord, and that chord was important enough to be exploited. After all, the text was plastic enough to permit the grafting on of various reformed doctrines and messages of consolation addressed to the true faithful. Furthermore, the Apocalypse could be used to teach the faithful the rudiments of ecclesiastical history and so to firm up their convictions even more.

To Chytraeus and Selnecker, on the other hand, the Apocalypse was, in different ways and for different reasons, a book about the Last Judgment and the role of the Reformation in it. Luther's early skeptical remarks about the value of the Apocalypse as a biblical text were very deliberately forgotten. Chytraeus was thus quite open in stating that the Reformation was a crucial event, in that it brought about the full manifestation of the Antichrist just before the Last Judgment. Chytraeus saw it as a book for his time, so much so that he unhesitatingly used it to speculate in some detail on the date of the Last Judgment. Selnecker in his vernacular commentary for "the common man" actualized the text even more by making the woman (the church) of Apc 12 pregnant not with Christ or with all the faithful since the beginning of time but with Luther himself. The images and figures of the text correspond to diverse events in Luther's Reformation, and the papacy is no more than a manifestation of one of the lesser devils. Living immediately before the Last Judgment, Selnecker refused to speculate on its possible date.

It seems as if our Lutheran commentators felt a sense of triumph that for some reason was denied to the Protestants who commented on the text. This difference of attitude is at least partly to be accounted for by the commentators' views of the Reformation. Lutherans saw the Reformation as an upheaval ushering in the Last Judgment just as John had predicted. The Zurich reformers saw it mainly as a movement affecting the daily lives and behavior of states and individuals, which accounts for the practical tone of their exegesis. Neither they nor the Calvinists saw themselves as fulfilling John's prophecy to the letter in the sense that the Lutherans did. Indeed, commentators in or around Calvin's Geneva were writing with an eye on France, where the religious situation was very confused and where Roman Catholic theologians were rather reticent about the value of the Apocalypse. We thus saw that the Calvinist commentaries were a mixture of anti-papal propaganda and very traditional exegesis that would not have shocked French Catholic theologians. The sole common feature of all the commentaries is their unhesitating identification of the papacy as the apocalyptic adversary.

NOTES

Introduction

1. Among recent commentaries, those of Wilhelm Bousset (1906), Urich Müller (1984), and Pierre Prigent (1988) are probably the most helpful. Among histories of early exegesis of the Apocalypse, we might single out G. Kretschmar, *Die Offenbarung des Johannes: Die Geschichte ihrer Auslegung im I. Jahrtausend* (Stuttgart: Calwer, 1985), and W. Kamlah, *Apokalypse und Geschichtstheologie* (Berlin: Emil Ebering, 1935). Numerous studies by Bernard McGinn throw a light on the exegesis of Joachim of Fiore. See especially his *Apocalypticism in the Western Tradition* (Aldershot: Variorum, 1994). See also Joachim of Fiore's *Enchiridion super Apocalypsim*, ed. E. K. Burger (Toronto: Pontifical Institute of Medieval Studies, 1986). Among other works that throw a useful light on some aspect of medieval exegesis of the Apocalypse, we might mention John van Engen, *Rupert of Deutz* (Berkeley and Los Angeles: University of California Press, 1983), and Pierre Prigent, *Apocalypse 12. Histoire de l'exégèse* (Tübingen: J.C.B. Mohr, 1959).

2. On this, see Martine Dulaey, "Jérôme 'éditeur' du Commentaire sur l'Apocalypse de Victorinus Poetovio," *Revue des Etudes Augustiniennes* 37 (1991): 199–236, and Victorinus of Poetovio, *Sur l'Apocalypse et autres écrits*, ed. Martine Dulaey, vol. 423 of *Sources chrétiennes* (Paris: Cerf, 1997). Hereafter cited as Victorinus of Poetovio, *In Apc.*

3. First published in 1543 in an appendix to Johannes Lonicer's edition of Theophylactus' *Enarrationes in Pauli Epistolas.*

4. First published in 1558 by B. Millanius in Bologna.

5. On this, cf. F. C. Burkitt, *The Book of Rules of Tyconius*, Texts and Studies 3, part 1 (Cambridge: Cambridge University Press, 1894).

6. Kamlah, *Apokalypse und Geschichtstheologie.*

7. Joachim of Fiore, *Expositio magni prophetie abbatis Joachimi in Apocalypsim. Opus illud celebre* . . . in aedibus Francisci Bindoni ac Matthei Pasini socii (Venice, 1527).

8. Cf. R. Manselli, *La 'Lectura super Apocalipsim' di Pietro di Giovanni Olivi. Ricerche sull'escatologismo medievale* (Rome: Istituto Storico Italiano per il Medio Evo [Studi Storici, 19–21], 1955).

9. Richard Bauckham, *Tudor Apocalypse: Sixteenth-Century Apocalypticism, Millenarianism and the English Reformation, from John Bale to John Foxe and Thomas Brightman* (Appleford: Sutton Courtenay Press, 1978).

10. Cf. Prigent, *Apocalypse 12*, 57–58.

11. Cf. E. A. de Boer, "The Book of Revelation in Calvin's Geneva," in *Calvin's Books. Festschrift Dedicated to Peter de Klerk on the Occasion of His Seventieth Birthday*, ed. W. H. Neuser, H. J. Selderhuis, and W. van't Spijker (Heerenveen: J. J. Groen en Zoon, 1997), 23–62.

12. I include a brief and synoptic chapter on Colladon's commentary in my pamphlet *Les sept visions et la fin des temps. Les commentaires genevois de l'Apocalypse entre 1539 et 1584*, Cahiers de la Revue de théologie et de philosophie 19. (Geneva: Revue de théologie et de philosophie, 1997), 65–73.

Chapter 1

1. Cf. Marjorie Reeves, *The Influence of Prophecy in the Later Middle Ages: A Study in Joachimism* (Oxford: Oxford University Press, 1969); McGinn, *Apocalypticism in the Western Tradition*; Howard Kaminsky, *A History of the Hussite Revolution* (Berkeley: University of California Press, 1967).

2. The MS in question (no. 2814), according to the twenty-seventh edition of E. Nestle and K. Aland's *Nouum Testamentum graece* (Stuttgart: Deutsche Bibelgesellschaft, 1993), 711, is held nowadays by the Augsburg University Library (Cod. I 1.4.1.). Jerry Bentley, *Humanists and the Holy Writ* (Princeton, N.J.: Princeton University Press, 1983), 128, calls it mistakenly MS. 1 in what is otherwise an extremely reliable section on New Testament manuscripts used by Erasmus.

3. Desiderius Erasmus, *Erasmus' Annotations on the New Testament. Galatians to the Apocalypse. Facsimile of the final Latin Text with all earlier Variants*, ed. Anne Reeve, introduction by M. A. Screech (Leiden: E. J. Brill, 1993), 782: "Testatur diuus Hieronymus Apocalypsin ne sua quidem aetate fuisse receptam a Graecis." Hereafter cited as Erasmus, *Annotations*.

4. Erasmus, *Annotations*, 782: "Perinde quasi syngrapham scriberet non librum. . . . At hic tam arcana cum angelis colloquia describens, quot locis inculcat 'ego Ioannes'. Ad haec in Graecis quos ego viderim codicibus non erat titulus Ioannis Euangelistae sed Ioannis theologi, vt ne commemorem stilum non parum dissonantem ab eo qui est in Euangelio et Epistola. Nam de locis quos quidam calumniati sunt, velut haereticorum quorundam dogmata redolentes, non magni negocii sit diluere. Haec inquam, me nonnihil mouerent quo minus crederem esse Ioannis Euangelistae, nisi me consensus orbis alio vocaret, praecipue vero autoritas ecclesiae, si tamen hoc opus hoc animo comprobat ecclesia vt Ioannis Euangelistae velit haberi et pari esse pondere cum caeteris canonicis libris."

5. Ibid.: "Iam Dorotheus Tyri episcopus ac martyr in Compendio vitarum prodidit Ioannem Euangelium suum scripsisse in Insula Patmo. 'Etiamsi Eusebius tradit Ephesi scriptum' [add. 1519]. Caeterum de Apocalypsi nullam omnino facit

mentionem. Ne Anastasius quidem graecus in suo Catalogo audet affirmare opus hoc illius esse, tantum ait receptum a quibusdam, tanquam illius opus." On Dorotheus of Tyre, an author of the sixth century or even later, not to be confused with the fifth-century bishop of the same name, cf. Theodor Schermann, *Propheten- und Apostellegenden. Nebst Jüngerkatalogen des Dorotheus und verwandte Texte* (Leipzig: J. Hinrichs, 1907).

6. *Synopsis Sacrae Scripturae* 3, PG 28:289–294. Cf. *CPG* 2249.

7. Cf. ASD 9:2.265–266: "Adduxeram rationes aliquot, quare Apocalypsis mihi non videretur esse Ioannis euangelistae, quarum vnam improbat et in me retorquet Stunica. Ea est: in peruetusto codice quo tum vtebar non erat asscriptus titulus Ioannis euangelistae sed Ioannis theologi. Imo, inquit Stunica, theologi cognomen proprie tribuitur Ioanni. Adducit Suidam qui vocat eum theologum, sed addit καὶ ἐμαγγελιστῆσ. Similiter et Dionysius illi scribens: Ἰωάννῃ θεολόγῳ ἀποστόλῳ καὶ εὐαγγελιστῇ. Nec mirum si Origenes aut quisquis alius earum homiliarum est autor, Ioannem θεόλογον appellet, hoc est deiloquum, quod sublimiter scripserit de natura Christi diuina, quum eundem multis aliis huic similibus titulis honestet. Videt igitur Stunica rationem hanc in me non posse retorqueri."

8. Erasmus, *Annotations*, 782: "Equidem video veteres theologos magis ornandae rei gratia hinc aducere testimonia quam vt rem seriam euincant."

9. Erasmus, *Annotations*, 782: "Dionysius Alexandrinus episcopus qui candidissime sensisse videtur de hoc opere, dissentit quidem ab his qui censebant esse Cerinthi haeretici, cuius erat dogma in terris futurum aliquando regnum Christi ac tum quicquid voluptatum pro Christo contemptum fuerat, vbere cum foenore rediturum, redituras opes, redituras victimas ac festos dies legis Mosaicae. Atque hoc consilio operi alieno Ioannis apostoli titulum praefixisse vt suos errores huic libro admixtos apostolici nominis suco commendaret simplicibus, tamen suspicatur librum ab alio quopiam Ioanne viro sancto conscriptum, et in hac sententia fuisse complures Christianos, quorum iudicio commotus non ausus sit librum aspernari."

10. Erasmus, *Annotations*, 783: "At rursum mihi non potest persuaderi Deum passurum fuisse vt diaboli techna tot seculis impune deluderet populum Christianum."

11. Jerome, *In Hiezechielem* 11, ad 36.1–15, in *S. Hieronymi presbyteri Opera. Corpus Christianorum. Series Latina*, vol. 75 (Turnhout: Brepols, 1964), 500–501. Cf. Erasmus, *Annotations*, 783: "Idem [Hieronymus] rursus exponens Ezechielis cap. 36 fatetur Irenaeum non omnino fuisse alienum ab opinione Chiliastarum, quemadmodum nec Tertullianum, Lactantium et Victorinum et Apollinarium."

12. On this, see especially Hans-Ulrich Hofmann, *Luther und die Johannes-Apokalypse* (Tübingen: J. C. B. Mohr, 1982).

13. Luther's 1522 preface *D. Martin Luthers Werke. Kritische Gesammtausgabe.* Abt. 3: *Deutsche Bibel* (Weimar, 1883–), 7:404. His 1530 preface, ibid., 406–421 (with the textually identical 1546 preface opposite). Hereafter cited as WA *Bibel*.

14. WA *Bibel* 7:404: "[M]eyn geyst kan sich ynn das buch nicht schicken. Und ist myr die Ursach gnug, das ich seyn nicht hoch achte, das Christus drynnen widder geleret noch erkandt wirt."

15. Ibid., 404: "Dazu dunckt mich das allzu viel seyn, das er so hartt solch seyn eygen buch . . . befilht. . . . Widderumb sollen selig seyn, die da halten, was drynnen stehet, so doch niemant weys was es ist, schweyg das ers halten sollt, und eben so viel ist, als hatten wyrs nicht. Auch wol viel edler bucher furhanden sind, die zu halten sind."

16. Cf. WA 28:123–124. Printed in Wittenberg by Nickel Schirlentz.

17. WA 28:124: "Hanc praefationem ideo factam a nobis intelligas, optime lector, vt orbi notum faceremus, nos non esse primos qui Papatum pro Antichristi regno interpretentur."

18. WA *Bibel* 7:408: "Umb solcher ungewissen auslegung und verborgens verstands willen, haben wirs bis her auch lassen ligen, sonderlich weil es auch bey etlichen alten Vetern, geachtet, das nicht S. Johannes des Apostels sey, wie in libro iii. Hist. ecclesi. xxv stehet. Inn welchem zweiuel wirs fur uns auch noch lassen bleiben. Damit doch niemand gewehret sein sol, das ers halte fur S. Johannis des Apostels, odder wie er wil."

19. Ibid.: "Es haben wol viel sich dran versucht, aber bis auff den heutigen tag, nichts gewisses auffbracht, ettliche viel ungeschickts dinges, aus jrem kopff hinein gebrewet."

20. *Commentarius*, 1528, *Prologus*, A4v.: "Quia hic continentur quae Deus reuelauit Iohanni et Iohannes ecclesiae: quanta scilicet ecclesia passa sit in tempore primitius et nunc patiatur et in nouissimis temporibus Antichristi passura sit."

21. WA *Bibel* 7:410: "Im siebenden und achten Capitel, gehet an die offenbarung von geistlichen trübsalen, das sind mancherley ketzerey. Und wird abermal vorher ein trost bilde gestellet, da der Engel die Christen zeichent und den vier bösen Engeln weret, auff das man abermal gewis sey, die Christenheit werde auch unter den ketzern frume Engel und das reine wort haben, wie auch der Engel mit dem reuch fass, das ist, mit dem gebet zeigt. Solche gute Engel sind die heiligen Veter, als Spiridion, Athanasius, Hilarius und das Concilium Nicenum und der gleichen."

22. WA *Bibel* 7:416: "Inn des nu solchs alles gehet, kompt im 20. Capitel auch her zu der letze tranck, Gog und Magog, der Turcke, die roten Juden, welche der Satan so vor tausent iaren gefangen geweset ist, und nach tausent iaren widder los worden, bringet. Aber sie sollen mit jm auch bald inn den feurigen pful, denn wir achten, das dis bilde [Gog und Magog] als ein sonderlichs von den vorigen, umb der Türcken willen gestellet sey, und die Tausent iar anzufahen sind, umb die zeit, da dis buch geschrieben ist, und zur selbigen zeit auch der Teuffel gebunden sey. Doch mus die rechnung nicht so genaw alle minuten treffen. Auff die Türcken folget nu flugs das jungst gericht am ende dieses Capitels, wie Daniel vii. auch zeiget."

23. Enrico Norelli, "The Authority Attributed to the Church in the *Centuries of Magdeburg* and in the *Ecclesiastical Annals* of Caesar Baronius," in *The Reception of the Church Fathers in the West*, ed. Irena Backus (Leiden: E. J. Brill, 1997), 2:745–774.

24. Cf. R. Bodenmann, *Bibliotheca Lambertiana*, in *Pour retrouver François Lambert. Bio-bibliographie et études*, ed. P. Fraenkel (Baden-Baden: V. Körner, 1987), 11–213.

25. Ibid., nos. 17a–c, 136–139.

26. Ibid., 17 bis, a–e, 140–147.

27. Lambert, François. *Exegeseos Francisci Lamberti Auenionensis in sanctam Diui Ioannis Apocalypsim libri VII. In Academia Marpurgensi praelecti* (Marburg: Franz Rhode, 1528), A2v.–A3r.: "[C]upis ab animo vt Regni ecclesiae sanctae administrator in concreditis tibi populis per verbum suum regnet. Nam et de hac regni administratione, a Christo passo, vsque in saeculi consummationem hoc libro agitur. Raro praeterea inter principes dono ex illis, Dei misericordia, factus es regibus qui suam in

ciuitatem illam sanctam Hierusalem nostram descendentem de coelo, gloriam attulere, prout huius libri capite 21. Et afferent, inquit, gloriam suam in illam." Hereafter cited as Lambert, *In Apc*, 1528.

28. Lambert, *In Apc*, 1528, A5v.: "De illius authore, cum Iustino Martyre et Origene sentimus, quod a Ioanne Apostolo conscripta est."

29. *Ibid.*: "Persuasi quoque ad id sumus et spiritu scribentis et vetustissimo exemplari graeco, sine consuetis spiritibus scripto, ex quo apud inclytam Hyspaniarum Academiam Complutensem plurima sunt exscripta, e quibus vnum habeo in quo sic ad verbum haec reuelatio inscribitur: Apocalypsis sancti Apostoli et Euangelistae et Theologi." Lambert is referring to the *Complutensian Polyglot*.

30. Frans Titelmans, *Libri duo de authoritate libri Apocalypsis. In quibus ex antiquissimorum authorum assertionibus scripturae huius dignitas et authoritas comprobatur aduersus eos qui nostra hac tempestate siue falsis assertionibus siue non bonis dubitationibus, canonicae et diuinae huius scripturae authoritati derogarunt. Per fratrem Franciscum Titelmannum Hasselensem, ordinis fratrum Minorum Sacrarum Scripturarum apud Louanienses praelectorem* (Antwerp: Michael Hillenius, 1530). Hereafter cited as: *De authoritate Apocalypsis*.

31. On Frans Titelmans, cf. Erika Rummel, *Erasmus and His Catholic Critics*, vol. 2, *1523–1536* (Nieuwkoop: de Graaf, 1989), 14–22, 102–103. Cf. also the entry "Titelmans," in *Contemporaries of Erasmus*, ed. P. Bietenholz and T. B. Deutscher, vol. 3 (Toronto: University of Toronto Press, 1987), 326–327, and the literature cited.

32. Rummel, *Erasmus and His Catholic Critics*, 2:14–22.

33. The first complete edition of Irenaeus was that of François Feu-ardent, also a Franciscan. It appeared in Paris in 1575: *Diui Irenaei episcopi Lugdunensis et martyris Aduersus Valentini et similium Gnosticorum haereses libri quinque . . . studio et opera Francisci Feuardentii ordinis Fratrum minorum, in S. Facultate Parisiensi theologi . . .*, (Parisiis, 1575). Hereafter I cite the work in Migne PG edition as Irenaeus, *Adv. haer.*

34. Lorenzo Valla cast doubts upon Dionysius' identity in his *Collatio Noui Testamenti* ad *Acts* 17.34. Cf. Lorenzo Valla, *Opera omnia con una premessa di Eugenio Garin* (Turin: Bottega d'Erasmo, 1962; reprint of the 1540 Basel edition), 1:852, col. A. For Erasmus' view of pseudo-Dionysius, cf. *Annotationes in nouum Testamentum* ad *Acts* 17.34 in LB6:503. Valla was also the first to question the apostolic origin of the *Apostles' Creed*. Cf. Valla, *Apologia ad Eugenium III* in *Opera omnia*, 1:80. He never overtly questioned the canonicity or the apostolic authorship of the book of Revelation, but it could be argued that his philological exegesis of the book first caused Erasmus to closely examine its style and so to note the linguistic discrepancy between the Apocalypse and the Fourth Gospel.

35. Cf. Jean-Louis Quantin, "The Fathers in Seventeenth-Century Roman Catholic Theology," in *The Reception of the Church Fathers in the West*, ed. Irena Backus (Leiden: E. J. Brill, 1997), 2:978; Eric Wilberding, "A Defense of Dionysius the Areopagite by Rubens," *Journal of the History of Ideas* 52 (1991), 19–34.

36. *De authoritate Apocalypsis*, lib. 2, cap. 6, fol. E1r.–v.: "Absurditatem profecto maximam imperitis ac rudibus animis imprimant arcanae illius sapientiae (significatiuam theologiam loquitur) patres cum per obscura quaedam aenigmata diuinam illam plenamque mysteriis ac prophanis inacessam veritatem enunciant. Atque ea ratio est quur plurimi diuinorum mysteriorum verbis difficile credimus. Ea enim cum adhaerentibus sibi tantum vernaculis et carnalibus signis aspicimus, cum his amotis,

ipsa in semetipsis nuda atque ad purum liquida intueri debeamus." Cf. PG 3:1103–1104.

37. *De authoritate Apocalypsis*, lib. 2, cap. 6, fol. E1v., cap. 7, fol. E2v.: "Post quae tandem duplicis theologiae traditionem ponit his verbis: 'et hoc propterea operae pretium est animaduertere, duplicem esse theologorum traditionem, arcanam alteram et mysticam, alteram vero manifestam atque notiorem; et alteram quidem significatiuam ac perficientem, alteram vero sapientiae esse studiosam et demonstratiuam." Cf. PG 3:1105–1106.

38. *De authoritate Apocalypsis*, lib. 2, cap. 7, fol. E3r.: "Cuius patris verba quisquis intelligit, facile videt non ideo hunc librum debere vel nihili vel minoris quam oportet reputari quod totus figurarum inuolucris sit plenus, neque ob hoc non esse ipsum apostolicae grauitatis iure cuique videri debet."

39. Cf. J.-G. Bougerol, "The Church Fathers and *auctoritates* in Scholastic Theology to Bonaventure," in *The Reception of the Church Fathers*, ed. Backus, 1:289–336.

40. *De authoritate Apocalypsis*, lib. 2, cap. 11, fol. E5r.–E6v. On Rupert of Deutz and his commentary, cf. van Engen, *Rupert of Deutz*.

41. *De authoritate Apocalypsis*, lib. 2, cap. 19, fol. F3r.–v.: "Ex qua primum superscriptione quis non prima facie videt eundem esse quem Dionysius et theologum et apostolum et Euangelistam nominauit?" Cf. PG 3:1117.

42. *De authoritate Apocalypsis*, lib. 2, cap. 22–23, fol. F7r.–F8r.: "Qui enim suum sensum vel suum etiam ingenium iudicio praeponunt ecclesiae, propter suas coniecturas aut rationes . . . illius determinationibus submittere sese recusantes, hos certum est ad synagogam Satanae spectare, quantumuis se Christianos profiteantur. . . . Atqui authoritate certissima tum ex vetustissimis sanctissimisque orthodoxis patribus, tum ex ipsius eccclesiae decretis et conciliorum determinationibus atque adeo ex antiquissimo ecclesiae vsu ostendimus hunc librum ab ecclesia haberi vt Scripturam canonicam sicque pari pondere cum caeteris canonicis haberi libris, cum absque vlla discretione aut separatione hunc cum aliis connumerant." Erasmus had already said in the 1516 *Annotations*: "Haec inquam me nonnihil mouerent quo minus crederem esse Ioannis Euangelistae, nisi me consensus orbis alio vocaret, praecipue vero autoritas eccclesiae, si tamen hoc opus hoc animo comprobat ecclesia vt Ioannis Euangelistae velit haberi et pari esse pondere cum caeteris canonicis libris."

43. *De authoritate Apocalypsis*, lib. 2, cap. 23, fol. F8r.

44. *De authoritate Apocalypsis*, lib. 2, cap. 24, fol. F8r.–v. A modern edition of the preface is to be found in Eugene F. Rice, *The Prefatory Epistles of Jacques Lefèvre d'Etaples and Related Texts* (New York: Johns Hopkins University Press, 1972), no. 20, 60–61.

45. The quarrel between Lefèvre and Erasmus over the interpretation of Hebrews 2.7 (Lefèvre proposed "lower than God," claiming that *elohim* in Ps. 8.6 was wrongly translated by the LXX and referred in fact to the hypostatic union; Erasmus agreed with Aquinas: Christ was made lower than the angels in his *human* nature) has received much scholarly attention recently. Cf. Rummel, *Erasmus and His Catholic Critics*, 1:48–58, and the literature cited there; Guy Bedouelle, "Lefèvre et Erasme: Une Amitié critique," in *Jacques Lefèvre d'Etaples (1450?–1536). Actes du colloque d'Etaples les 7 et 8 novembre 1992*, ed. Jean-François Pernot (Paris: Honoré Champion, 1995), 23–42.

46. *De authoritate Apocalypsis*, lib. 2, cap. 24, fol. G1r.

47. Cf. Cornelis Augustijn, *Erasmus. Der Humanist als Theologe und Kirchen-reformer* (Leiden: E. J. Brill, 1996),164–166.

48. In-fol. Tiguri, in officina Froschoviana, s.d.

49. See Sabastian Meyer, *In Apocalypsim Johannis Apostoli D. Sebastiani Meyer ecclesiastae Bernensis commentarius, nostro huic saeculo accommodus, natus et aeditus* (Zurich: Froschouer, s.d.), *Ad lectorem*, Q4r.–v.: "Sunt autem illi in primis diebus ille Beda Venerabilis, Albertus Magnus, Nicolaus de Lyra, Rupertus Tuitensis, Dionysius Carthusianus, Iohannes quidam Viterbiensis. Scripsit et Haymo in hunc librum, item Iohannes Huss et vt audio Franciscus Lamberti Auinioniensis. Verum hos tres ego non vidi."

50. Henri Vuilleumier, *Histoire de l'Eglise réformée du pays de Vaud sous le régime bernois*, vol. 1: *L'Age de la Réforme* (Lausanne: La Concorde, 1927), 261–264.

51. Wilhelm Bousset, *Die Offenbarung Johannis* (Göttingen: Vandenhoeck und Ruprecht, 1906), 86–87.

52. Meyer, *In Apc*, a2r.: "Verum apud ecclesiasticos, praesertim Latinos, fere obtinuit a Iohanne apostolo fuisse conscriptum. De qua Tertul.lib. aduersus Marcio. 4. sic scribit: habemus et Iohannis alumnas ecclesias. Nam etsi Apocal. eius Marcion respuit, ordo tamen episcoporum ad originem recensus in Iohannem stabit autorem." Cf. Tertullian, *Adv. Marcionem* 4.5.2, *Corpus Christianorum Latinorum* 1 (Turnhout: Brepols, 1954), 551.

53. Meyer, *In Apc*, a2r.: "Neque solum Iohannis apostoli esse sed et de Canone Scripturarum hunc esse librum, adeo inter ecclesiasticos scriptores obtinuit vt per omnes orbis ecclesias eius celebrata sit autoritas et plures magni nominis viri illum cum miris commendarint eulogiis, tum etiam aeditis commentariis illustrarint."

54. Meyer, *In Apc*, a2r.: "Quod si eam, inquit, nempe ad Hebraeos epistolam, Latinorum consuetudo non recipit inter Scripturas canonicas, nec Graecorum quidem ecclesiae Apocalypsim Iohannis eadem libertate suscipiunt, et tamen nos vtramque suscipimus, nequaquam huius temporis consuetudinem sed veterum scriptorum autoritatem sequentes, qui plerumque vtriusque abutuntur testimoniis, non vt interdum de Apocryphis facere solent, quippe qui et gentilium literarum raro vtantur exemplis, sed quasi canonicis et ecclesiasticis."

55. E.g., Irenaeus, *Adu. haer.*, 5.30, PG 7:1203–1207; Eusebius, *Hist. Eccl.*, 3.18, PG 20:251–252; Jerome, *De vir. ill.*, 9, PL 23:623–626.

56. Meyer, *In Apc*, a2v.: "Ex quibus omnibus consequitur, sic huius libri autoritatem nobis esse habendam vt in loco vsui esse possit, non, vt quidam adsolent, in totum reiiciendam, quando sibi tamen permittunt in re admodum contentiosa eius autoritate abuti."

57. Meyer, *In Ap*, a3v.: "Postremo aiunt: nusquam in toto libro neque docetur neque agnoscitur Christus, cum tamen per totum librum, ita Christi cum sacerdotium tum regnum ac iudiciaria eius potestas magnificentissime adeo describitur, vt vix in alio augustius et magnificentius."

58. Meyer, *In Apc*, a4r.: "Sed vindicanda est, inquies, sanctarum Scripturarum autoritas ne incerta pro certis recipientur. Fateor vindicandam esse sed neque reiiciendum est quod plurimorum eorundemque probatissimorum patrum magno consensu receptum est."

59. On du Pinet (Pignet), cf. E. Haag and E. Haag, *La France Protestante*, 2nd ed. (Paris: Fischbacher, 1886), 5:853–862. The first edition of his commentary appeared anonymously under the title *Familière et brieve Exposition sur l'Apocalypse de sainct*

Jehan l'apostre. Nouuellement imprimé à Geneue par Iehan Girard, 1539. The second (1543) and third (1545) editions, identical to one another, bore the title *Exposition sur l'Apocalypse de sainct Jean. Extraicte de plusieurs docteurs tant anciens que modernes.* (The 1545 edition adds "reveue et augmentee de nouueau," although this not true.) The edition of 1557 also bore the mention "*avec Preface de Theodore de Beze,* 1557" (cf. Bodenmann, *Bibliotheca Lambertiana,* 140–147).

60. Du Pinet, *Exposition,* 1545, aIv.: "A quoy tous les docteurs sont tellement conformes que tous d'une bouche luy attribuent. Et mesme le consentement de l'Eglise, tant grecque que latine, y est; attendu que certaines leçons de ce liure estoyent ordinaires au seruice de l'Eglise, soubz le nom de sainct Iehan."

61. E.g., Sixtus of Siena, *Bibliotheca sancta,* 1st ed., 1566 (Paris: ex typographia Rolini Theodorici, 1610), lib. 7.600–605: "De Apocalypsi Ioannis haeresis X. Apocalypsim nec esse Ioannis Apostoli nec inter Canonicas Scripturas recipiendam."

62. Beza's preliminary note on the Apocalypse remained unchanged in all the editions of his New Testament published between 1557 and 1598. I shall be referring here to the posthumous 1642 edition, which reproduces the text of the 1598 edition without alterations: *Iesu Christi Domini nostri Nouum Testamentum siue Nouum Fœdus, cuius Graeco contextui respondent interpretationes duae: vna vetus, altera Theodori Bezae . . .* Cambridge: Roger Daniel, 1642. Hereafter cited as: Beza, *N.T.,* 1642.

63. Beza, *N.T.,* 1642, 743 col. A: "Deinde sicut a quibusdam fuit repudiatus [hic liber], ita fuisse a plerisque receptum, adeo quidem vt Epiphanius illos a quibus reiiciebatur aperte inter haereticos recensuerit, vt interim omittam antiquissimos scriptores, Iustinum philosophum et Irenaeum Lugdunensem episcopum, martyrem vtrumque, non modo illum comprobasse sed etiam commentariis illustrasse."

64. The *editio princeps* of Justin's works came out in 1551 from the presses of Robert Estienne in Paris. Three Latin translations followed: Joachim Perionius OSB, Paris, J. Dupuys, 1554; Sigismund Gelenius, Basel, H. Froben and N. Episcopius, 1555 (repr. Paris, 1575); Johannes Lange, Basel, Ambrose and Aurelius Froben, 1565. Cf. Irena Backus, "Some Fifteenth- and Sixteenth-Century Latin Translations of the Greek Fathers, c. 1440–1565," in *Studia Patristica,* vol. 18:4, *Papers of the 1983 Oxford Patristic Conference,* ed. E.A. Livingstone (Kalamazoo: Cistercian Publications, 1990), 305–321 (esp. 317–321).

65. Beza, *N.T.,* 1642, 743 col. A.

66. Beza, *N.T.,* 1642, 743 col. B.

67. Beza, *N.T.,* 1642, 743 col. B: "Nam historiae veritas aliunde potius quam a scriptore pendet: in prophetia vero, quia res futurae praedicuntur nulla nisi reuelantis et annunciantis autoritate innixae, quis non videt hoc requiri imprimis vt vnde tandem illarum praedictio emanet, quis patefecerit, quis scripserit intelligamus?"

68. Beza, *N.T.* 1642, 744 col. A: "Itaque mirum nemini videri debet quod non ita culto sermone vtatur, vt qui a prophetarum qui hebraice scripserunt ne verbis quidem nedum charactere discedere voluit."

69. Beza, *N.T.,* 1642, 744 col. B: "Quid vero quod vbi de mille annis loquitur nihil eorum narrat, de quibus Cerinthus tam impie garriebat? Vbi enim luxus ille?"

70. Beza, *N.T.,* 1642, 744 col. B: "Venio in eam sententiam vt existimem Spiritum sanctum in hunc pretiosissimum librum congerere voluisse quae ex superiorum prophetarum praedictionibus implenda post Christi aduentum superarent ac nonnulla etiam addidisse quatenus nostra interesse cognouit."

71. E. Haag and E. Haag, *La France Protestante*, 1st ed. (Paris: J. Cherbuliez, 1857), 7:256–259, s.v. "Marlorat."

72. [A. Marlorat], *Noui Testamenti Catholica Expositio ecclesiastica, id est, ex vniuersis probatis theologis excerpta, a quodam verbi Dei ministro . . . siue Bibliotheca expositionum . . .* (Geneva: H. Estienne, 1570), 136 (hereafter cited as: Marlorat, *Noui Testamenti Expositio*).

73. Marlorat, *Noui Testamenti Expositio*, 236: "Docet enim (quanquam sub typis, clarius tamen quam ipsi Prophetae) quaenam sit regni Christi conditio, quae sors ecclesiae et quibus persequutionibus exponantur quotquot Christianae religioni serio addicti sunt. . . . Aperit nobis ipsum etiam coelum et quaenam vera sit fidelium spes luculentissime ostendit; asserit et veram vniuersae carnis resurrectionem; ostendit et copiosissime quis tandem electorum et reproborum, fidelium et infidelium finis sit futurus . . . et dictante Spiritu sancto scriptum commonstret adeoque et euincat."

74. On this, cf. Enrico Norelli, "Pertinence théologique et canonicité: Les premières Apocalypses chrétiennes," *Apocrypha* 8 (1997): 147–164.

75. Marlorat, *Noui Testamenti Expositio*, 236: "Sed quum papisticae doctrinae peruersitas totiusque cleri papalis mores corruptissimi nullum alium praecipuum Antichristum venturum clament quam qui dudum venit in pontificibus Romanis, qui interim iuguletur gladio verbi Dei in cordibus fidelium et breui totus sit abolendus glorioso Christi aduentu in iudicium, hoc ipsum si nos premere et subticere voluerimus, lapides clamabunt."

76. Zwingli, *Auslegugng des 20. Artikels*, in *Huldreich Zwinglis sämtliche Werke* (Berlin: Theologischer Verlag, 1905–), 2:208–209. Cf. also W. P. Stephens, *The Theology of Huldryh Zwingli* (Oxford: Oxford University Press, 1986), 56.

77. Leo Jud, *Paraphrasis oder Postille teutsch. Die Offenbarung Sant Johanns des Theologi* (Zurich: C. Froschouer, 1542). In 1549, Jud's *Paraphrase* was translated into English and published as an integral part of the English version of Erasmus' *Paraphrases*. Cited hereafter as Jud, *Offenbarung*. Cf. Bauckham, *Tudor Apocalypse*, 44–45.

78. Printed in Bibliander's *Ad omnium ordinum reipublicae christianae principes viros populumque christianum Relatio fidelis* (Basel: [Ioh. Oporinus], 1545), 114–161. Hereafter cited as Bibliander, *Relatio fidelis*.

79. Heinrich Bullinger, *In Apocalypsim Iesu Christi reuelatam quidem per angelum Domini, visam vero vel exceptam atque conscriptam a Ioanne apostolo et euangelista. Conciones centum* (Basel: n.p., 1557). French translation: *Cent sermons sur l'Apocalypse de Iesus Christ, reuelee par l'ange du Seigneur, veue et escrite par S. Iean Apostre et Euangliste. Mis en lumiere par Henri Bullinger, ministre de l'Eglise de Zurich* (Geneva: Jean Crespin, 1558) (reprinted in 1565 by Jean Bonnefoy, for Guillaume Fournet). Hereafter cited as: Bullinger, *Cent sermons*, 1565.English translation: *A hundred sermons upon the Apocalips of Jesus Christe, reveiled in dede by Thangell of the Lorde: but seen or receyved and written by thapostle and Evangelist S. John* (London: n.p., 1561). Cf. also Richard Bauckham, "Heinrich Bullinger, the Apocalypse, and the English," in *The Swiss Connection. Manchester Essays on Religions Connections between England and Switzerland between the Sixteenth and Twentieth Centuries*, ed. Henry D. Rack (Manchester: n.p., 1995), 9–54.

80. *Biblia sacrosancta Testamenti Veteris et Noui e sacra Hebraeorum lingua Graeconimque fontibus, consultis simul orthodoxis interpretibus religiosissime translata in sermonem Latinum* (Zurich: C. Froschouer, 1543), γιv.

81. Jud, *Offenbarung*, cc 4v.: "Deshalb die übel sündend, die das gantz buch hinwerffend, als ob es Apocryphus wäre, so man doch dises buch gantz von anfang zum end in den Christenlichen Kirchen offentlich gesungen unnd geläsen hat, wie das kundtbar ist nach Osteren am anderen Sonntag angefangen. So doch Apocryphi allein die heissend, die man wol mag ausswendig der Kirchen und heimlich läsen, aber nit in der gemeind."

82. Bibliander, *Relatio fidelis*, 116: "Hominum certe iudicium sequimur et autoritate humana ducimur, non diuina, quamdiu non intrepide assentimur scripto propter seipsum et propter Dei maiestatem, quem agnoscimus et sentimus loqui in eo scripto."

83. Bibliander, *Relatio fidelis*, 125: "Sed optimum fuerit, totum librum strictim percurrere vt appareat euidentius claritas Verbi diuini eo etiam in libro qui omnium iudicio videtur obscurissimus."

84. Bullinger, *Cent sermons*, 1565, 18v.–19r.: "Il y a treize ans passez qu'iceluy a leu publiquement et auec grande louange ce liure de la Reuelation de saint Iean, et si ie ne confessoye que i'ay esté grandement aidé de lui, ie seroye vilainement ingrat. On trouve de lui vne Relation fidele, imprimee à Basle, l'an 1545, en laquelle il met ce liure par ordre l'ornant de breues Annotations."

85. Bullinger, *Cent sermons*, 1565, 6v.–7r.: "Or pource que ce liure de l'Apocalypse est du tout euangelique et apostolique, il est certain qu'en toute ceste siene exposition il entremesle souuentesfois des choses tristes auec des ioyeuses et la ioye auec la tristesse. . . ."

86. Bullinger, *Cent sermons*, 1565, 34r.: "Or si ces bien-heureux Peres ont en leur temps exposé l'Apocalypse à leurs Eglises, pourquoy ne nous sera-il loisible de nostre temps, à nous qui sommes venus ès fins des siècles, l'exposer aussi à nos gens et declarer les choses qui sont plus plenement accomplies qu'elles n'estoyent alors?"

87. Cf. C. de Jonge, *De irenische Ecclesiologie van Franciscus Junius* (Nieuwkoop: de Graaf, 1980).

88. We shall be referring here to the third Latin edition in: François du Jon, *Francisci Iunii Biturigis, Sacrarum literarum in Academia Heidelbergensi et Lugduno-Bataua professoris eruditissimi Opera theologica duobus tomis . . . digesta . . .* (Geneva, 1607): *primus tomus*, col. 1305–1367 (hereafter referred to as du Jon, *Apocalypsis*, 1607).

89. Du Jon, *Apocalypsis*, 1607, col. 1305: "[E]t haec [Apocalypsis] quoque nostra inde a priore aduentu Christi, in expectatione secundi illius et gloriosi aduentus, per optimos quosque illius seruos, inprimis vero per sanctissimum illum Apostolum et Euangelistam Ioannem, illum discipulum quem diligebat Christus aduersus similes aut grauiores etiam tempestates . . . obtecta est."

90. Du Jon, *Apocalypsis*, 1607, col. 1307.

91. [Dauidis Parei], *In Heidelbergensi Academia doctoris et professoris primarii, Operum theologicorum exegeticorum pars secunda. . . .* Geneua: Pierre Chouet, 1642, p. 1069–1335 (hereafter referred to as: Pareus, *In Apocalypsim*, 1642). On David Pareus, cf. the entry "Pareus" in *Realencyklopädie für Protestantische Theologie und Kirche*, ed. J. J. Herzog and A. Hauck (Leipzig: 1904), 14:686–689.

92. Pareus, *In Apocalypsim*, 1642, 1072.

93. Pareus, *In Apocalypsim*, 1642, 1072: "Quae in contrarium afferri solent argumenta breuitatis causa nunc non referam. Operose ea Erasmus collegit. Eadem vero Theodorus Beza in notis ad hunc librum solide refutauit."

94. Matthias Flacius Illyricus commented on the entire New Testament, including the Apocalypse (*Glossa compendaria* [Basil: 1570]). Nikolaus Selnecker wrote a Commentary on Daniel and the Apocalypse in German: *Der Prophet Daniel und die Offenbarung Johannis* (Leipzig: Jacob Berwaldt, 1567). We shall be discussing Chytraeus' and Selnecker's commentaries in chapter 5.

95. David Chytraeus, *Explicatio Apocalypsis perspicua et breuis. Tradita a Davide Chytraeo* (Wittenberg: Ioh. Crato, 1564).

96. Cf. David Steinmetz, "The Superiority of Pre-Critical Exegesis," *Theology Today* 27 (1980): 27–38.

Chapter 2

1. Cf. entry "du Pinet" in E. Haag and E. Haag, *La France Protestante*, 2nd ed., vol. 5, col. 852–863.

2. John Calvin, "*La vraie piété.*" *Divers traités de Jean Calvin et la Confession de foi de Guillaume Farel*, ed. I. Backus and C. Chimelli (Geneva: Labor et Fides, 1986), 59–61.

3. Calvin "*La vraie piété*," 60.

4. Cf. Du Pinet, *Exposition*, 1557.

5. Du Pinet, *Exposition*, 1552. Cf. de Boer, "The Book of Revelation," 23–62.

6. Theodore Beza, *Correspondance de Théodore de Bèze, recueillie par Hippolyte Aubert*, ed. F. Aubert, H. Meylan, A. Dufour, et al. (Geneva: Droz, 1960–) 2: 231–236. Antoine du Pinet, *Familière et brève Exposition sur l'Apocalypse de sainct Jehan l'apostre* (Geneva: Jean Girard, 1539).

7. De Boer, "The Book of Revelation," 47–52.

8. E. Haag and E. Haag, *La France Protestante*, 2nd ed., vol 5, col. 858: extract from du Pinet's preface to his translation of Pliny's *History* (Lyon: Claude Senneton, 1562): "Joint aussi que durant 15 mois j'ay esté souvent malade et pressé de quelques affaires pour le service d'aucuns grans seigneurs à la dévotion desquels je suis. . . ."

9. Cf. du Pinet, *Familière et brève Exposition*, 1539, a1v.: "L'imprimeur au Lecteur fidele . . . Assauoir ce present commentaire sur l'Apocalpe de sainct Iehan, ne voulant estroitement lier personne à nostre sentence, laquelle nous offrons seulement au iugement de l'Eglise."

10. Backus, *Les sept visions*, 51.

11. Bede, *Explanatio Apocalypsis, Epist. ad Eusebium*, PL 93:130–131.

12. Du Pinet, *Familière et brève Exposition*, 1539, 3: "Ce present liure dict Apocalypse, c'est adire reuelation, est vne epistre qui commence ou est dict: Iehan aux sept églises etc. Et ce qui est deuant, est le proëme dudict liure."

13. Du Pinet, *Familière et brieve Exposition*, 1539, 3: "La premiere vision et premier liure, commence au premier chapitre, ou est dict: i ay esté en esperit etc. Et en ceste vision y a sept epistres partiales, enuoyées aux sept eglises d'Asie, lesquelles contiennent tout ce qui appartient à la chrestienté. La seconde vision et liure s'estend depuis le commencement du quatriesme chapitre jusqu'au huictieme. Et en icelle sont les mysteres des seaulx. La tierce vision et liure commence au douziesme chapitre, ou est traicté d'une femme vestue du soleil, d'un dragon et de deux bestes, l'une montant de la terre et l'aultre de la mer. La cinquiesme vision et livre commence au quinziesme chapitre, ou est parlé de l'effusion des sept phyoles pleines de l'ire de Dieu viuant. La sixiesme vision et liure commence au disseptiesme chapitre; en laquelle

est parlé de Babilone et de la condamnation d'icelle, du dragon et des bêtes. La septiesme et derniere vision et liure commence au vingt et uniesme chapitre, laquelle compete et appartient au sabbat repos et gloire des esleuz au royaume aduenir. Cf. Bede, *Expl. Apc, Epist. ad Eusebium*, PL 93: 130–31: "In quarum prima, post praefationem copiosam … commemoratis his quae specialiter in septem Asiae gesta vel gerenda sint ecclesiis, generales totius ecclesiae luctas describit et palmas. . . . In secunda autem periocha . . . agnum videt apertis septem libri signati sigillis conflictus et triumphos ecclesiae reserare futuros. . . . Tertia vero periocha sub specie septem angelorum tuba canentium varios ecclesiae describit euentus. Quarta sub figura mulieris parturientis et draconis eam persequentis eiusdem ecclesiae labores et victorias aperit et vtrique militiae praemia digna rependit. Vbi septem quoque angelorum dicta commemorantur et facta, etsi non pariter, vt supra. Hunc enim mystica solertia numerum pene vbique seruat, cum et moris sit eiusdem Ioannis in Euangelio quoque et Epistolis, nihil tepide et breuiter dicere. Quinta autem periocha per septem angelos septem plagis nouissimis terram perfudit. Sexta, damnationem meretricis magnae, id est impiae ciuitatis. Septima, ornatum vxoris agni, sanctae videlicet Jerusalem de coelo a Deo descendentis, ostendit."

14. Du Pinet, *Familière et briève Exposition*, 1539, 4: "Donc chascune vision est diuisée en sept parties, selon les diverses manieres des persecutions et persecuteurs et selon les sept éages qui sont depuis Christ iusques en la fin du monde. Et sommes de present au sixiesme éage. Au premier, a esté la rebellion des iuifz. Au second, la persecution et tyrannie des princes gentilz. Au troisiesme, les principaux heretiques. Au quatriesme, a commencé la beste à monter de la mer. Au cinquiesme, le regne de la beste qui est antechrist. Au sixiesme, la bataille de la beste contre les fideles chrestiens. Au septiesme, le repos celeste et sabbat perdurable de l'Eglise chrestienne."

15. The best brief introduction is by Andrea Tagliapetra in his Latin-Italian edition of Joachim's *Enchiridion* (a summary version of the *Expositio*): *Gioacchino da Fiore sull'Apocalisse* (Milan: Feltrinelli, 1994), 79–84. Cf. also bibliography *ibid.*, 395–411.

16. Cited here from the 1545 edition, the text of which is identical to that of 1543. The only difference is the change of date at the end of the prefatory epistle by du Pinet to "Simon Siluius."

17. Du Pinet, *Exposition*, 1545, a2v.: "Et premierrement ayant veu l'accueil des fideles faict a la premiere édition de ce present liure et le iugement de plusieurs bons personnages sur iceluy, consideré aussi qu'il estoit requis de plusieurs, comme souuentes fois m'auez testifié et que les boutiques des libraires en estoyent despourueues, ie n'ay regardé aux calumnies de ceux qui se delectent a mesdire d'autruy, ny mesmes au danger d'exposer mon nom en public . . . ."

18. Du Pinet, *Exposition*, 1545, a3v.–a4v.: "Vous scavez combien de brocardz ont été gettez sur la première édition et sortye de ce livre et de quelz collyres ces manieres de gens ont vsé pour esclaircir leur veuë, afin de mieux cercher s'il y auroit quelque chose à mordre. Ie me taiz des beaux propos qu'ilz en tenoient, desquelz la plus part estoyent directement contumelieux au Sainct Esprit et à l'apostre autheur de ceste Prophetie. Car si ceste escriture ne se peut interpreter sans songer et resver, que celuy qui la vouldra declarer est songeur et resueur, sur quoi dirons nous qu'elle est fondée, sinon sur songes et resueries? Qui sesbahyra donc de les voir tant eloquens à detracter d'autruy, quand mesmes ils n'espargnent la sapience de Dieu qu'ilz ne la blasonent par leurs parolles? Que si parauenture ilz s'arrestent sur ce que ce liure est compilé et prins

de plusieurs docteurs tant aunciens que modernes, le labeur desquelz ne conuiendroit (comme ils disent) ainsi temerairement mesler ny confondre et tant moins y adiouster son nom: que ilz se contentent de ceste response comme peremptoire et suffisante.

"Ie ne nye pas, ains comme tousiours ay confessé aussi de present ie confesse auoir assemblé en ce petit traicté l'opinion de tous ceux que i'ay congneu auoir escrit tant sur le total de l'Apocalypse que sur aucuns poincts et passages d'icelle et y auoir mis leur sentences de mot à mot: toutefois plus de modernes que des anciens, comme de Françoys Lambert et Sebastien Meyer. . . ."

19. Bede, *Expl. Apc, Epist. ad Eusebium*, PL 93:131–33.

20. Meyer, *In Apc*, a6r.–a6v.: "Tyconii regulae prae oculis habendae, de quibus Augustinus li. de Doctr. christ. 3 et Beda in huius libri praefatione. Quarum prima est ea quae capitis Christi sunt, plerumque illius corpori, quod est ecclesia, tribui et contra, quae corporis sunt, capiti Christo. Atque eodem modo de Sathana et suo corpore, hoc est ecclesia malignantium, sentiendum. Secunda est de bipartito Christi corpore, altero quidem vero, hoc est ecclesia interna, nimirum in spiritu congregata, quae coram Deo est ecclesia, nec videtur sed creditur; altero permixto, propter externam sacramentorum communionem, de quo in Cant. 1.ca. *fusca sum et speciosa* etc. . . . Tertia est, in specie genus intelligi et econtra. Eodem modo de toto et parte per synecdochen. Quarta recapitulationis item et anticipationis habendam esse rationem. De quibus illi [Augustinus et Beda] fusius."

21. Du Pinet, *Exposition*, 1545, b2r.–v.: "[F]aut auoir les quatre regles de Tyconius tousiours deuant les yeux: la premiere, ce qui appartient à Christ, comme Chef, est souuent attribué au corps d'iceluy, qui est l'Eglise; et au contraire, ce qui appartient à l'Eglise, est souuent attribué à Christ. Le semblable faut sentir de Satan et de son corps, qui est la congregation des malins. La seconde regle est, de prendre l'Eglise de Christ en deux sortes: c'est assauoir, veritablement et spirituellement, en laquelle sorte l'Eglise est deuant Dieu et ne la voyons pas, mais la croyons et charnellement qui est ceste Eglise uisible, en laquelle y a administration de parolle et de sacremens. La tierce regle est que par le special, le general est quelquesfois entendu et au contraire; pareillement aussi le total est prins aucunesfois pour vne partie et la partie pour le tout. La quatriesme regle est que plusieurs choses sont dites en ce livre par recapitulation ou anticipation."

22. Meyer, *In Apc*, a6r.–a6v.

23. Lambert, *In Apc, Praefatio*, A6r.: "Praeterea non est opus, omnes rerum quae typice ponuntur naturas seu, vt loqui solent, proprietates conuertere ad allegoriam. . . ." A6r.–v.: "Summe autem vitandum ne contra spiritus iudicium typicum sermonem pro aperto, aut apertum pro typico enarremus."

24. In his 1530 preface (WA *Deutsche Bibel* 7, in Martin Luther, *D. Martin Luther's Werke. Kritische Gesammtausgabe* [*Weimar, 1883*–], 406–408), Luther took the self-evident prophecy (or revelation), or one needing no interpretation, to be the superior. In this category, he placed the prophets' revelations of the coming of Christ. The second, inferior, type of prophecy is one requiring interpretation (such as Daniel's dream), with the prophet himself providing it. The third, very inferior, type of prophecy is one which is not self-evident and for which the prophet does not provide any interpretation. In this last category, he placed the Apocalypse. Meyer, by changing the classification of revelations in general, also altered the status of the book.

25. Meyer, *In Apc*, a6r.: "Nimirum per visiones, hoc est per figuras quasdam diuina virtute siue angelico ministerio formatas."

26. Du Pinet, *Exposition*, 1545, b4v.–b5r.:"Aucuns diuisent ceste Reuelation en trois choses principalement, c'est assauoir, en sept seaux, sept trompettes et sept phioles. Et entendent par les sept seaux les principales persequutions, que les empereurs Romains ont faites à l'Eglise de Christ, depuis le temps des Apostres, iusqu'a l'Empire de Constantin le Grand, cha. iiii, v, vi et vii. Par les sept trompettes entendent les principales heresies suruenues apres la paix donnee à l'Eglise, desquelles elle a este fort vexee, depuis le temps de Constantin, iusqu'à Mahomet, qui a amené la dernière, chap. viii, ix, x, xi, xii, xiii, xiiii, xv, xvi. Et par les sept phioles, entendent les dernieres playes qui sont à venir au monde, par la beste, qui est l'Antechrist, chap. xvii, xviii etc.

"Toutefois, sans n'en contemner il est plus raisonnable le diuiser en sept parties, selon les sept diuisions principales escrites en iceluy.Desquelles la premiere contient ce qui se faisoit adonc es sept Eglises d'Asie, en l'absence de sainct Iean et ce qui leur deuoit auenir un peu après, chap. i, ii et iii. La seconde est de l'exaltation, gloire et Royaume uniuersel de Christ, de la clarté de science, de la victoire et presente felicite du peuple de Dieu, chap. iiii, v, vi, et vii. La tierce traite de la diligence et constance des disciples du seigneur, touchant la promotion et auancement de son Royaume et aussi du profit de la predication. Item des diuerses punitions des incredules et principalement des Juifs contemnans la predication de l'Euangile, chapit. viii, ix, x, xi, quasi pres de la fin. La quatriesme est de plusieurs afflictions et calamitez que l'Eglise se deuoit souffrir et des Gentils et des Juifs, faux apostres et heretiques agitez de Satan, desquelles toutes, elle seroit sauuée par Jesus Christ son Protecteur et par les anges, chap. xii, xiii, xiiii. La cinquiesme est de la derniere persecution que l'Eglise souffre et a a souffrir sous la tyrannie d'Antechrist. Item, des diuerses playes, desquelles Dieu frappera ceux qui delaissent la foy de Christ, cha. xv et xvi. La sixieme est du iugement et damnation finale de la grande putain Babylone, l'Eglise des mauuais et de la ioye que les bons fideles auront sur la ruine d'icelle, chap. xvii, xviii et xix. La septiesme est des nopces de Christ et de son Eglise, et de la perpetuelle felicite des bons, apres que Satan et tout son Royaume sera triomphamment abbatu, chap. xx, xxi et xxii."

27. Victorinus of Poetovio, *In Apc*, 98–99. The only *influential* Western commentator to partly adopt the Marial interpretation of the passage was Rupert of Deutz (cf. his *Ruperti abbatis Tuitiensis In Apocalypsim Johannis Apostoli Commentariorum libri XII* [Cologne: Johannes Soter, 1533], 109: "Sicut econtra mulier illa sole amicta, signum erat ecclesiae totius, cuius beata virgo Maria portio maxima."). Cf. Joachim of Fiore, *Expositio in Apc*, 1527, 154r.: "Mulier ista generaliter matrem designat ecclesiam . . . specialiter vero ecclesiam heremitarum et virginum." Lambert, *In Apc*, 199r.: "Mulier non Maria sed ecclesia. Mariae siquidem haec non competunt etiam si Christus sit filius eius. Verum Maria est huius mulieris, id est ecclesiae, portio nobilissima." Meyer, *In Apc*, 45r., 48r.: "Mulier illa ecclesia credentium quae per fidem Christo desponsata ac multa prole foecunda est. . . . Ecclesia apostolica et initialis mulieri recte comparatur, quae licet ex sui natura fragilis, modica et sterilis, tamen per sponsum suum Christum multa prole foecunda et magna redditur."

28. Lambert, *In Apc*, 205r.

29. Du Pinet, *Exposition*, 1545, 230–231.

30. Lambert, *In Apc*, 208r.; Meyer, *In Apc*, 50r.

31. Du Pinet, *Exposition*, 1545, 237–238.

32. Bede, *Expl. Apc*, PL 93: 168; Primasius, *In Apc*, PL 68:876.

33. Meyer, *In Apc*, 47v.: "Duorum Testamentorum, Veteris ac Noui intelligentia in altum subuolans, impetuosum flumen curiosarum disputationum facile euadit, de

vtroque proferens duarum in Christo naturarum testimonia, fide recta et syncera alitur."

34. Du Pinet, *Exposition*, 1545, 241–242.

35. Backus, *Les sept visions*, 50–51.

36. Lambert, *In Apc*, 284r.–v.

37. Meyer, *In Apc*, 79r.–80v.

38. Bede, *Expl. Apc*, PL 93:192–193: "Porro Gog et Magog vel a parte totum signifi-cant, vel, iuxta interpretationem nominum que *tectum* et *de tecto* dicuntur, occultos et apertos indicant hostes." Cf. Augustine, *De ciuitate Dei*, 20.11, PL 41:676–677.

39. Du Pinet, *Exposition*, 1545, 367.

40. Du Pinet, *Exposition*, 1545, 369–371.

41. Victorinus of Poetovio, *In Apc*, 102–103; Primasius, *In Apc*, PL 68:873; Bede, *Expl. Apc*, PL 93:166; Joachim of Fiore, *In Apc*, 156v. col. B; [Nicholas of Lyra], *Sexta pars biblie cum glosa ordinaria et expositione Lyre litterali et morali: necnon additionibus ac replicis* (Basel: J. Amerbach, J. Petri, J. Froben, 1502), 257v. Herafter cited as Lyra.

42. Lambert, *In Apc*, 202r.–204v.

43. Rupert of Deutz, *In Apc*, 111: "Quia videlicet vnum ex regnis supradictis regnum Macedonicum in reges quatuor diuisum fuit."

44. Du Pinet, *Exposition*, 1545, 228–229.

45. Victorinus of Poetovio, *In Apc*, 100–101.

46. Primasius, *In Apc*, PL 68:874; Bede, *Expl. Apc*, PL 93:166; Joachim of Fiore, *In Apc*, 157r.; Lyra, 257v.

47. Lambert, *In Apc*, 204v.–205v.

48. Meyer, *In Apc*, 46r., 49r.

49. Du Pinet, *Exposition*, 1545, 230–231.

50. Bede, *In Apc*, PL 93:191; Primasius, *In Apc*, PL 68:914; Rupert of Deutz, *In Apc*, 178; Joachim of Fiore, *In Apc*, 210v.; Lyra, 270r.

51. Lambert, *In Apc*, 283r.–285r.

52. Meyer, *In Apc*, 80r.–81v.

53. Cf. Backus, *Les sept visions*, 31–41. On Pürstinger, cf. Joseph Schmuck, *Die Prophetie "Onus eccclesiae"* (Vienna, n.p.: 1973) and the unpublished Ph. D. thesis by Michal Milway: *The Burden and the Beast: Berthold Pürstinger, Bishop of Chiemsee, and Apocalyptic Reform in Early Sixteenth-Century Salzburg* (University of Arizona, Tucson, 1996).

54. Meyer, *In Apc*, 81v.: "Verum de pace illa et securitate quam pollicetur ipse, cum de medio Christi aduentu, tum ante iudicium finale post interitum gentium Gog, ac decem regum hoc dico: vtinam tum firmiter, adstipulantibus scripturis, id sperare liceret, quam optabile omnino est quod tradunt. Sunt enim plaereque Scripturae quae huic opinioni aperte aduersari videntur, vt Dan. 12."

55. PL 68:915.

56. Du Pinet, *Exposition*, 1545, 358–361.

Chapter 3

1. Haag and Haag, *La France Protestante*, 1st ed., 10 vols. (Paris: Cherbuliez, 1857), 7:256–259.

2. Marlorat, *Noui Testamenti Expositio*, 1570, 189 col. A: "ᴬAgitur hoc capite de certamine quod suscipit ecclesia Christi aduersus Satanam et impios et de victoria

quae ipsi ecclesiae confertur, Satana interim in filiis contumacibus agente.[M] Vt autem caput istud facilius explicetur, operae pretium est notare ecclesiam tripliciter accipi apud sanctos doctores. Vno modo secundum quod a synagoga distinguitur et sic tota secta Christianorum siue verorum siue falsorum, fidem tamen profitentium, vocatur ecclesia. Alio modo accipitur pro quacunque congregatione fidelium et hoc siue professione fidei et opere sint fideles, siue sint fideles nomine tenus, scilicet professione sola fidei. Tertio accipitur ecclesia pro toto numero praedestinatorum et haec sola ecclesia vera est et Catholica, cuius pars non est aliquis praescitus ad aeternam poenam. Aduersus hanc ecclesiam diabolus continuo belligeratur et eam a fide sponsi Christi reuocare nititur, quemadmodum mox videbimus."

3. Meyer, *In Apc*, 45r., 48r.

4. Marlorat, *Noui Testamenti Expositio*, 1570, 189 col. B: "[A]Item, tales sitis vt nemo de vobis quaeri possit sincerique filii Dei, irreprehensibiles in medio nationis prauae ac tortuosae, inter quos lucete tanquam luminaria in mundo, sermonem vitae sustinentes, Philip. 2, 15. Item, quicunque baptizati estis, Christum induistis, Gal. 3, 27.[M] Certe ecclesia quae Christum induit in sua conuersatione et doctrina, multo clarius illustratur spiritualiter quam aer a sole."

5. Marlorat, *Noui Testamenti Expositio*, 1570, 189 col. B: "Caeterum etsi duodecim illi apostoli quos primitiua ecclesia habuit, nobiscum iam minime versantur quia tamen eorum doctrina veluti per manus nobis tradita est, non caret Christi ecclesia splendido hoc ornamento quod Iohannes illi tribuit. Neque enim ad personas apostolorum restringi debent quae de illis praedicat Scriptura, sed ad eos omnes extenduntur qui veri sunt apostolorum successores, hoc est qui vnum Christum et eundem crucifixum aliis annuntiant."

6. Meyer, *In Apc*, 82v.

7. PL 68:914–915; PL 93:191.

8. Marlorat, *Noui Testamenti Expositio*, 1570, 224 col. A: "*Et vidi angelum descendentem.* Quo propinquior erit dies iudicii, eo maioribus insultibus Satan Christianam Ecclesiam adorietur vt eam penitus opprimat. Verum Christus ecclesiae sponsus et rex omnium supremus, eam omnino in die resurrectionis liberabit, horrendamque de hostibus ipsius vltionem sumet, sicuti hoc capite docet Iohannes. Hic angelus Christum designat qui fortis est ille heros, de quo dicitur: si fortior illo superueniens vicerit eum, vniuersa arma eius auferte, in quibus confidebat, etc, Luc. Cap. 11, 22."

9. Cf. Meyer, *In Apc.*, 80r.–81v.

10. Cf. Haag and Haag, *La France Protestante*, 2nd ed., 4: 512–513, and *Registres de la Compagnie des Pasteurs de Genève*, vol. 3, *1565–1574*, ed. Olivier Fatio and Olivier Labarthe (Geneva: Droz, 1969), viii–xii, and the literature cited there. There is no modern biography of Colladon. Useful information on his indexes to the 1559 edition of Calvin's *Institutes* appears in Richard Muller, "In the Light of Orthodoxy: The 'Method and Disposition' of Calvin's *Institutio* from the Perspective of Calvin's Late-Sixteenth-Century Editors," *Sixteenth Century Journal* 28:4 (1997): 1203–1211.

11. I have used the copy held by the Bodleian Library, Oxford. 8°. Shelfmark: Th 8° C 181.

12. Morgiis. Excudebat Ioannes le Preux, Illustrissimorum D. Bernens. Typographus, 1581.

13. Nicolas Colladon, *Methodus facilima ad explicationem sacrosanctae Apocalypseωs Ioannis theologi ex ipso libro desumpta. Authore N. Colladone Biturige,*

sacrarum literarum professore in Schola Lausannensi. 2 Thessal., 2 vers. 5. An non meministis me cum adhuc essem apud vos, haec dixisse vobis? Nunc vero quid obstet nostis vt is suo tempore retegatur, etc. (Morges: Jean Le Preux, 1581, 3d ed., 1584), *iv–v.: "Quare sicut priore libello Christum vobis depingi audiistis, ita hac Apocalypsi detegit vobis Christianisque omnibus principibus ac proceribus ipse Deus horrendam illam abominationem Antichristi." Hereafter cited as: *Methodus,* 1581, and *Methodus,* 1584.

14. *Methodus,* 1581, * ijr.–v.: "[S]pem faciebam studiosis sacrarum literarum huius vestrae Academiae Lausannensis, adolescentibus fore, vt quem tum ingrediebar cursum, prosequerer in publicam etiam ipsorum vtilitatem. Eo pertinebat illud consilium institutumque nostrum vt in lucem emitterem quae in sacra penu nostra literaria recondita apud me habebam, id est, ad sacrarum literarum interpretationem et multiplex studium pertinentia. Verum aliter placuit Domino, in cuius manu sunt viae omnes nostrae et vt nihil aliud impedierit, variae tamen pestes hic etiam grassatae, quae necdum ipsae prorsus conquieuere, typographicam officinam multis intermissionibus afflixerunt."

15. *Methodus,* 1581, *iv.v–vr.: "Me scilicet (prout debeo, alioqui erga Deum et a Deo institutum magistratum ingratissimus) quotidie precari toto corde vt Deus vos magis ac magis confirmet et stabiliat in sanctae vocationis cursu . . . vt vim omnem externam eorum qui seruiunt illi homini peccati, filio perditionis et Antichristo illo Romano longissime a vobis vestrisque propulsare pergat."

16. *Methodus,* 1584 (verso of title page): "Si papa suae et fraternae salutis negligens deprehenditur, inutilis et remissus in suis operibus et insuper a bono taciturnus quod magis officit sibi et omnibus nihilominus innumerabiles populos cateruatim secum ducit primo mancipio gehennae, cum ipso plagis multis in aeternum vapulaturus. Huius culpae isthic redarguere praesumit mortalium nullus, quia cunctos ipse iudicaturus, a nemine est iudicandus, nisi deprehendatur a fide deuius. C. Si Papa, distinct. 40."

17. *Methodus,* 1584, 452: "Ergo lege et gaudeat mater nostra Ecclesia Romana, magis ac magis innotescere toti mundo suam immanem Romanitatem."

18. For further information about the Riario family, cf. D. S. Chambers, *A Renaissance Cardinal and His Worldly Goods: The Will and Inventory of Francesco Gonzaga (1444–1483)* (London: Warburg Institute, 1992), index; John D'Amico, *Renaissance Humanism in Papal Rome* (Baltimore: Johns Hopkins University Press, 1983); P. Farenga, "*Monumenta memoriae.* Pietro Riario fra mito e storia," in *Un pontificato e une città. Sisto IV (1471–84)*, ed. M. Miglio, et al. (Vatican City: 1986), 179–216.

19. Cf. Chambers, *A Renaissance Cardinal,* 67–70, 118.

20. *Methodus,* 1584, 454: "O prodiga rerum luxuries, nunquam paruo contenta paratu / . . . Nobilis ignoto diffusus consule Bacchus, / Non auro gemmisque bibunt sed gutture puro / Vita redit." Lucan, *Pharsalia* 4, 374. Cf. *L. Aennaei Lucani Pharsalia,* ed. C. M. Francken (2 vols., Leiden: A. W. Sijthoft, 1896–1897), 1:205.

21. *Methodus,* 1584, 463: "Sponda se mediam locat Diana / Gemmis splendidulis decora virgo." Colladon's note: "Apoc. Cap. 18 v. 16: Ciuitas illa magna quae amicta erat bysso et purpura et cocco et deaurata erat auro et lapidibus pretiosis et margaritis."

22. *Methodus,* 1584, 465–466: "Bio haec seriola optime redundat. / Plena haec aurea defruto metreta est. / Mulsum haec crinea dulcius recondit." Colladon's note: "Non tanta vini varietate diffluebat nuptiale conuiuium in Cana Galileae, vbi praesens aderat Dominus cum Maria matre et discipulis. Sed haec non curat Ascanius cardinalis cum sua Diana sydereisque ephebis et comatulis."

23. On Christ's presence in the church, cf. I. Backus, "Nicolas Durand de Villegagnon contre Calvin: Le *Consensus Tigurinus* et la présence réelle," in *Calvin et ses contemporains*, ed. Olivier Millet (Geneva: Droz, 1998), 163–178. On Calvin and Revelation, cf. de Boer, "The Book of Revelation," 26–35.

24. Cf. de Boer, "The Book of Revelation," 40–42.

25. *Methodus*, 1584, 41–42: "Boni enim etiam quidam viri iidemque eruditionis et doctrinae eximiae approbant primum quasi a Caluino, deinde vt non minus vrbane quam prudenter dictum (nescio ex quorum hominum relatu) de hoc Apocalypseωs libro et eius scriptore se penitus ignorare quid velit tam obscurus scriptor, qui quis qualisque fuerit nondum constet inter eruditos. Ego vero optime quidem certe memini et recordor, cum aliquoties in eum Caluinus incidisset sermonem, mentio inquam fieret Apocalypseωs apud eum a quibusdam familiaribus, me quoque praesente, longe aliam fuisse eius sententiam de sanctissimo hoc libro, quam fortassis eo nunc mortuo aliqui in aliorum aures insusurrent. Non nego rogatum nonnunquam a fratribus quibusdam vt Apocalypsin publice exponeret, vel in schola apud literatos, vel in templo toti ecclesiae, respondisse, nec dum a se totam intelligi, quemadmodum et hac de causa cum in sacris concionibus enarraret Ezechielis librum, postrema quaedam capita reliquit intacta. Ego vero non dubito, quin si vel maiore otio abundasset . . . vel ei ad hunc vsque diem viuere datum esset, quamuis valde afflicta valetudine, non dubito, inquam, quin haberemus eximii illius serui Dei in Apocalypsim et in totum Ezechielem aliosque nonnullos Scripturae libros vtilissimas lucubrationes."

26. Cf. Beza's dedicatory epistle to Gaspard de Coligny in the posthumous edition of 18 January 1565: "Mais la mort dont il a esté prevenu l'a empesché de parachever Ezechiel au dommage de l'Eglise d'autant plus grand, qu'on sçait qu'il est le plus obscur de tous les Prophetes, principalement vers la fin." Cf. Theodore Beza, *Correspondance de Théodore de Bèze, recueillie par Hippolyte Aubert*, ed. F. Aubert, H. Meylan, A. Dufour, et al. (Geneva: Droz, 1960–), 6:18.

27. For further details of the *Epinicion*, cf. Erik de Boer, *Loflied en Hekeldicht. De geschiedenis van Calvijn's enige gedicht. Het Epinicion Christo cantatum van 1 januari 1541* (Haarlem: Aca Media, 1986).

28. *Methodus*, 1584, 362–364.

29. *Methodus*, 1584, *Prima pars libri Christiano lectori salutem*, 23–24: "Caeterum, quoties (vt modo dixi) instituti nostri ratio tulit vt contextus totius alicuius loci legendus proponeretur, vulgatam illam veteris interpretis Latini versionem inserere placuit, non quia sit optima, sed vt hoc vnum saltem gratificaremur Romano pontifici, cardinalibus, praelatis, canonicis, sacrificulis, monachis vtriusque sexus, curatis et in genere clericis omnibus, Romanensibus, coronam (vt loquuntur) siue tonsuram habentibus, de quibus multo antequam exorirentur depingendis, huius libri non minima parte agi videmus . . . legant ergo libere et resipiscant a simulachrorum cultu et omnibus operibus suis malis. . . ."

30. Cf., e.g., Pierre Prigent, *L'Apocalypse de Saint Jean*, 380–383.

31. *Methodus*, 1584, *Breuis partitio*, 4–5: "[H]abere etiam sua quaedam prooemia tria, quae praeparent lectorem ad varium hoc et triplex genus visionum et deinde partim interseri et media poni multa, partim postponi et vltimo loco subiici alia non pauciora quae omnia simul spectent ad expositionem trium illarum praecipuarum visionum." [sigilla, tubae, phialae]

32. *Methodus*, 1584, *Breuis partitio*, 3: "[A]b initio capitis quarti ad vigesimum vsque primum caput, totus libri contextus consumitur in varie describenda,

graphice depingenda saepius et ob oculos omnium ponenda Romani papatus abominatione. . . ."

33. *Methodus*, 1584, 78–104.

34. *Methodus*, 1584, 104–110.

35. *Methodus*, 1584, 110–113.

36. *Methodus*, 1584, 114–129.

37. *Methodus*, 1584, 121: "Nicolaitae scilicet Carpocrates, Cerinthus, Ebion suo tempore, Marcion postea et alii pessima haeresi inficiebant ecclesias. Nero et alii Romani saepe post eum principes igni ferroque Christianos persequebantur, sed non deerant sui ecclesiis ministri et strenui duces gregis industriique pastores qui illorum pestiferos errores refutarent. . . ."

38. *Methodus*, 1584, 130–136.

39. *Methodus*, 1584, 137–156.

40. *Methodus*, 1584, 255: "Non sunt haec sic capienda quasi tempore subsequantur praecedentem narrationem, imo pertinent ad expressiorem descriptionem quorundam quae antea dicta fuere."

41. *Methodus*, 1584, 257: "Siquidem mulier, id est ecclesia, iam nunc est in coelo quia per fidem et spem certissimam illic versatur et eo tandem tota maxime praesens evehetur, sicut et filii eius aliqui quotidie eo rapiuntur, vt est scriptum vers. 5. Qui autem nominatur draco rufus antea angelus erat sanctus et angelus lucis habitabat in coelo antequam peccaret. Ideo non absurde dicit etiam de eo loquens Ioannes, vidisse se signum in coelo."

42. *Methodus*, 1584, 255–256.

43. *Methodus*, 1584, 259–260.

44. *Methodus*, 1584, 19: "Ergo versus tres primi feliciora illa secula ecclesiae Christi depingunt, cum non esset adhuc prorsus extincta Dei veritas et maneret ministerii ecclesiastici sacrosancta forma aliqua."

45. *Methodus*, 1584, 20: "Versus quartus vna eademque periodo comprehendit cruentas omnes persecutiones, quibus subinde varie afflicta fuit Christi ecclesia ipseque Christus in suis membris, praecipue tamen sub papatu Romano . . . vt autem vixit et regnauit cum Christo in his terris per fidem et spem tota Christi ecclesia, sic praesentem regnaturam apud Deum in aeternum dicit versus sextus."

46. *Methodus*, 1584, 20–22.

47. *Methodus*, 1584, 435: "[N]empe quod Deus ipse facit suapte vi per Euangelii praedicationem, quam efficacissimam reddit per Spiritum sanctum. . . ."

48. *Methodus*, 1584, 433: "Si de Romani papatus tempore intelligitur istud (vt est indubium) quaeret aliquis quomodo dicatur exiguum tempus."

49. *Methodus*, 1584, 434: "Respondeo: exiguum dici tempus vt est reuera, si comparetur cum infinita illa aeternitate seculorum regni Christi."

50. *Methodus*, 1584, 437: "Quemadmodum vixerunt et regnarunt cum Christo mille annis, id est toto huius seculi cursu fideles, qui primae resurrectionis scilicet sunt omnes participes, ita post primam mortem (corporis scilicet et naturalem, id est externam) regnabunt . . . cum Christo mille annis, id est toto futuro saeculo."

51. For Bullinger's interpretation, see chapter 4. Beza, *N.T.*, 1642, 763 col. B: "Viuentque. Connectitur hoc verbum non cum proximo verbo *acceperunt* sed cum *sederunt* et *datum est*, sicut Paulo ante dictum fuit. Deinde obseruandum et etiam positum esse praeteritum pro futuro ex Prophetarum more." (The same note appears in his 1557 edition of the *Nouum Testamentum*.)

52. *Methodus*, 1584, 437: "Item quum dixisset v. 4 τὰ χίλια ἔτη dicit v. 6 χίλια ἔτη quasi illud prius cum articulo significet tempora quae finem sunt habitura, hoc posterius temporum immensitatem et saeculorum infinitatem."

53. *Methodus*, 1584, 439–442. Colladon's interpretation of the sack of Rome is nothing more than another piece of antipapal invective. Cf. Judith Hook, *The Sack of Rome* (London: Macmillan, 1972).

54. The best study of Gagny is by André Jammes, "Un bibliophile à découvrir, Jean de Gagny," *Bulletin du bibliophile* (1996): 35–81. Cf. also I. Backus, *Les sept visions*, 17–22.

55. *Breuissima et facillima in omnes D. Pauli Epistolas scholia, vltra priores editiones ex antiquissimis Graecorum authoribus abunde locupletata. Itidem in septem Canonicas Epistolas et D. Ioannis Apocalypsin, breuissima scholia recens edita* (Paris: V. Gaultherot, 1550). Hereafter cited as Gagny, *Scholia*, 1550.

56. Gagny, *Scholia*, 1550: *Praefatio in Apocalypsin Joannis Apostoli*, 245r.

57. Gagny, *Scholia*, 1550: *In Apocalypsin Joannis Apostoli*, 247r.: *"Fui* inquam *die dominica*, hinc constat sola apostolorum auctoritate sine scriptura, imo praeter scripturae auctoritatem exclusum sabbatum et introductam diem dominicam, ne quis putet ea tantum tenenda quae habentur in Scripturis."

58. Gagny, *Scholia*, 1550: *In Apocalypsin Joannis Apostoli*, 270v.–271r.

59. Gagny, *Scholia*, 1550: *In Apocalypsin Joannis Apostoli*, 274r.–278r.

60. Gagny, *Scholia*, 1550: *In Apocalypsin Joannis Apostoli*, 297 r.–v.

61. Gagny, *Scholia*, 1550: *In Apocalypsin Joannis Apostoli*, 297 r.–v.: *"Et ligauit eum per mille annos*. Hoc fecit per passionem suam Christus quando principem daemonum . . . compescuit ne adeo vt antea nocere posset per baptismum aduersum eius saeuitiam et fraudem Dei gratiam communitis. Mille annos autem omnes tempus legis euangelicae vsque ad Antichristum significare aiunt, quo medio tempore in abysso inferni tanquam clausus . . . detinetur Sathanas ne pro suo arbitrio noceat *donec consumentur mille anni* i.e., donec Antichristus venerit et tunc soluetur *modico tempore*, tribus annis scilicet cum dimidio, quamdudum regnabit Antichristus."

Chapter 4

1. Cf. Carl Pestalozzi, *Leo Jüda: Nach handschriftlichen und gleichzeitigen Quellen* (Elberfeld: Friderichs, 1860); Karl-Heinz Wyss, *Leo Jud, Seine Entwicklung zum Reformator, 1519–1523* (Bern: Peter Lang, 1976).

2. Cf. Backus, *Les sept visions*, 55, and the literature cited there.

3. Jud, *Offenbarung*, 1542, ad 1.1–3, yy3r.: "Unserm herren Jesu Christo nach menschlicher natur ist vom vatter geben nit allein aller gnaden überfluss unnd volkommenheit, sonder auch offenbarung der heimligkeiten Christenlichs stands in zukunfftige zeyt, biss zu der anderen zukunfft an das gericht. Soliche heimligkeiten hat Christus der Herr geoffenbaret durch seine Engel, seinen knechten, besonder aber Johanni."

4. Cf. Victorinus of Poetovio, *In Apc.*, 78–85.

5. Jud, *Offenbarung*, 1542, ad 6, 1, zz1v.: "Die sieben fürnaemen artickel und heimligkeiten Christlichs gloubens mögend als die siben sigel aufthon werden durch den Geist Gottes in der heiligen geschrifft des alten Testaments, wie auch das selbig mit vil zeugnuss anzeigt Luce am 24. cap. der hochgeleert Erasmus in disem buch der ausslegung des neüwen Testaments."

6. Jud, *Offenbarung*, 1542, ad 6.2–17, zz2r.

7. *Ibid.*, zz3v.

8. Jud, *Offenbarung*, 1542, aaa 2r.

9. Jud, *Offenbarung*, 1542, aaa 2r.: "Wie in des alten Testaments propheten, die ersten klarlicher und verstenlicher geschriben habend dann die letsten, die vil vnuerstentlicher sind als Ezechiel, Daniel und Zacharias, dann Isaias und Jeremias, also im neüwen Testament in disem prophetischen buch die letsten propheceyen und offenbarungen sind etwas klarer dann die ersten, das also dise gesicht schier als ein ausslegung seyn mag der vorderigen gesichten."

10. Jud, *Offenbarung*, 1542, aaa 2v.: "Dann daz kind ist geboren, Gottes wort ist mensh worden, warheit hat überwunden, falschheit ist vndergelagen, teüfels betrug ist von Gottes weyssheit überlistiget und der welt bekannt word. Dises kind Christus, das ewig wort Gottes, mensh worden in dem heiligsten leyb Marie der jungkfrauwen ist auf und angenommen worden ausz gnaden von Gott dem vatter, für alle welt sünd. . . ."

11. Jud, *Offenbarung*, 1542, aaa 2v.

12. Jud, *Offenbarung*, 1542, aaa 3r.: "[A]ber der hochfliegend umbsichtig Adler des Göttlichen geists, an der Tauben statt, im streyt wider den Tracken verleycht krafft und maacht mit seinen gnaden der Christenlichen seel zefliehen an ein sicher ort, das da ist verachtung diser welt, und liebe der zukünfftigen, einsame der ruwigen conscientz im creütz Christi, vnd trost in betrachtung des Göttlichen worts, mit denen sie entfleücht dem Satan und allen seinen Gespanst und anfechtungen."

13. Cf. Lee Palmer Wandel, *Voracious Idols and Violent Hands* (Cambridge: Cambridge University Press, 1996), and the literature cited there.

14. Jud, *Offenbarung*, 1542, aaa 4v.: "Darausz nachmals volget, das wär den bilderen nit eer anhtun wolt, der muszt sterben, wie heüttigs tags das Pabsthumb haben wil, und mit ansähung der person maalzetchen anschlahend, das ist, in Bann thund, und der künigreychen entsetzend, die so nit wöllend anbätten, daz ist vereeren, die bilder. Hie muss man weysslich von der sach reden, das man niemants erzürne, das man leybs, läbens, eeren und guts möge sicher bleyben, aber Gottes wort vnd will heiszt anders, ist gar ein andere weyssheit. Gott wolle das diser bestien zal vnd irrthumb bald auszgange. Zell vom 1520. jar hindersich dise zal der jaren 666, vnd lug was zeyten dozemal gewesen ist bey den Päbsten und Keyseren."

15. Jud, *Offenbarung*, 1542, bbb 8r.: "Solichen gewalt hat Christus gewaltigklich dem Satan genommen, durch die gerechtigkeit und demut bis anns creütz, gnügthünde vmb die hochfart und unglauben Adams und Eve."

16. Jud, *Offenbarung*, 1542, bbb 8v.: "Unlangst vor dem letsten tag zum end der welt wird Satanas wider gewalt überkommen und brauchen, und mit ungloubigen menschen nach seiner art und bossheit handlen in der gantzen welt."

17. On his edition of the Koran, cf. Hartmut Bobzin, *Der Koran im Zeitalter der Reformation. Studien zur Frühgeschichte der Arabistik und Islamkunde in Europa*, Beiruter Texte und Studien 42 (Beirut: Franz Steiner, 1995), 159–262. On Bibliander himself, the most comprehensive study is still that of Emil Egli in *Analecta reformatoria* II. *Biographien Bibliander. Ceporin. Johannes Bullinger* (Zurich: Zürcher und Furrer, 1901), 1–144. Hereafter cited as: Egli.

18. Cf. Egli, 62–63. Oswald Bär (d. 1569) produced a commentary on the Apocalypse which was never published. Excerpts from it were copied by Bibliander himself when he wrote down his lectures on the Apocalypse (Zürich ZB: Ms. Car I 91).

19. Cf. Egli, 62.

20. *Relatio fidelis*, 114: "Agite principes et ciues vniuersi reipublicae christianae, expendamus breuiter vltimum scriptum codicis diuini, quod Dominus et Deus noster Iesus Christus post 64. annum ascensionis in coelos ministerio angelorum suorum per Ioannem Euangelistam et dilectum discipulum, ecclesiae suae exhibuit."

21. *Relatio fidelis*, 162: "Omniumque primum constat inter omnes theologos melioris notae, Apocalypsim Iesu Christi continere vaticinium de rebus Christi et ecclesiae, et hostium ecclesiae, ab vltimis temporibus imperatoris Domitiani vsque ad mundi finem, quatenus ecclesiae totius et piorum singulorum scire interest."

22. Cf. Bousset, *Die Offenbarung Johannis*, 87.

23. *Relatio fidelis*, 129.

24. *Relatio fidelis*, 129: "Secunda pars expositionis octo capitibus compraehenditur, quae rationem prouidentiae diuinae explicat, quinam homines ingrediantur in vitam aeternam aut qui damnentur et quibus de causis."

25. *Relatio fidelis*, 130: "Itaque vniuersum tempus ab origine mundi vsque ad seculi consummationem per septem sigillorum apertionem et per septem tubas distribuitur."

26. *Relatio fidelis*, 130–133.

27. *Relatio fidelis*, 140–141: "Sed non contentus fuit Satan hactenus in Iudaea Christianos afflixisse per Iudaeos furentes, nisi etiam in vrbibus gentium persequerentur, vt testantur Apostolorum Acta et Epistola ad Smyrnensem angelum, capite 2. Habet autem ecclesia locum et alitur inter gentiles quondam, et remotos a testamentis Dei vsque ad seculi consummationem. Quod tempus quantum futurum sit, abscondit Deus a notitia hominum. Ideoque dicitur: ad tempus et tempora et dimidium temporis."

28. *Relatio fidelis*, 144: "Eodemque tempore Mahumet, radix peccati et Satanae delicium prodiit, qui antichristianam tyrannidem extra ecclesiam exercens, antichristum in visceribus ecclesiae et populi Dei grassantem redargueret."

29. *Relatio fidelis*, 147: "Cernes anno salutis nostrae 763 adultum iam Antichristum, victorem trium regum et regibus formidabilem et insipientibus Christianis adorabilem."

30. *Relatio fidelis*, 147–148: "Inde si numeres rursum annos 666 eosque addas annis 763, cernes anno salutis 1429 in fine pontificatus Martini quinti, antichristum prominentibus cornibus et auribus praelongis et detracta larua nudatum et claritate verbi diuini manifestatum."

31. *Relatio fidelis*, 148–155.

32. *Relatio fidelis*, 155: "Quarta pars expositionis sequitur, quae describit finem bonorum hominum pariter et malorum, quaenam praemia proposita sint piis cultoribus Christi, et contra, quae supplicia parata sint diabolo et antichristo cum suis membris et vniuersis impiis."

33. *Relatio fidelis*, 157: "Venit enim lux euangelicae praedicationis in totum orbem per apostolos, in primis vero per doctorem gentium et organum electissimum Dei Paulum, qui ab ipso Christo coelitus ad euangelii munus vocatus neque ab hominibus neque per homines euangelium accepit et plus quam caeteri apostoli effecit. Ideoque per angelum coelo descendentem aptissime figuratur. Homines autem magis dilexerunt tenebras quam lucem, vt anno millesimo postquam Christus obtinuit regnum in terris, vtique a consummatione Iudaeorum, Satan imperitarit in mundo aeque atque ante praedicatum Christum."

34. Cf. Egli, 63.

35. Cf. Egli, 67. Several of Bibliander's contemporaries made copies of his lectures on the Apocalypse. The copies are still extant in Zurich, Zentralbibliothek, under the following signatures: MS D53–54 (Rudolf Gwalther, 1543); MS D70 (Gregor Mangold, 1549); MS S204m (anonymous); MS S204m (Heinrich Bullinger and Petrus Cholinus); MS Car XV 42 (anonymous).

36. *Relatio fidelis: "[Q]uod a solo Verbo filioque Dei tum exacta cognitio praesentium temporum et futurorum, atque ipsius etiam Antichristi, maximae pestis totius orbis, tum recta optimaque moderatio reipublicae et totius vitae Christianae petenda sit."*

37. Zurich, Zentralbibliothek, MS Car I 91, contains some 550 folios.

38. Zurich, Zentralbibliothek, MS Car I 91, 461r.: "Caeterum omnes gentes sunt Antichristi, verum tanto magis Hebraei, quanto maius lumen per Scripturas sacras et omnibus denique modis habuerunt, nec ipsum susceperunt sed acrius quam gentiles persequuti."

39. Zurich: Zentralbibliothek, MS Car I 91, 461r.: "Proinde quemadmodum omnium bonorum verorumque Christianorum Christus caput est, sic furatis atque improbis caput quodam habere conuenit, quod omnino Christo erit contrarium, quo peius neque imaginari quidam poterit."

40. Zurich, Zentralbibliothek, MS Car I 91, 461v.: "Praeterea quia vnicus homo non erit, non est ignorandum, quoniam cum vita nostra breuis sit, multum minime mali furere posset, sed plures erunt, vnus alteri succedentes eodem nihilominus nomine vocati, sicut quondam reges omnes Aegypti pharaones vocari solebant."

41. On Bullinger's *Sermons*, cf. also Bauckham, "Heinrich Bullinger," 9–54; Backus, *Les sept visions*, 55–63; Rodney Petersen, *Preaching in the Last Days. The Theme of Two Witnesses in the Sixteenth and the Seventeenth Centuries* (Oxford: Oxford University Press, 1993).

42. Bullinger, *In Apc.*

43. I shall be referring here to the second French edition published in Geneva in 1565 by Jean Bonnefoy and Guillaume Fournet: *Cent sermons.* Cf. Joachim Staedtke, ed., *Heinrich Bullinger: Werke,* vol. 1:1, *Bibliographie* (Zurich: Thelogischer Verlag, 1972), nos. 327, 341–345, 349. The first French edition (1598) was published by Jean Crespin. The first English translation of the *Sermons* appeared in 1561. The translator was John Daus.

44. *Cent sermons*, 1565, 1r.

45. *Cent sermons*, 1565, 25v.: "Or i'ay diuisé ceste miene exposition par Sermons, tant pource que i'ay publiquement exposé ce liure à l'Eglise fidele de Jesus Christ à laquelle ie sers, lequel i'ay exposé en ces deux annees 1555 et 1556 és Sermons que i'ay quasi ainsi faits au peuple, que pource qu'estant prié, i'ay voulou fournir vn tel quel exemple à ceux qui voudront exposer ou declarer ce mesme liure aux Eglises qui leur ont esté baillees en charge."

46. *Cent sermons*, 1565, 25v.

47. *Cent sermons*, 1565, 9v.–18r.

48. *Cent sermons*, 1565, 18v.: "M. Theodore Bibliander, professeur de théologie en l'escole de Zurich, homme de grand sauoir et diligent et adroit à exposer les sainctes Ecritures, m'a grandement aidé en ceci."

49. *Cent sermons*, 1565, 19r.–v.

50. *Cent sermons*, 1565, 20r.: "[M]ais mon affection a esté d'exposer simplement ce liure du nouueau Testament, excellent et fort vtile, ayant desia dés long temps fait des Commentaires sur tous les liures du nouueau Testament. Ioinct que plusieurs

gens de bien et sauans m'ont escrit de diuers lieux et requis que ie misse en lumiere ceste miene exposition sur l'Apocalypse."

51. *Cent sermons*, 1565, 30r.: "De l'autheur de ce liure, de l'argument, des parties et finalement du diuers vsage ou vtilité tressalutaire d'icelui."

52. *Cent sermons*, 1565, 35r.–v.

53. *Cent sermons*, 1565, 34v.–35r.

54. *Cent sermons*, 1565: sermons 30–33, 130r.–141v.

55. *Cent sermons*, 1565, 223r.

56. *Cent sermons*, 1565, 223r.: "La lumière de sa justice croist et descroist et finalement elle attire tousiours des taches du naturel de la chair, lesquelles elle n'oste point sinon en la mort."

57. *Cent sermons*, 1565, 223r.; Victorinus of Poetovio, *In Apc.* 98, 100: "Ecclesia est antiqua patrum et prophetarum et sanctorum apostolorum, quia gemitus et tormenta desiderii sui habuit. . . . *Stellarum duodecim coronam* <chorum> patrum significat secundum carnis natiuitatem, ex quibus erat Christus carnem sumpturus." Lambert, *In Apc*, 1528, 199v.: "Stellae ministri verbi sunt, supra capite 1." Cf. Bullinger, *Cent sermons*, 1565, 223r.: "Ici donc est signifiee la doctrine des ministres, comme au premier chapitre de ce livre."

58. Lambert, *In Apc*, 1528, 199v.: "Parturitio vero eius quod nitebantur vt Christus in vniuersis formaretur, prout Galatis Paulus scripsit, Gal. 4: filioli mei quos iterum parturio donec formetur Christus in vobis." Bullinger, *Cent sermons*, 1565: "L'Eglise donc a desiré d'vn grand zele et d'une affection tresardente, que Christ fust quelque fois engendré par la sainte Vierge, qui est un membre for excellent de l'Eglise. Dauantage Christ est engendré en ses fideles quand ils sont regenerez par sa vertu. Car S. Paul dit: mes petits enfans, lesquels i'enfante derechef jusqu'à ce que Christ soit formé en vous."

59. *Cent sermons*, 1565, 223r.: "Au surplus ceste femme est enceinte et non seulement est enceinte, mais aussi elle crie comme celles qui sont en travail d'enfant et en travaillant souffre tourment pour enfant. Ce qui ne convient point proprement à la vierge Marie, ains à l'Eglise." Cf. Primasius, *In Apc*, PL 68:874.

60. *Cent sermons*, 1565 (sermon 87), Apc 20.1–3, 356r.: "Comme ceci est de grand poids en la vraye religion, que nous cognoissions vrayement et entendions comme il appartient que c'est du dernier Jugement, ce que nous remonstrons souventesfois, saint Iean aussi traite ici diligemment de ce Iugement, et ce pour nostre grand profit et utilité."

61. *Cent sermons*, 1565 (sermon 87), 359r.: "Ie say que l'heresie des chiliastes ou des millenaires a este tiree de ceci, de laquelle heresie Papias fut autheur, comme Eusebe le recite au 3. liure de ses Histoires. De moy, ce ne'st mon intention de refuter les opinions des autres; comme aussi cela seroit trop long et de trop grand labeur et mesme cela n'apporteroit pas aux lecteurs fort grand profit."

62. *Cent sermons*, 1565, 357r.

63. Cardinal Benno, *Vita Hildebrandi*, was first published in 1516. I shall be referring here to the 1535 edition, published as part of the *Fasciculus rerum expetendarum ac fugiendarum*, in Köln. Hereafter cited as *Vita Hildebrandi* in *Fasciculus rerum*, 1535.

64. *Cent sermons*, 1565, 359v.: "Et pourtant s'il semble bon on pourra commencer la supputation de mille ans depuis le trente quatriesme an apres la natiuité de Iesus

Christ, auquel il monta au ciel, et saint Paul a esté appelé à faire son office d'Apostre et par la predication de la Parole attira les Gentilz à la société du peuple de Dieu et commença à reprimer Satan. Et pour faire les mille ans depuis cest an, on viendra jusqu'à l'an 1034, auquel temps Benois 9 estoit pape, lequel estant monté par finesses et meschantes pratiques à ce siege de pape (lequel on apelle le siege de S. Pierre ou Apostolique) exerça l'art magique et fit alliance auec le diable, lequel le fit mourir, mais ce fut apres qu'il eut vendu la papauté à Gregoire 6 de ce nom." (Cf. *Vita Hildebrandi* in *Fasciculus rerum*, 1535, 42r.).

65. Cf. *Vita Hildebrandi* in *Fasciculus rerum*, 1535, 42r.

66. *Cent sermons*, 1565, 359v.

67. *Cent sermons*, 1565, 359v.–360r.

68. *Cent sermons*, 1565, 360r.

69. *Cent sermons*, 1565, 360r.–v.

70. Cf. Augustine, *In Iohannem*, tract. 51, *Corpus Christianorum*. Series Latina 36:448; *Cent sermons*, 1565, 360v.

71. *Cent sermons*, 1565, 362v.: "[O]n dira de ces mille ans que c'ont esté autant de siècles d'or et d'argent et des nostres depuis 500 ans, que ce sont des siecles de fer ou de cuivre, ou de plomb ou de terre. Lactance au cha. 15 du 7 liure de ses Institutions dit: quand le terme de ce siecle approchera il faudra necessairement que l'estat des choses basses et humaines change et que la malice et iniquité croisse de plus en plus, comme aujourd'hui de nostre temps la malice et peruersité est montee iusqu'au plus haut degré. Tant y a neantmoins qu'en comparaison de ce mal incurable, on pourra iuger de nostre temps present, que c'est vn siecle heureux, ou vn siecle d'or." Cf. Lucius Caelius Firmianus Lactantius, *Institutiones diuinae* 7.15. *Opera omnia*, part 1, section 2, ed. S. Brandt and G. Laubmann (Prague: F. Tempsky, 1890; reprint, 1965), 631–634.

72. *Cent sermons*, 1565, 362v.–363r.

73. Irenaeus, *Adu. haer.* 5, 30. 2–4, PG 7:1203–1207.

74. *Cent sermons*, 1565, 271r.–v.: "Le s. Martyr Irenee parlant de ce roy en ce mesme liure 5 dit ainsi: a la venue de la beste se fait une recapitulation de toute iniquité et fraude, en sorte que toute la force apostatique s'assemblant et estant là enclose, est iettee en la fornaise de feu. Or il n'y aura personne qui ne confesse ouuertement qu'Irenee a dit cela d'vn esprit de prophetie, pourveu qu'il ait leu les vies des Papes . . . Italie, Espagne, France, Angleterre, Hongrie, Alemagne et les autres royaumes qui ont eu guerres mortelles l'vn contre l'autre, peuvent bien rendre tesmoignage de ce que de nostre temps et memoire ont faict les Iules, les Leons, les Clemens et Pauls. . . . Que reste-il donc, sinon que nous-nous gardions de cest homme de peché et que nous adherions au Fils de Dieu nostre Sauveur et Redempteur? Et le prions de bon cœur qu'il viene bien tost et qu'il nous deliure de toute oppression. . . ."

75. *Cent sermons*, 1565, 362r.: "Saint Iean a destiné vn certain nombre d'annees à l'Antechrist, assavoir 666, afin que par cela nous cognoissions le nom de l'Antechrist. Mais il ne sensuit pas pourtant que le diable ait esté alors du tout deslié, ou que la lumière de la vérité ait esté du tout esteinte."

76. *Cent sermons*, 1565, 364r.–367r.

77. *Cent sermons*, 1565, 363v.–364r.: "Et ils regneront mille ans auec lui. Et est signifié par cela, que tous les fideles viuront éternellement auec Christ et, principalement les ames, voire deuant le Iugement."

Chapter 5

1. Cf. especially Karl-Heinz Glaser, Hanno Lietz, and Stefan Rhein, eds., *David und Nathan Chytraeus: Humanismus im Konfessionellen Zeitalter* (Ubstadt-Weiher: Verlag Regionalkultur, 1993). Hereafer cited as *Chytraeus*, 1993.

2. Cf. Thomas Fuchs, "David und Nathan Chytraeus: Eine biographishe Annäherung," in *Chytraeus*, 1993, 33–48, and the literature cited *ibid.*

3. I shall be referring to the second edition: David Chytraeus, *Explicatio Apocalypsis Ioannis perspicua et breuis. Tradita a Davide Chytraeo* (Vitebergae: Excudebat Iohannes Crato, 1564). Hereafter cited as *Explicatio*, 1564.

4. Erik XIV (1533–1577) was king of Sweden from 1560 until 1568. Cf. Ingvar Andersson, *Erik XIV* (Stockholm: Wahstroem och Widstrand, 1948).

5. *Explicatio*, 1564, A3v.: "[L]uculentissimam descriptionem Regni Christi, quam a Iohanne Apostolo, ex sinu Christi depromtam et insignibus typis ac imaginibus venustissimis illustratam et a me in Academia vrbis Rosarum pro officii mei ratione publice propositam, regiae Maiestati tuae cum debita subiectione et reuerentia dedicare et offerre volui, non modo vt obseruantiae erga R.M.T. meae et amoris admirationisque virtutum, quibus prae aliis regibus a Deo ornatus es, in meo et multorum in Germania bonorum virorum pectoribus excitatae, testimonium qualecunque declararem, verumetiam vt me inclyto Regno tuo piam tranquillitatem et ecclesias Christi florentes, quam iudicio et hoc meum scriptum et alia prius edita reuerenter subiicio, gratulari ostenderem. . . ."

6. *Explicatio*, 1564, B5r.–v.: "Semper itaque nobis in conspectu versentur diuinae praedictiones Matth. 24: 'multi falsi doctores exorientur et multos seducent. . . .' Denique totus liber Apocalypsis tale vaticinium est de secuturis in ecclesia Christi confusionibus et corruptelis doctrinae et aliis calamitatibus. Quas non casu, non temere et fortuito accidere, sed Deum patrem et agnum ac redemtorem et dominum nostrum Iesum Christum sapientissimo consilio et iustissimo iudicio, omnia quae in ecclesia eueniunt bona et mala regere et gubernare asseuerat."

7. *Explicatio*, 1564, A4v.–A5r.

8. There is absolutely no reason why Chytraeus, given his knowlege of history, should think that the Council of Nicea took place in 230 AD! Cf. *Explicatio*, 1564, A5r.–A6v.

9. *Explicatio*, 1564, A6v.–B3v.

10. *Explicatio*, 1564, B1r.: "Quam haeresim nostra aetate renouauit Michael Seruetus Hispanus qui anno Christi 1553, die 27 octobris Geneuae in Subaudia combustus est."

11. *Explicatio*, 1564, B2r.–v.

12. *Explicatio*, 1564, B1v.: "Ita nostris etiam temporibus illucescente vera Euangelii doctrina et per salutare organon Dei, D. Martinum Lutherum, taxatis erroribus pontificiis et renouata coelesti doctrina diabolus inter ipsa initia variis distractionibus, sectis et seditionibus excitatis salutarem Euangelii lucem iterum accensam obscurare et paulatim extinguere conatus est."

13. *Explicatio*, 1564, B3r.: "Nec vllum aliud scandalum nostris ecclesiis nocentius fuit et plurium, bonorum etiam et sapientium animos a puriore euangelii doctrina deterruit et cursum euangelii magis impediuit, quam tristis illa praecipuorum doctorum de sacramento coenae Domini dissensio."

14. *Explicatio*, 1564, B4r.: "Primum itaque perpetua Historia Ecclesiae ab initio vsque ad nostram aetatem consideretur."

15. *Explicatio*, 1564, B5v.–B6r.: "Denique totus liber Apocalypsis tale vaticinium est de secuturis in ecclesia Christi confusionibus et corruptelis doctrinae et aliis calamitatibus. Quas non casu, non temere et fortuito accidere, sed Deum patrem et Agnum ac Redemtorem et Dominum nostrum Iesum Christum sapientissimo consilio et iustissimo iudicio, omnia quae in ecclesia eueniunt, bona et mala regere et gubernare asseuerat. Cum igitur sapientia diuina mirando consilio permittat diabolis et petulantibus ingeniis vt falsa dogmata et haereses in ecclesia spargant et hos euentus tot seculis antea ecclesiae suae praemonstrauerit, facilius se aduersus hoc triste scandalum munire et confirmare et placidius acquiescere mentes piae possunt."

16. *Explicatio*, 1564, B6v.–B8r.

17. *Explicatio*, 1564, B8v.

18. *Explicatio*, 1564, C1r.: "Non itaque mirum est varias et multiplices sectas et haereses et efficaces errores inter nos existere et late propagari, praesertim hoc postremo mundi tempore, quo vt in effoeto corpore naeui omnes et morbi praecipue sese exerunt, ita errores et infirmitates omnis generis multifariam augentur."

19. *Explicatio*, 1564, C1v.–C2r.: "Atqui defendit et conseruauit Filius Dei ecclesiam suam inde ab initio generis humani aduersus diaboli et omnium sectarum furores iam annis 5525. Tot enim anni a condito mundo vsque ad hunc currentem 1563 effluxerunt. Idem Filius Dei deinceps etiam hoc exiguo tempore quod vsque ad finem mundi superest ecclesiam suam aduersus sectas et omnes inferorum portas incolumem tuebitur, sicut promittit: ecce ego vobiscum sum omnibus diebus vsque ad consummationem seculi."

20. *Explicatio*, 1564, C3r.: "Sunt autem duplices fructus qui falsum doctorem seu impostorem pelle ouina tectum aliis ostendunt et arguunt. Primum, manifesta corruptela alicuius articuli doctrinae christianae. Secundo, manifesta scelera in exteriori consuetudine vitae, quae tanquam pia et recte facta praetextu euangelii aut nominis ecclesiae defenduntur, vt externa idolatria, seditiones, caedes, diuortia, libidines, etc."

21. *Explicatio*, 1564, 6–7: "Ideo autem visionibus et figuris pleraque huius libri vaticinia pingit Iohannes quia hae picturae et imagines ad perspicuitatem et euidentiam rerum ac memoriam plurimum adiumenti adferunt, sicut Christum videmus in docendo saepissime parabolis et figuris vsum esse."

22. *Explicatio*, 1564, 7–8.

23. *Explicatio*, 1564, 8–11.

24. *Explicatio*, 1564, 11: "Quarum [visionum] prima luculentam descriptionem Christi regis et pontificis ecclesiae supremi et statum ac formam totius gubernationis ecclesiasticae in hac vita, cernendam exhibet, cap. 1, 2, 3."

25. *Explicatio*, 1564, 12: "Secunda visio ab initio capitis quarti vsque ad octauum, imaginem regni et iustissimae gubernationis diuinae et praedictiones de secuturis ecclesiae aerumnis corporalibus et simul consolationem de perpetua ecclesiae conseruatione et gloria aeterna continet."

26. *Explicatio*, 1564, 12: "Tertia visio cap. 8, 9,10, 11 corruptelas dogmatum et haereses in ecclesia grassaturas, imagine septem tubarum depingit."

27. *Explicatio*, 1564, 12: "Quarta visio cap. 12, 13, 14 certamen ecclesiae cum dracone et veteri ac nouo imperio Romano et descriptionem ac reuelationem Antichristi Romani luculentam comprehendit."

28. *Explicatio*, 1564, 12: "Sequens pars Apocalypsis vsque ad caput 21 tantum est repetitio et illustratio et velut commentarius 13. et 14. capitis."

29. *Explicatio*, 1564, 12–13.

30. *Explicatio*, 1564, 15–18.

31. *Explicatio*, 1564, 19: "In tota fere Apocalypsi per angelos et stellas significari ministros Euangelii, seu pastores et doctores ecclesiae siue pios, siue impios. Cf. Luther, WA Bibel 7, 408: "Uber das lernen wir draus, durch das wert, Engel, hernach inn andern bilden und gesichten, verstehen, Bisschoue oder lerer inn der Christenheit, etliche gut, als die heilige Veter und Bisschoue, etliche böse. . . ."

32. *Explicatio*, 1564, 20. Cf. Luther, WA *Bibel* 7:410.

33. *Explicatio*, 1564, 20. Cf. Luther, WA *Bibel* 7:414.

34. *Explicatio*, 1564, 20. Cf. Luther, WA *Bibel* 7:410.

35. *Explicatio*, 1564, 20. Cf. Luther, WA *Bibel* 7:412.

36. *Explicatio*, 1564, 21. Cf. Luther, WA *Bibel* 7:412.

37. *Explicatio*, 1564, 21. Cf. Luther, WA *Bibel* 7:414.

38. *Explicatio*, 1564, 21–22.

39. *Explicatio*, 1564, 130: "Primus equus candidus et eques arcu et sagittis armatus ac corona insignitus et victor significat purae et sincerae Euangelii doctrinae felicem ac victricem toto orbe terrarum propagationem ac cursum, qua Christus rex ecclesiae . . . omnes diabolos, peccatum, mortem et infernum vincit. . . ." Cf. Bullinger, *Cent sermons* 130r.–131v.

40. *Explicatio*, 1564, 130–131: "Secundus equus ruffus . . . belli pictura est, quo Euangelii sui pacem et omnia bona diuina offerentis, contemtum et alia scelera principum et subditorum Deus iustissimo iudicio punit . . . Similes poenas vniuersae Germaniae propter horribilem ingratitudinem et contemtum verbi Dei, Lutherus saepe praedixit. Quae et ipsius mortem secutae sunt et maiores imminere non dubitemus."

41. Bullinger, *Cent sermons*, 130v.–131r.

42. Bullinger, *Cent sermons*, 130v.–132v.

43. *Explicatio*, 1564, 132–134; Bullinger, *Cent sermons*, 133r.–135r.

44. Bullinger, *Cent sermons*, 135v.–141r.

45. *Explicatio*, 1564, 135–137.

46. *Explicatio*, 1564, 147: "Has poenas beatae animae etiam, accensae zelo iusticiae et amore gloriae Dei, iuxta voluntatem Dei pie expetunt, etiamsi perditionem et interitum impiorum non praecipue intendunt."

47. *Explicatio*, 1564, 147; Bullinger, *Cent sermons*, 141v.–142v.

48. *Explicatio*, 1564, 148; Bullinger, *Cent sermons*, 142v.–143r.

49. *Explicatio*, 1564, 165: "Initio autem facta silentii mentione, lectores ad diligentiam et accuratam attentionem exuscitat."

50. *Explicatio*, 1564, 233.

51. *Explicatio*, 1564, 234–235: "[P]arturit et cruciatur vt pariat, hoc est ardenti desiderio inde vsque ab edita prima promissione expetit et optauit, semen mulieris conterens caput serpentis ex virgine nasci."

52. *Explicatio*, 1564, 357: "Cum igitur doctrina de extremo iudicio non tantum in hoc capite 20, verum etiam in tota fere Apocalypsi praecipuum locum obtineat et in vniuersum ad veram pietatem, timorem Dei, fidem, diligentiam et intentionem in omnibus vitae consiliis et actionibus honeste et sancte regendis vtilissima sit, paulo copiosius eam in praesentia explicabo, distributam in 8 capita, quae omnia fere in hac Iohannis visione contineri, attentus lector ipse perspiciet."

53. *Explicatio*, 1564, 357.

54. *Explicatio*, 1564, 358.

55. *Explicatio*, 1564, 358–359.

56. *Explicatio*, 1564, 364: "Hos mille annos Theodorus Bibliander in 13 tabula Chronologiae suae, non ab ipsa Christi resurrectione, sed a consummata iam plerorumque apostolorum circa annum Christi 73. praedicatione incipiens, peruenit ad annum Christi 1073. Et initia pontificatus Gregorii septimi Hellebrandi, quo nullus priorum pontificum furiosius Antichristi tyrannidem in orbe Christiano et praecipue in Imperio Germanico opprimendo, exercuit."

57. *Explicatio*, 1564, 368.

58. *Explicatio*, 1564, 381–382.

59. Cf. Ebel Jobst, "Die Herkunft des Konzeptes der Konkordienformel," *Zeitschrift für Kirchengeschichte* 91 (1980): 237–282, and Franz Dibelius, "Selnecker," *Realencyklopädie für protestantische Thelogie und Kirche*, vol. 18, ed. Albert Hauck (Leipzig: C. Hinrichs'sche Buchhandlung, 1906), 184–191. Cf. also Robert Kolb, "Selnecker," *Oxford Encyclopedia of the Reformation*, vol. 4, ed. Hans Hillerbrand (New York: Oxford University Press, 1996), 43.

60. Nikolaus Selnecker, *Der Prophet Daniel and die Offenbarung Johannis* (Leipzig: Jacob Berwaldt, 1567), A2r–v.: "Weil es mir aber an zeit und auch gesundheit gemangelt, das ich mit mühe kaum die ersten drey Capitel habe verfertigen können . . . so sende ich wo viel ich verfertigen hab können. . . ." Hereafter cited as *Daniel und Offenbarung*, 1567.

61. *Daniel und Offenbarung*, 1567, A2v.: "[W]eill sie auffeinander sehen und die bepstischen grewel miteinander gewaltiglich anzeigen und straffen."

62. *Daniel und Offenbarung*, 1567, A2r.: "So habe ich auch in der Offenbarung sonderlich diese drey punctlin gemerkt. Erstlich, das man sich nicht sol kranck oder zu tod bekümmern, wenn man teglich erferet und sihet, wie so grosse gewaltige leut, bapst, könige, fürsten und dergleichen voller Abgötterey, halstarrigkeit und bosheit stecken. Zum andern, das man sich frewen sol, wenn man von wegen rechter, erkanter und bekanter warheit leiden, und sein eigen Blut vergiessen sol. Zum dritten, das das Jüngste gericht gewiss nicht fern mehr sey."

63. *Daniel und Offenbarung*, 1567, A3r.

64. *Daniel und Offenbarung*, 1567, [462]: "Die 12. sterne hie auch bedeuten alle Lehrer, die von Christo durch die lieben Apostel erleuchtet sind. Und weil die Figur des Weibes in sonderheit bedeut die Christenheit der letzten zeit, bedeuts hie die 12. Sterne jre Lehrer, die zu jrer zeit jre ehr und kron sind, als die der Apostel lehre recht und rein füren, unnd unverfelscht, jrer sey viel oder wenig."

65. *Daniel und Offenbarung*, 1567, [463]: "Aus der rechten Kirchen Gottes solte kommen ein für trefflicher, geistreicher Lehrer wie gewest ist zu unser zeit, Lutherus, der solte blitzen und donnern, und seinen Mund auffthun als ein küner Helt. Aber sein anfang sol schwerlich zugehen, wie man denn gesehen hat. . . ."

66. *Daniel und Offenbarung*, 1567, [464].

67. *Daniel und Offenbarung*, 1567, [465]: "Ein jeder gedencke bey diesem Text, was er wolle oder könne, mir zweyffelt gar nicht, denn das es sey der handel wider den anfang Lutheri von dem Ablass, den er anfeht mit seinen conclusionibus im jar Christi 1517. . . . Da hat sich warlich der Drach angefangen zu erzeigen, das diese geburt so verhanden war, nicht an das liecht komen möchte."

68. *Daniel und Offenbarung*, 1567, [466–467].

69. *Daniel und Offenbarung*, 1567, [606]: "Diese, davon die heilige Schrift zeuget, ist die erste Aufferstehung. Und gehöret in diese aufferweckung alles, das von dem Jüngsten tage zum ewigen leben wird aufferweckt."

70. *Daniel und Offenbarung*, 1567, [607]: "[D]as Christus alle zeit seiner geliebten etliche habe bey sich im Himel haben wollen, und freude mit jnen haben. Und ist auch nichts seltzams, so wir es dafür hattten, das der liebe Lutherus auch deren einer sey."

71. *Daniel und Offenbarung*, 1567, [609]: "Das ist aber seine Gefengnis, das jme geweret ist, die Christenheit gantz und gar mit dem Schwert aus zu rotten durch die ungleubigen, als durch den Türcken, Moscoviter, etc."

72. *Daniel und Offenbarung*, 1567, [610]: "Aber vor Machomets zeiten (nicht lang zuuor) umb den angang der 1000. Jaren lese man derselbigen zeiten historien. Und sonderlich was der Gottloser und hoffertige heyde Cosroes der Perser könig dem Keyser Heraclio zumutet in seinen Artickeln, die zwischen jm und dem Römischen Reich solten gehalten werden, so er anders friede von jme haben wolte."

73. *Daniel und Offenbarung*, 1567, [610–611]: "Der Oberste Teuffel ist wolgefangen gelegen, das er niemands hat müssen verführen 1000 Jar lang, aber die andern Teufel sind nicht also gefangen gelegen, sondern haben für und für verführet, wie man vielfeltiger weise ohne zal bewisen kan, und sonderlich wie unter dem Bapstumb haben regieret allerley Irthumb des glaubens und allerley sünde und laster. Denn wir wissen, das eben die Namen und Tittel, so diesem gefangnem Teuffel in diesem Capitel gegeben, werden jme auch gegeben, oben cap. 12. Da er unter der geheimnis eines roten Drachens wird aus dem himmel der Christenheit geworffen. Und ist das geschehen unter der zeit der 1000. jar und der zeit seiner gefengnis."

74. *Daniel und Offenbarung*, 1567, [616–617]: "Und hie am Ende dieses capitels weren wir wol zu ermanen, Gott dem Herren zu dancken, das er uns seine gleubige Kinder vor dem Gog und Magog, den Türcken, Bapst und Moscowiter etc. hat bewaret. Also das wir zu diesen unsern zeiten sein komen zu rechter erkentnis seiner gnade in Christo unserm Herren, welche erkentnis er uns durch Luthertum hat ernewert. Denn das hat der Teuffel sonderlich im sinn gehabt, solchs zuverkommen."

BIBLIOGRAPHY

Primary Sources

Beza, Theodore. *Iesu Christi Domini nostri Nouum Testamentum siue Nouum Fœdus, cuius Graeco contextui respondent interpretationes duae: vna vetus, altera Theodori Bezae*. . . . Cambridge: Roger Daniel, 1642.

Beza, Theodore. *Correspondance de Théodore de Bèze, recueillie par Hippolyte Aubert*. Ed. F. Aubert, H. Meylan, A. Dufour, et al. Geneva: Droz, 1960—.

Biblia sacrosancta Testamenti Veteris et Noui e sacra Hebraeorum lingua Graecorumque fontibus, consultis simul orthodoxis interpretibus religiosissime translata in sermonem Latinum (Zürich: C. Froschouer, 1543).

Bibliander, Theodor. *Ad omnium ordinum reipublicae christianae principes viros populumque christianum Relatio fidelis*. Basel: [Ioh. Oporinus], 1545.

Bullinger, Heinrich. *In Apocalypsim Iesu Christi, reuelatam quidem per angelum Domini, visam vero vel exceptam atque conscriptam a Ioanne apostolo et euangelista. Conciones centum*. Basel: n.p., 1557.

Bullinger, Heinrich. *Cent sermons sur l'Apocalypse de Iesus Christ, reuelee par l'ange du Seigneur, veue et escrite par S. Iean Apostre et Euangeliste. Mis en lumiere par Henri Bullinger, ministre de l'Eglise de Zurich*. Geneva: Jean Crespin, 1558. Reprinted under the same title, Geneva: Jean Bonnefoy, for Guillaume Fournet, 1565.

Bullinger, Heinrich. *A hundred sermons upon the Apocalips of Jesus Christe, reveiled in dede by Thangell of the Lorde: but seen or receyved and written by thapostle and Evangelist S. John*. London: n.p., 1561.

Calvin, John. *"La vraie piété." Divers traités de Jean Calvin et la confession de foi de Guillaume Farel*. Ed. I. Backus and C. Chimelli. Geneva: Labor et Fides, 1986.

Chytraeus, David. *Explicatio Apocalypsis Ioannis perspicua et breuis. Tradita a Davide Chytraeo*. Wittenberg: Iohannes Crato, 1564.

Clavis patrum graecorum. Ed. Maurice Geerard. 4 vols. Turnhout: Brepols, 1974–1983.

Colladon, Nicolas. *Methodus facilima ad explicationem sacrosanctae Apocalypseos Ioannis theologi ex ipso libro desumpta. Authore N. Colladone Biturige, sacrarum literarum professore in Schola Lausannensi. 2 Thessal., 2 vers. 5. An non meministis me cum adhuc essem apud vos, haec dixisse vobis? Nunc vero quid obstet nostis vt is suo tempore retegatur,* etc. Morges: Jean Le Preux, 1581. (Third edition, 1584).

Corpus Christianorum. Series Latina. Turnhout: Brepols, 1954—.

David and Nathan Chytraeus. Humanismus im konfessionellen Zeitalter. Ed. Karl-Heinz Glaser, Hanno Lietz, Stefan Rhein. Ubstadt-Weiher: Verlag Regionalkultur, 1993.

Du Jon, François. *Francisci Iunii Biturigis, Sacrarum literarum in Academia Heidelbergensi et Lugduno-Bataua professoris eruditissimi Opera theologica duobus tomis . . . digesta. . . .* Geneva, 1607.

Du Pinet, Antoine. *Familière et brieve exposition sur l'Apocalypse de sainct Jehan l'apostre.* Geneva: Jean Girard, 1539.

Du Pinet, Antoine. *Exposition sur l'Apocalypse de sainct Jean. Extraicte de plusieurs docteurs tant anciens que modernes, reveue et augmentée de nouveau.* Geneva: Jean Girard, 1545. Reproduces the text as in the 1543 edition.

[Du Pinet, Antoine]. *Exposition de l'Apocalypse de sainct Jean l'apostre reuuë, augmentée et diligemment corrigée tout de nouveau. Par Jean Marcorelles.* [Geneva?], 1552.

Du Pinet, Antoine. *Exposition sur l'Apocalypse de sainct Jean. Extraicte de plusieurs docteurs tant anciens que modernes. Avec Preface de Theodore de Beze.* Geneva: Jean Girard, 1557.

Erasmus, Desiderius. *Opera omnia emendatiora et auctiora, ad optimas editiones, praecipue quas ipse Erasmus postremo curauit, summa fide exacta doctorumque virorum notis illustrata. Tomus sextus, complectens Nouum Testamentum, cui in hac editione subiectae sunt singulis paginis Adnotationes.* Leiden: Petrus vander Aa, 1705.

Erasmus, Desiderius. *Opera omnia.* Amsterdam: North Holland, 1969.

Erasmus, Desiderius. *Erasmus' Annotations on the New Testament. Galatians to the Apocalypse. Facsimile of the final Latin text with all earlier Variants.* Ed. Anne Reeve. Introduction by M. A. Screech. Leiden: E. J. Brill, 1993.

Fasciculus rerum expetendarum ac fugiendarum. Cologne, 1535.

Gagny, Jean de. *Breuissima et facillima in omnes D. Pauli Epistolas Scholia, vltra priores editiones ex antiquissimis Graecorum authoribus abunde locupletata. Itidem in septem Canonicas Epistolas et D. Ioannis Apocalypsin, breuissima scholia recens edita.* Paris: V. Gaultherot, 1550.

Glossa ordinaria. See Nicholas of Lyra.

Joachim of Fiore. *Expositio magni prophetie abbatis Joachimi in Apocalypsim. Opus illud celebre . . .* in aedibus Francisci Bindoni ac Matthaei Pasini socii. Venice, 1527.

Joachim of Fiore. *Enchiridion super Apocalypsim.* Ed. E. K. Burger. Toronto: Pontifical Institute of Medieval Studies, 1986.

Joachim of Fiore. *Gioacchino da Fiore sull' Apocalisse. Traduzione e cura di Andrea Tagliapietra. Testo originale a fronte.* Milan: Feltrinelli, 1994.

Jud, Leo. *Paraphrasis oder Postille teütsch. Die Offenbarung Sant Johanns des Theologi.* Zurich: C. Froschouer, 1542.

Lactantius, Lucius Caelius Firmianus. *Opera omnia.* Part 1. Section 2. Ed. S. Brandt and G. Laubmann. Prague: F. Tempsky, 1890. Reprint: New York: Johnson Reprint, 1965.

Lambert, François. *Exegeseos Francisci Lamberti Auenionensis in sanctam Diui Ioannis*

Apocalypsim libri VII. In Academia Marpurgensi praelecti. Marburg: Franz Rhode, 1528.

Lucan. *L. Aennaei Lucani Pharsalia.* Ed. C. M. Francken. 2 vols. Leiden: A. W. Sijthoff, 1896–1897.

Luther, Martin. *D. Martin Luthers Werke. Kritische Gesammtausgabe.* Abt. 1: *Werke*, vol. 1–58; Abt. 2: *Tischreden*, vol. 1–7; Abt. 3: *Deutsche Bibel*, vol. 1–12; Abt. 4: *Briefwechsel*, vol. 1–6, 9–15. Weimar, 1883–.

[Marlorat, Augustin]. *Noui Testamenti Catholica Expositio ecclesiastica, id est, ex vniuersis probatis theologis excerpta, a quodam verbi Dei ministro . . . siue Bibliotheca expositionum . . .* Geneva: H. Esteinne, 1570.

Meyer, Sebastian. *In Apocalypsim Johannis Apostoli D. Sebastiani Meyer ecclesiastae Bernensis commentarius, nostro huic saeculo accommodus, natus et aeditus.* Zurich: Froschouer, s.d.

Migne, Jacques-Paul, general editor. *Patrologiae cursus completus.* Series Latina. 221 vols. Paris, 1844–1890.

Migne, Jacques-Paul, general editor. *Patrologiae cursus completus.* Series graeca. 161 vols. in 166. Paris, 1857–1866.

Nestle, E., and Aland K. *Nouum Testamentum graece.* Stuttgart: Deutsche Bibelgesellschaft, 1993.

[Nicholas of Lyra]. *Sexta pars biblie cum glosa ordinaria et expositione Lyre litterali et morali: necnon additionibus ac replicis.* Basel: J. Amerbach, J. Petri, J. Froben, 1502.

Pareus, David. *In Heidelbergensi Academia doctoris et professoris primarii, Operum theologicorum exegeticorum pars secunda. . . .* Geneva: Pierre Chouet, 1642.

Registres de la Compagnie des Pasteurs de Genève. Vol 3, *1565–1574.* Ed. Olivier Fatio and Olivier Labarthe. Geneva: Droz, 1969.

Rupert of Deutz. *Ruperti abbatis Tuitientis In Apocalypsim Iohannis Apostoli commentariorum libri XII.* Cologne: Johannes Soter, 1533.

Selnecker, Nikolaus. *Der Prophet Daniel und die Offenbarung Johannis.* Leipzig: Jacob Berwaldt, 1567.

Sixtus of Siena. *Bibliotheca sancta* [1st ed., 1566]. Paris: Ex typographia Rolini Theodorici, 1610.

Titelmans, Frans. *Libri duo de authoritate libri Apocalypsis. In quibus ex antiquissimorum authorum assertionibus scripturae huius dignitas et authoritas comprobatur aduersus eos qui nostra hac tempestate siue falsis assertionibus siue non bonis dubitationibus, canonicae et diuinae huius scripturae authoritati derogarunt. Per fratrem Franciscum Titelmannum Hasselensem, ordinis fratrum Minorum Sacrarum Scripturarum apud Louanienses praelectorem.* Antwerp: Michael Hillenius, 1530.

Valla, Lorenzo. *Opera omnia con una premessa di Eugenio Garin.* Turin: Bottega d'Erasmo, 1962. Reprint of the 1540 Basel edition.

Victorinus of Poetovio (Victorin de Poetovio). *Sur l'Apocalypse et autres écrits.* Ed. Martine Dulaey. Vol. 423 of *Sources chrétiennes.* Paris: Cerf, 1997.

Zwingli, Ulrich. *Huldreich Zwinglis sämtliche Werke.* Berlin, Zurich: Theologischer Verlag, 1905—

Secondary Sources

Andersson, Ingvar. *Erik XIV.* Stockholm: Wahstroem och Widstrand, 1948.

Augustijn, Cornelis. *Erasmus. Der Humanist als Theologe und Kirchenreformer.* Leiden: E. J. Brill, 1996.

Backus, Irena. "Some Fifteenth- and Sixteenth-Century Latin Translations of the Greek Fathers, c. 1440–1565." In *Studia Patristica 18:4. Papers of the 1983 Oxford Patristic Conference.* Ed. E. A. Livingstone. Kalamazoo, Mich.: Cistercian Publications, and Leuven: Peeters Press, 1990, 305–321.

Backus, Irena. *Les sept visions et la fin des temps. Les commentaires genevois de l'Apocalypse entre 1539 et 1584.* Cahiers de la Revue de théologie et de philosophie 19. Geneva: Revue de théologie et de philosophie, 1997.

Backus, Irena, ed. *The Reception of the Church Fathers in the West.* 2 vols. Leiden: E. J. Brill, 1997.

Backus, Irena. "The Church Fathers and the Canonicity of the Apocalypse in the Sixteenth Century: Erasmus, Frans Titelmans, and Theodore Beza." *Sixteenth Century Journal* 29 (1998): 651–665.

Backus, Irena. "Apocalypse 20.2–4 et le millenium protestant." *Revue d'histoire et de philosophie religieuses,* 79 (1999): 101–118.

Backus, Irena. "The Beast: Interpretations of Dan. 7:2–9 and Apc. 13:1–4, 11–12 in Lutheran, Calvinist and Zwinglian Circles in the late Sixteenth Century." *Reformation and Renaissance Review,* forthcoming.

Barnes, Robin. *Prophecy and Gnosis. Apocalypticism in the Wake of the Lutheran Reformation.* Stanford, Calif.: Stanford University Press, 1988.

Bauckham, Richard. *Tudor Apocalypse. Sixteenth Century Apocalypticism, Millenarianism, and the English Reformation. From John Bale to John Foxe and Thomas Brightman.* Appleford, Eng.: Sutton Courtenay Press, 1978.

Bauckham, Richard. "Heinrich Bullinger and the English." In *The Swiss Connection. Manchester Essays on Religious Connections between England and Switzerland between the Sixteenth and the Twentieth Centuries.* Ed. Henry D. Rack. Manchester: n.p., 1995, 9–54.

Bentley, Jerry. *Humanists and the Holy Writ.* Princeton: Princeton University Press, 1983.

Bobzin, Hartmut. *Der Koran im Zeitalter der Reformation. Studien zur Frühgeschichte der Arabistik und Islamkunde in Europa.* Beiruter Texte und Studien 42. Beirut: Franz Steiner, 1995.

Bousset, Wilhelm. *Die Offenbarung Johannis.* Göttingen: Vandenhoeck und Ruprecht, 1906.

Burkitt, F. C. *The Book of Rules of Tyconius.* Texts and Studies 3, part 1. Cambridge: Cambridge University Press, 1894.

Chambers, D. S. *A Renaissance Cardinal and His Wordly Goods: The Will and Inventory of Francesco Gonzaga (1444–1483).* London: Warburg Institute, 1992.

D'Amico, John. *Renaissance Humanism in Papal Rome.* Baltimore: Johns Hopkins University Press, 1983.

De Boer, Erik. *Loflied en Hekeldicht. De geschiedenis van Calvijn's enige gedicht. Het Epinicion Christo cantatum van 1 januari 1541.* Haarlem: Aca Media, 1986.

De Boer, Erik. "The Book of Revelation in Calvin's Geneva." In *Calvin's Books. Festschrift Dedicated to Peter de Klerk on the Occasion of His Seventieth Birthday.* Ed. W. H. Neuser, H. J. Selderhuis, and W. van't Spijker. Heerenveen: J. J. Groen en Zoon, 1997.

De Jonge, C. *De irenische Ecclesiologie van Franciscus Junius.* Nieuwkoop: De Graaf, 1980.

Dulaey, Martine. "Jérôme 'éditeur' du Commentaire sur l'Apocalypse de Victorin de Poetovio." *Revue des Études Augustiniennes* 37 (1991): 199–236.

Egli, Emil. *Analecta reformatoria II. Biographien Bibliander. Ceporin. Johannes Bullinger.* Zurich: Zürcher und Furrer, 1901.

Farenga, P. *"Monumenta memoriae.* Pietro Riario fra mito e storia." In *Un pontificato e una città. Sixto IV (1471–84).* Ed. M. Miglio et al. Vatican City: 1986.

Fraenkel, Pierre, ed. *Pour retrouver François Lambert. Bio-bibliographie et études.* Bibliotheca Bibliographica Aureliana 108. Baden-Baden: Valentin Koerner, 1987.

Haag, E., and Haag, E. *La France Protestante.* 1st ed. 10 vols. Paris: J. Cherbuliez, 1846–1859.

Haag, E., and Haag, E. *La France Protestante.* 2nd ed. 6 vols. Paris: Fischbacher, 1877–1888.

Hauck, Herbert, ed. *Realencyclopädie für Protestantische Theologie und Kirche. Begründet von J. J. Herzog.* 3rd edition. 23 vols. Leipzig: J. C. Hinrichs, 1896–1913.

Herminjard, A. L. *La correspondance des réformateurs dans les pays de langue française.* 9 vols. Geneva: H. Georg, 1866–1897.

Hofmann, Hans-Ulrich. *Luther und die Johannes-Apokalypse.* Tübingen: J.C.B. Mohr, 1982.

Hook, Judith. *The Sack of Rome.* London: Macmillan, 1972.

Jammes, André. "Un bibliophile à découvrir, Jean de Gagny." *Bulletin du bibliophile* (1996): 35–81.

Jobst, Ebel. "Die Herkunft des Konzeptes der Konkordienformel." *Zeitschrift für Kirchengeschichte* 91 (1980): 237–282.

Kamlah, W. *Apokalypse und Geschichtstheologie.* Berlin: Emil Ebering, 1935.

Kretschmar, Georg. *Die Offenbarung des Johannes: Die Geschichte ihrer Auslegung im I. Jahrtausend.* Stuttgart: Calwer, 1985.

Millet, Olivier, ed. *Calvin et ses contemporains. Actes du colloque de Paris 1995.* Geneva: Droz, 1998.

Milway, Michael. *The Burden and the Beast: Berthold Pürstinger, Bishop of Chiemsee, and Apocalyptic Reform in Early Sixteenth Century Salzburg.* Ph.D. diss, University of Arizona, Tucson, 1996.

Müller, Ulrich. *Die Offenbarung des Johannes.* Gütersloh: G. Mohr, 1984.

Muller, Richard. "In the Light of Orthodoxy: The 'Method and Disposition' of Calvin's *Institutio* from the Perspective of Calvin's Late-Sixteenth-Century Editors." *Sixteenth Century Journal* 28 (1997): 1203–1211.

Norelli, Enrico. "Pertinence théologique et canonicité: Les premières Apocalypses chrétiennes." *Apocrypha* 8 (1997): 147–164.

Oxford Encyclopedia of the Reformation. Ed. Hans Hillerbrand. 4 vols. New York: Oxford University Press, 1996.

Pernot, Jean-François, ed. *Jacques Lefèvre d'Étaples (1450?-1536). Actes du colloque d'Étaples, les 7 et 8 novembre 1992.* Paris: Honoré Champion, 1995.

Pestalozzi, Carl. *Leo Jüda: Nach handschriftlichen und gleichzeitigen Quellen.* Elberfeld: Friderichs, 1860.

Petersen, Rodney. *Preaching in the Last Days. The Theme of Two Witnesses in the Sixteenth and Seventeenth Centuries.* Oxford: Oxford University Press, 1993.

Prigent, Pierre. *Apocalypse 12. Histoire de l'exégèse.* Tübingen: J.C.B. Mohr (Paul Siebeck), 1959.

Prigent, Pierre. *L'Apocalypse de Saint Jean.* Geneva: Labor et Fides, 1988.

Reeves, Marjorie. *The Influence of Prophecy in the Later Middle Ages: A Study in Joachimism.* Oxford: Oxford University Press, 1969.

Rice, Eugene F. *The Prefatory Epistles of Jacques Lefèvre d'Etaples and Related Texts.* Baltimore: Johns Hopkins University Press, 1972.

Rummel, Erika. *Erasmus and His Catholic Critics.* 2 vols. Nieuwkoop: De Graaf, 1989.

Scherman, Theodor. *Propheten- und Apostellegenden. Nebst Jüngerkatalogen des Dorotheus und verwandte Texte.* Leipzig: J. Hinrichs, 1907.

Schmuck, Josef. *Die Prophetie "Onus ecclesiae."* Vienna: n.p., 1973.

Staedtke, Joachim, ed. *Heinrich Bullinger. Werke.* Vol. 1:1. *Bibliographie.* Zurich: Theologischer Verlag, 1972.

Steinmetz, David. "The Superiority of Pre-Critical Exegesis." *Theology Today* 27 (1980): 27–38.

Stephens, W. P. *The Theology of Huldrych Zwingli.* Oxford: Oxford University Press, 1986.

Van Engen, John. *Rupert of Deutz.* Berkeley: University of California Press, 1983.

Vial, Marc. "Luther et l'Apocalypse d'après les préfaces de 1522 et 1530." *Revue de Théologie et de Philosophie* 131 (1999): 25–37.

Vuilleumier, Henri. *Histoire de l'Eglise réformée du pays de Vaud sous le régime bernois.* Vol. 1, *L'âge de la Réforme.* Lausanne: La Concorde, 1927.

Wandel, Lee Palmer. *Voracious Idols and Violent Hands.* Cambridge: Cambridge University Press, 1996.

Wilberding, Eric. "A Defense of Dionysius the Areopagite by Rubens." *Journal of the History of Ideas* 52 (1991): 19–34.

Wyss, Karl-Heinz. *Leo Jud. Seine Entwicklung zum Reformator, 1519–1523.* Bern: Peter Lang, 1976.

INDEX